How to say Mass
in the Anglican Rite

BY
THE MOST REVEREND RUTHERFORD JOHNSON, PhD

A.D. MMIX

How to say Mass in the Anglican Rite

BY THE MOST REVEREND RUTHERFORD JOHNSON, PHD.

ARCHIDIOECESIS METROPOLITANA ANGLICANA-CATHOLICA
MERIDIONALIS-OCCIDENTALIS, SEDES METROPOLITANA ECCLESIAE
TRADITIONALIS ANTIQUAE ANGLICANAE-CATHOLICAE

ANGLO-CATHOLIC ARCHDIOCESE OF THE SOUTHWEST
METROPOLITAN SEE OF THE
TRADITIONAL OLD ANGLO-CATHOLIC CHURCH

PRO DEO ET MARIA.

ISBN: 978-0-557-25655-6

FIRST EDITION

COPYRIGHT © 2009. ANGLO-CATHOLIC ARCHDIOCESE OF THE SOUTHWEST, INC.
ALL RIGHTS RESERVED.

This publication conforms to the standards and traditions of the Anglo-Catholic Rite under general Sarum Tradition, and the Canons and Ceremonial of this Metropolitan See, and is further consistent with traditional Catholic doctrine.

Imprimatur
Most Rev. ✠Rutherford Johnson
Metropolitan

TABLE OF CONTENTS

Introduction iii
Churches and Altars 1
Layout of the Church 1
Altar 4
Altar Linens 10
Sacristy 11

Objects for Sacred Use in the Mass 13
Elements for Consecration 13
Sacred Vessels 13
Mass Linens 15
Stacking a Chalice 19
Other Objects for the Mass 26
Blessings of Objects 36
Purifying and Cleaning Mass Linens and Sacred Objects 36
Paschal Candle 37
Disposal of Sacred Objects 38

Vestments 39
Color of Vestments 39
Low Mass 40
Pontifical Low Mass 41
High Mass 42
Sung Mass 45
Pontifical High Mass 45
Pontifical Sung Mass 49
Putting on an Amice 50
Tying a Cincture 52
Vesting Prayers 55

Altar Servers 57
Specific Duties of Servers 57
At a Pontifical Mass 60
Bows and Genuflections *(for everyone)* 61
Postures of the Body *(for everyone)* 63
Uniformity of Action 65

Masses..67
Low Mass..67
High Mass...141
Sung Mass...185
Mass with a Bishop Presiding but not Celebrating....................187
Mass in the Presence of the Exposed Sacrament.......................189

Pontifical Masses..191
Pontifical Low Mass..191
Pontifical High Mass...193
Pontifical Sung Mass...227
Pontifical Mass with a Greater Prelate Presiding but not Celebrating.....229
Pontifical Mass in the Presence of the Exposed Sacrament
  (See under "Masses" above.)

Requiem Mass..231
Changes for a Requiem Mass..231
Absolution...233
Requiem Mass Celebrated by a Bishop.....................................235
Absolution by Five Bishop...237
Absolution in the Absence of the Body....................................239
Dress of Priests for Burial...239

Special Occasions and Circumstances...............................241
Holy Week Rites...241
    Palm Sunday..241
    Monday, Tuesday, & Wednesday of Holy Week....................248
    Chrism Mass..249
    Maundy Thursday..259
    Good Friday..267
    Masses of Saints on Holy Saturday...................................280
    Holy Saturday and Easter Vigil..280
Ordinations.. 297
Nuptial Masses..299
Celebrating without a Server...301
Celebrating Alone..303
Public Veneration of a Relic..305

LITURGICAL RESOURCES
OF THE ARCHDIOCESE OF THE SOUTHWEST

Missale Anglicanum 2009 – *Latin-based Anglican mass with English parts*

Rituale Anglicanum – *Prayer Book in English and Latin for priests, with blessings, prayers, psalms, litanies, and other rituals.*

Rituale Breve – *Prayer Book in English and Latin for the people, including a detailed section for following and participating in the mass.*

Pontificale Anglicanum – *Collection of rites proper to Bishops in large print with easy-to-follow ceremonial cues.*

Evangeliarium – *Book of Gospels in side-by-side Latin and English, with instructions for chant.*

Epistolarium – *Book of Epistles in side-by-side Latin and English, with instructions for chant.*

Liber Processionalis – *Contains everything needed for all major processions of the church, including complete chant and prayers in Latin and English.*

Daily Offices – *Complete chancel edition of the Daily Offices, including Morning Prayer, Noonday Prayer, Afternoon Prayer, Evening Prayer, and Compline, with all readings for the major offices and the complete psalter.*

Ordo-Kalender – *Contains the masses for each day of the year, including secondary masses and potential votive masses, as well as other special instructions.*

AND

The Southwest Anglo-Catholic Catechism – *A catechism for Anglo-Catholics based on the venerable Baltimore catechism; a concise statement of faith.*

This book is dedicated to my parents, Dr. R. Barry and Marianne Johnson, who first brought me to the Church, and to my wife, Anya, for her constant patience as I wrote this book.

Introduction

ಬಿಂ

This book is intended to help priests understand the ceremonies of the Anglican Rite. The rites of the Church are a beautiful thing, designed to involve all the senses in the highest form of prayer and worship we have. All aspects of the ceremonies given in this book are well grounded in history, faith, doctrine, and theology. Each part either has a theological purpose or a practical purpose. This is the key test for correctness of liturgy.

This not to say, however, that there is only one correct way. Rituals of the church, of course, evolve as all things evolve. This is the normal way of life. Revolutionary changes and modernistic innovations that seek to destroy the link to our heritage and past, however, must be avoided. Variations and local use can make sense, under proper authority, provided they maintain the truth they are intended to teach. If we lose our traditional liturgy, then we lose our faith. The traditional liturgy and the Holy Spirit working through it are our link to the earliest days and even the very founding of our Church.

This book represents over a decade of work, beginning when I was Master of Ceremonies for my Bishop at the time. He taught me to love the liturgy as a means of reflecting the love of God. More than that, he instilled in me an understanding of why the liturgy is as it is. I hope and pray that this book will inspire a similar love and understanding in each person who reads it.

Pax Domini sit semper vobiscum,

✠ Rutherford Johnson

HOW TO SAY MASS IN THE ANGLICAN RITE

THE CHURCH AND ALTAR

LAYOUT OF THE CHURCH

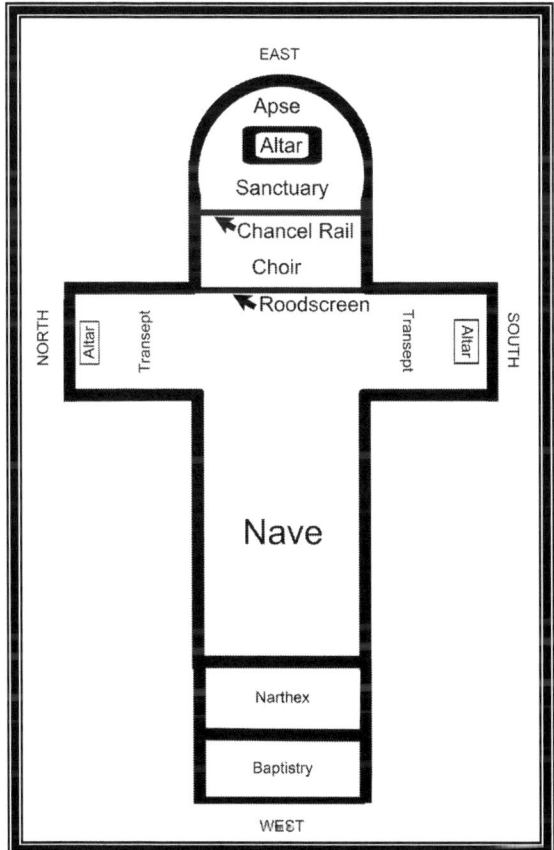

Fig. 1.1 – A layout of a church

Observe Fig. 1.1. This is a classic design for a church layout. Of course, not every church looks the same, or necessarily even close. However, this layout is good for illustrating the principals of traditional church layout.

Directions:

The altar faces east. This is liturgical east, and may or may not correspond to the geographical direction. The opposite end of the building is liturgical west. The two transepts (or sides of the building, if there are no transepts) are north and south.

The Nave:
The nave is the part of the church where the laity sits.

Transept:
The transepts give the church is cruciform shape. They may provide seating for the faithful for liturgy at the main altar. They may also provide seating for masses at small chapel altars contained within them.

Narthex:
The area before the Nave.

Baptistery:
The area containing the Baptismal font. This is in different locations in different churches, but is generally considered most appropriately located near the entrance for reasons of symbolism.

Choir:
Where the clergy who are attending the mass (but not officiating or serving) sit. This is not to be confused with the location where the lay choir sit, which is quite typically in the back of the church in a choir loft.

Roodscreen:
This is not always present. However, its function is to separate the areas for the clergy from the areas for the laity. The clergy areas are the choir, chancel, and sanctuary. The lay areas are the nave and transepts.

Chancel Rail:
The railing marking the entrance to the sanctuary.

THE CHURCH AND ALTAR

Chancel:

The area immediately before the chancel rail.

Sanctuary:

The area of the church containing the altar, sedilia, credence table, etc. If it is a cathedral, it is also the location of the throne. See Fig. 1.2 for a close-up of a typical sanctuary.

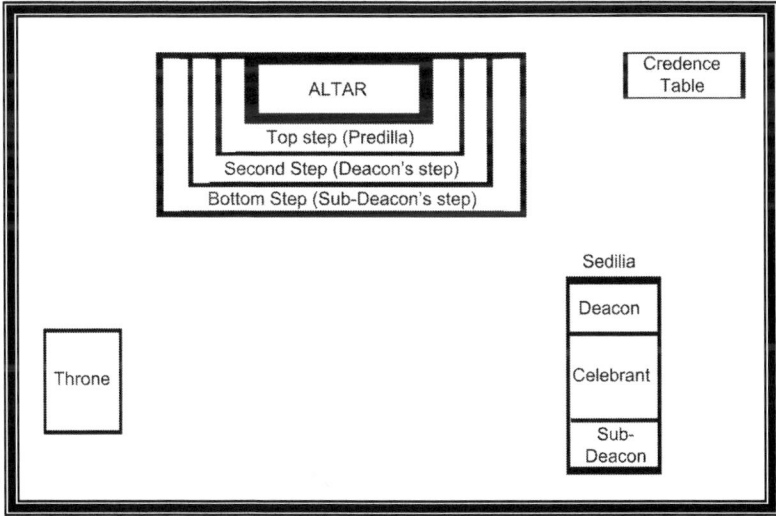

Fig. 1.2 – Close-up of a typical sanctuary layout, including location of the throne if a cathedral, and the sedilia.

In Fig. 1.2., the typical positions are given for the sanctuary. The top step is the one that the Celebrant stands on. It is also called the predella. The second step is also called the Deacon's step because at times in a sung or high mass, he is appointed to stand on that step. The third, or bottom step is also called the Sub-Deacon's step, because he is appointed to stand there at times in the high mass. When there are insufficient steps, the Deacon and Sub-Deacon merely stand on the pavement (the main floor of the sanctuary).

THE ALTAR

The altar should ideally be made of stone or have a stone top. A wooden altar works just as well, though. In the case of a wooden altar, an altar stone (see below) is prescribed to be housed within the altar. This may be dispensed by episcopal authority. The altar should be sufficient in size to accommodate the actions of the mass, and ideally should be of sufficient height to permit the priest to kiss it and bow down with hands resting upon it without being at an awkward angle.

Altar Stone:

The altar stone should be made of natural stone and of a size sufficient that a chalice and paten could be placed upon them. There should be five crosses carved into the top of it (but need not be). See Fig. 1.3. There should also be a sepulchre inside for the housing of the three grains of incense and the sacred relics, if there are to be any enclosed inside. A particularly useful style is one that is effectively a stone box with a lid, which is then closed with mortar according to the rite in the Pontificale Anglicanum. Such an altar stone may be enclosed within a permanent altar, or it may be used as a portable altar. In the case of a portable altar, the stone itself may be moved from table-top to table-top as needed, or may have its own tabletop.

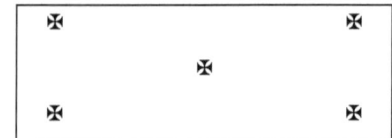

Fig. 1.3 – Position of crosses on the top of an altar stone

A stone altar itself may also function as the altar stone. What applied in the above description applies there as well. There is need for the 5 crosses (though not required) and a sepulchre for the 3 grains of incense and the relics, if any.

Relics:

The altar, where the bread and wine are consecrated into the Precious Body and Blood of our Lord Jesus Christ, is a fitting place for relics to be housed. The relics may be first, second, or third class, approved by episcopal authority. They are permanently enclosed in the altar stone in the rite of consecrating an altar (see the Pontificale). With episcopal permission, relics need not be housed in the altar, and in such a case may be added later. If there are no relics, the prayers upon arrival at the altar (*Aufer a nobis*, etc.) are still said due to tradition, the need to indicate the altar as a fitting resting place for the relics of saints, and as honor to the communion of all saints in general.

The sepulchre should be sealed with red cord, tied in any convenient manner, and a wax seal bearing the seal of the episcopal authority consecrating the altar or certifying the relics. There should be a document certifying the relics enclosed in the stone, along with the document of consecration of the altar. These should be either enclosed within the altar or stored in a safe and honorable place.

Altar Top:

The altar top, if it is not also the top of the altar stone, should ideally have the five crosses on it, as in Fig. 1.3. If it is a permanent altar, then the anointing of the top of the altar in the Pontificale is done on the top of the altar. If it is a portable altar with its own top, then the same is true. If it is a portable altar consisting only of the altar stone, then the stone itself only is anointed.

Altar Cross:

There must be a cross/crucifix on the altar. It may be on the altar itself, hung on the wall or screen behind the altar, or both. The cross should be blessed according to the forms in the Rituale Anglicanum.

Candles on the Altar:

Candles must be used on the altar during the mass. Candles are always used in even numbers, with half on each side of the altar cross. They are used in the following numbers:

A) Two candles – Low mass
B) Four candles – Low mass celebrated by a bishop
C) Six candles – High mass or sung mass

For a high mass or sung mass celebrated by a bishop, a seventh candle may be lit and placed in the center of the altar. This candle, known as the Pontifical Candle, goes immediately in front of or behind the altar cross, depending on the size of the cross and physical arrangement of the altar. See the section below on the layout of the altar to see the position of the candles.

Layout of the Altar:

Fig. 1.4 gives the typical layout of the altar in an aerial view.

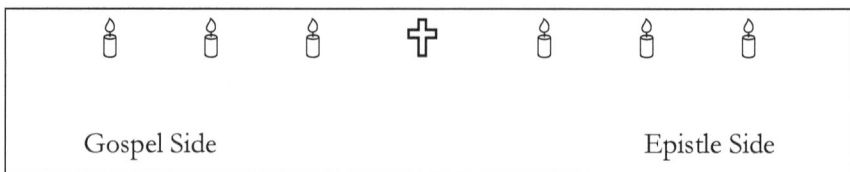

Fig. 1.4 – Layout of the altar.

Where the cross is indicated above in Fig. 1.4, the tabernacle also goes, with the cross above it. In front of the cross is the location where the corporal is spread.

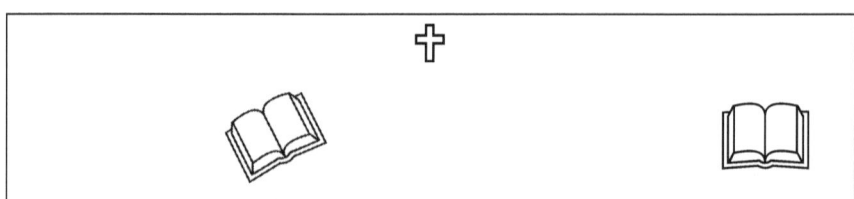

Fig. 1.5 – Positions of the missal on the altar.

The missal is in two positions on the altar during any mass. In Fig. 1.5, the missal is shown in the right of the figure at the Epistle corner. This is its location until after the gradual and from the Thanksgiving to the end. The other position shown in Fig. 1.5 is on the Gospel side just to the left of the corporal. This is the position from the Gospel until after the Ablutions. The missal is angled to make it easier to read while the priest is standing in the center of the altar, as the sacred vessels are in front of him. Nota bene: In a pontifical high or sung mass from the throne, the missal is on the altar only in the position in the Gospel side in Fig. 1.5. Otherwise it is at the throne.

THE CHURCH AND ALTAR

Moving the Missal:

When the altar server moves the missal, he follows the pathway in Fig. 1.6 below. After the Epistle he says *Deo gratias* (A). He rises from the Credence table and approaches the Epistle corner (B) and waits for the Celebrant to finish reading the Gradual. He then takes the missal on its stand (holding it by the stand), follows the arrows back down to the pavement, and genuflects in the center (C), holding the missal, or else bows if the sacrament is not reserved. Then he follows the path back up the steps to the predella (D) and places the missal back on the altar in its proper position as shown in Fig. 1.6 on the Gospel side. He follows the pathway on the pavement back to the credence table, where he stands for the Gospel. When he passes in front of the cross (E), he genuflects, or bows if the sacrament is not reserved.

Fig. 1.6 – Pathway for the altar server to transfer the missal from the Epistle to the Gospel side

After the Ablutions, while the priest is stacking the chalice, the altar server again moves the missal. This time it is moved from the Gospel-side position to its original position on the Epistle side. He follows the same pathway as in Fig. 1.6, only in reverse. Once he has placed the missal back on the Epistle corner, he returns to the credence table and waits for the General Thanksgiving.

Altar Cards:

Altar cards are optional, but facilitate better flow and ease for the priest during the mass. They come in various forms. The central altar card goes in front of the tabernacle, just behind the corporal. It contains what a priest says before and after the Gospel in the center of the altar, and typically the text for the Offertory and Consecration, as well as the *Placeat Tibi*, said in the center of the altar after the Dismissal and before the Blessing.

Other altar cards contain text where they are needed. In the center of the altar, usually to the Gospel side, may be a card containing the *Aufer a nobis* and the prayers for incensing the altar at the offertory. To the Epistle side may be another card containing the Absolution and Comfortable Words, which may be held by the server as the priest gives absolution in the mass. On the Epistle corner may be a card containing the *Deus qui*, for blessing the water, and the *Lavabo*. On the far Gospel side may be a card containing the Last Gospel.

Lighting Candles:

Candles are lit before the procession (or if there is no procession, then before the priest enters the sanctuary to say mass). They are lit by acolytes or altar servers. They are lit starting with the candle on the Epistle side closest to the cross and then, working outward, all the Epistle candles are lit. Then the candles on the Gospel side are lit in the same manner, starting with the candle nearest to the cross. Observing Fig. 1.7, the candles are lit in the order shown, 1-6.

Fig. 1.7 – Order of lighting candles.

If there are two acolytes, then one lights the Epistle side, the other lights the Gospel side. If there is only one, then he lights the Epistle side first, descends all the way to the pavement, crosses in front of the cross (point A in Fig. 1.8), genuflecting if the Sacrament is reserved, else bowing, and

THE CHURCH AND ALTAR

ascending to the Gospel side, lights the candles on the Gospel side. See Fig. 1.8 for the pathway for a single acolyte lighting all the candles.

If there are Benediction candles present on the altar, then all the altar candles on the Epistle side are lit first as above. Then all the Benediction candles are lit on the Epistle side, beginning with the one closest to the cross and working out, just as for the altar candles. Then when all the Epistle-side candles have been lit, the Gospel-side candles are lit in the same manner. See Fig. 1.8 below.

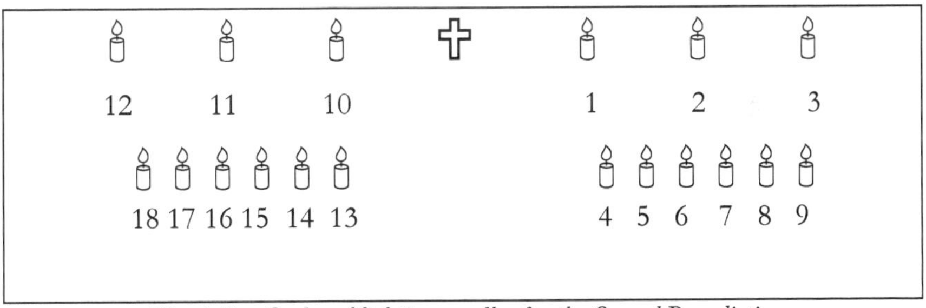

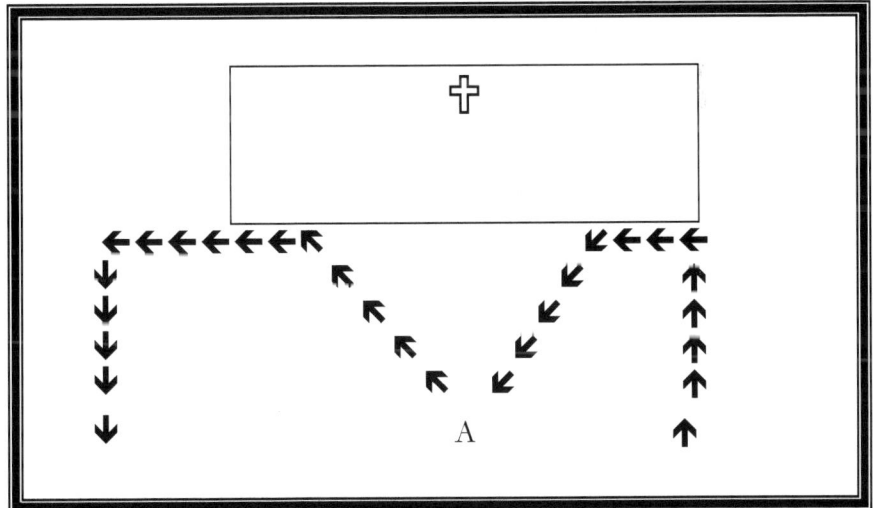

Fig. 1.7 – Order of lighting candles for the Sacred Benediction

Fig. 1.8 – Pathway for a single altar server lighting all the candles

Flowers:

Flowers are appropriate on the altar at any time except during Lent (though they are permitted during Laetare week). They should be of a style appropriate to the season or occasion. When the color is purple or black, they should be few in number and not overly grand or joyous, due to the penitential nature of such masses.

Consecration of the Altar:

An altar must be consecrated by a bishop. With episcopal permission and for just cause, mass may be said on a temporary, unconsecrated altar. More preferably, though, is the practice of using a portable consecrated altar if a permanent/fixed altar is not currently possible. The consecration of the altar follows the rites in the Pontificale.

ALTAR LINENS

On the altar should be an under-cloth, white in color, which may or may not cover the front of the altar. On top of this goes the altar cloth proper, which must cover the entire width of the altar, and the depth sufficient to accomodate a corporal being spread over it without any of the corporal hanging over. It must be made of linen and may be embellished on the front edge with lace, which hangs over the front.

The altar cloth is blessed according to the form in the Rituale. If it must be cleaned, it must first be cleaned by hand by a priest if there is any chance that any sacrament is on it or has been spilled on it. Then it may be laundered regularly.

Frontals:

A frontal is an optional covering for the front of the altar. It is made in the liturgical color of the day and usually of a similar nature to vestments. It hangs over the front of the altar, but underneath any overhang of the altar cloth.

SACRISTY

The sacristy is the area in the church for storing and preparing the sacred vessels, vestments, and other objects for mass. It is typically where the priest and other ministers vest for mass, and is usually immediately adjoining the sanctuary of the church. It is also where the mass linens are typically purified after mass.

For the purpose of cleaning mass linens, the sacristy typically has a sacrarium, also known as a piscina. This is a sink, the drain pipes of which go to bare earth, not into the sewer. If this is not present, then other methods of purification should be used, as described in the section on mass linens.

The sacrarium is also an acceptable location for disposal of ashes from burning bread or cloths used for cleaning holy oils. Holy oils themselves, though, are typically burned rather than being poured down the piscina. Ashes from burning anything sacred may be disposed of in the sacrarium if they are not properly buried or scattered.

HOW TO SAY MASS IN THE ANGLICAN RITE

OBJECTS FOR SACRED USE IN THE MASS
※

ELEMENTS FOR CONSECRATION

The three elements needed for consecration are as follows:

Wine:

Any wine containing alcohol from a fermentation process is sufficient. Due to their preservability, the fortified wines are recommended, such as port and sherry. Due to their red color, the darker fortified wines like port have particular appeal. However, the lighter-color fortified wines like sherry are easier to clean from purificators.

Bread:

Unleavened bread only is used for the host. "Standard" available communion wafers come in three sizes. The small ones (around 1 inch in diameter) are for the servers, other clergy, and the people. The middle and large ones (around 3 inches and around 5 inches in diameter respectively) are for the Celebrant. Except where called for in the rubrics, there is only one priest's host per mass, and the Celebrant consumes the entire host.

Water:

For the co-mingling, pure, clean water should be available in the water cruet.

SACRED VESSELS

The Sacred Vessels are those used directly in the consecration of the elements. The chalice and the paten are essential, while the ciborium in its various forms are optional depending on immediate need.

The chalice and paten should be made out of metal only. If they are not made out of gold or silver, then they should be plated in gold or silver, at least on the top side of the paten and the inside surface of the bowl of the chalice. Even silver chalices and patens are best gold plated on the top surface of the paten. Furthermore, the chalice and paten should be of a beautiful, conservative design fitting for our Lord.

In some locations, provisions are made by proper episcopal authority to permit chalices and patens to be made of another precious substance inherent to the local area. These instances are highly rare and localized. The underlying issue is that the substance touching the Precious Body and Blood of our Lord Jesus Christ should be a precious substance.

Fig. 2.1 – A Chalice

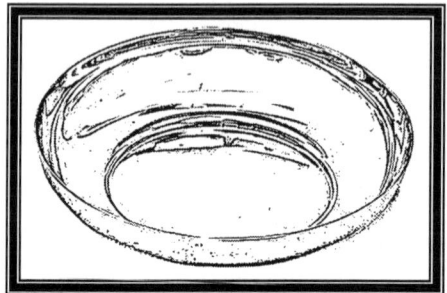

Fig. 2.2 – A Paten

The paten may be quite flat, as is often the case, or it may have a depression in the center, as in Fig. 2.2 above.

OBJECTS FOR SACRED USE IN THE MASS

Fig. 2.3 – A Ciborium

The Ciborium:

Ciboria have two uses. One is for holding additional hosts to be consecrated during the mass for distribution to the faithful. The other use is for reserving the sacrament (and for communicating people from the reserved sacrament during mass). In the later case, it is generally considered good practice to communicate fresh hosts during mass, communicate the people from the reserved sacrament in the ciborium, and then place the newly-consecrated hosts in the ciborium. In this manner, the hosts reserved in the tabernacle (see the section on Other Equipment) are kept fresh. Fig. 2.3 gives an example of a ciborium suitable both for holding hosts to be consecrated during the mass and for reserving the sacrament. There exists also a type of ciborium similar to a bowl, usually without a cover, and sometimes on a very short stem. This type is only for holding hosts to be consecrated during mass.

Mass Linens:

Accompanying the sacred vessels are the mass linens. These are:

> Corporal: This is unfolded on the altar. The consecration takes place over the corporal, and it holds the host. The chalice also sits on it.
>
> Purificator: The purificator is used to purify the chalice and paten after the mass.
>
> Lavabo Towel: This is a small finger towel used to dry the priest's finger after the Lavabo.

Corporal:

The corporal is a square piece of white linen fabric. It may be, with episcopal authority, made of a linen blend, provided the other material is natural, such as cotton or muslin. It should have no fringe, trim, embroidery, or other adornment, except that it may have a single, small cross embroidered in white or red to the front of center, where the host will be placed during the mass.

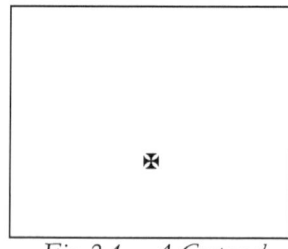

Fig. 2.4 – A Corporal

Folding the Corporal:

1	2	3
4	5	6
7	8	9

Fig. 2.5 – A Corporal with the squares numbered

First the corporal is ironed flat. and placed facing up as it would be on the altar. Then it is folded and ironed into 9 even squares, as in Fig. 2.5 above. It is unfolded on the altar in the opposite order. The order for *folding* the corporal is as follows:

1. The top row (squares 1, 2, & 3) are folded down over the second row (squares 4, 5, & 6).
2. The bottom row (square 7, 8, & 9) are folded up over the top and second rows.

OBJECTS FOR SACRED USE IN THE MASS

3. The right third (now squares 3, 6, & 9) are folded over the middle portion (now squares 2, 5, & 8).
4. The left third (now squares 1, 4, & 7) are folded over the middle portion (now squares 2, 3, 5, 6, 8, & 9).

Purificator:

The purificator is made of the same material as the corporal. It is oblong in shape. Like the corporal, it must be white, without fringe, embroidery, or other adornment, except that there may be a single white or red cross in the center. See Fig. 2.6.

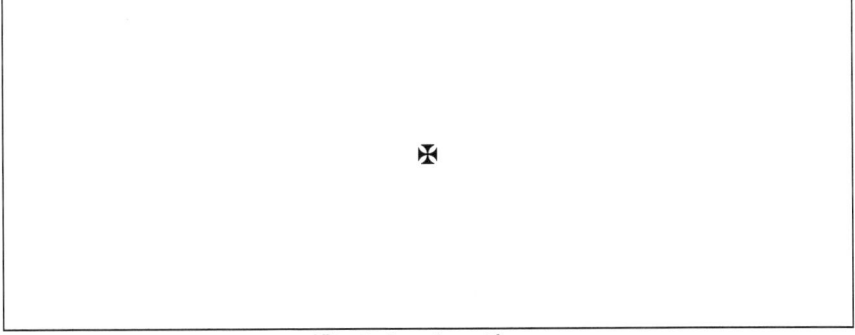

Fig. 2.6 – A purificator

Folding a Purificator:

First the purificator is ironed flat and then folded and pressed into 9 sections. See Fig. 2.7 and the following instructions.

1	2	3
4	5	6
7	8	9

Fig. 2.7 – A purificator with the sections numbered

First place the purificator flat and *face down*. Then fold and press in the following order:

1. The top row (sections 1, 2, &3) over the second row (sections 4, 5, & 6).
2. The bottom row (sections 7, 8, & 9) over the top row (now in the middle).
3. The right half (sections 3, 6, & 9) over the middle (sections 2, 5, & 8).
4. The left half (sections 1, 4, & 7) over the middle (now sections 2, 3, 5, 6, 8, & 9).

Lavabo Towel:

The lavabo towel is made of the same material as the corporal and purificator. It is very similar in style and shape to the purificator, but is usually smaller. It should also be plain, without adornment, except for an optional white or red cross embroidered either in the center or on the center end of the towel (see Fig. 2.8 below).

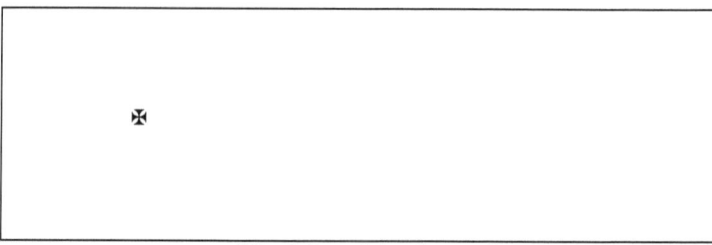

Fig. 2.8 – A lavabo towel

Folding the Lavabo Towel:

The lavabo towel is folded exactly the same as the purificator in the beginning, but then is folded into two parts left and right instead of three. Observe Fig. 2.9 and the following instructions.

OBJECTS FOR SACRED USE IN THE MASS

1	2
3	4
5	6

Fig. 2.9 – A lavabo towel with sections numbered

First, iron the lavabo towel flat and place it *face down*, just as with the purificator. Then fold and press the towel in the following order:

1. The top row (sections 1 & 2) over the middle (sections 3 & 4)
2. The bottom row (sections 5 & 6) over the top row (now in the middle)
3. The right half (sections 2, 4, & 6) over the left half (sections 1, 3, & 5)

The Pall:

The pall is made of the same material as the other mass linens. It is square with a rigid insert, and it used to cover the paten in the stacked chalice (see below), and the chalice during mass. It may have a red or white embroidered cross in its center. It is usually approximately 6 inches in width.

Stacking a Chalice:

The Sacred Vessels must be properly arrayed before the mass, whether it is a low mass, high mass, or sung mass. Once the mass linens are properly folded, follow this procedure to stack the chalice.

Fig. 2.10 – Chalice with purificator draped over it.

The purificator is laid over the top of the chalice from right to left with the embroidered cross, if any, centered over the middle of the chalice. The purificator remains folded lengthwise, but the other two folds are allowed to drape over the edges of the chalice as in Fig. 2.10 above.

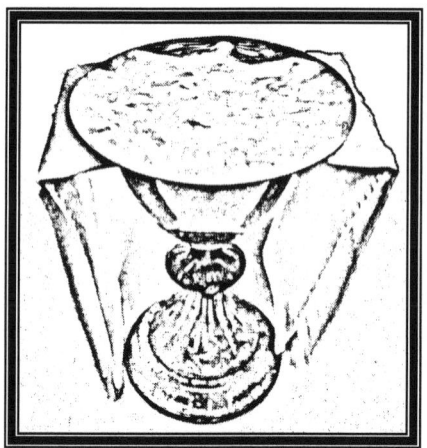

2.11 – Paten on top of purificator and chalice

Next the paten is placed on top of the purificator and chalice, as in Fig. 2.11 above.

OBJECTS FOR SACRED USE IN THE MASS

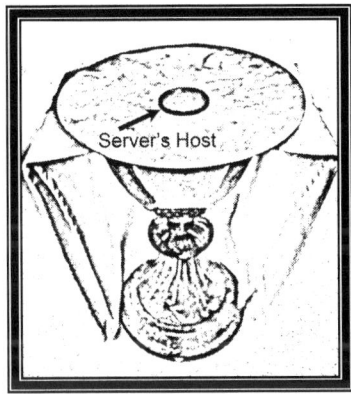

Fig. 2.12 – Server's Host in the middle of the paten

If there is a single server or a very small number of servers or communicants to be communicated from new hosts (not reserved sacrament), then this host (or these hosts) may be placed on the paten. This must be a sufficiently small number of people's hosts that the priest will be able to manage, as they will be placed on the corporal to the right of the chalice after the offering of the host. A single host for a server is the ideal number for this approach. If a ciborium is to be used, or no new sacrament, other than the priest's host, is to be consecrated, then this step is omitted.

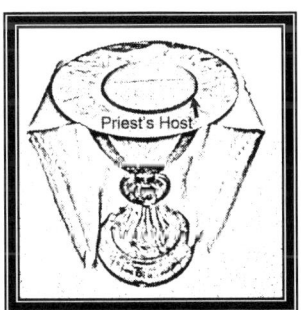

2.13 – The priest's host placed in the center of the paten (over the server's host, if any)

Next the priest places the priest's host in the center of the Paten. See Fig. 2.13 above.

HOW TO SAY MASS IN THE ANGLICAN RITE

Fig. 2.14 – Pall on top of the paten

Next the pall is placed on top of the paten, as in Fig. 2.14 above. In the event that there is no chalice veil available, this is the final step.

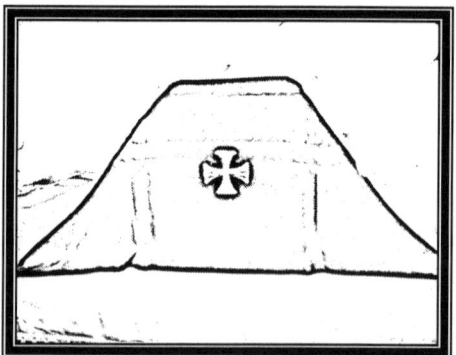

Fig. 2.15 – Chalice veil over the stacked chalice

Next the chalice veil is placed over the entire stack. The chalice veil is in the liturgical color for the mass.

The burse (see Fig. 2.16) is a small flat "wallet" in the color matching the chalice veil. The corporal is placed inside the burse, and the burse is placed on top of the chalice. (See Fig. 2.17.)

OBJECTS FOR SACRED USE IN THE MASS

*Fig. 2.16 – The corporal is placed in the burse.
In this figure, this action is shown as later in the mass when
the priest places the corporal in the burse after communion.*

*Fig. 2.17 – The burse is placed on top of the veiled chalice.
In this figure, as in Fig. 2.16 above, this action is shown
as later in the mass when the priest places the corporal
in the burse after communion.*

Next a priest, deacon, or sub-deacon carries the Sacred Vessels to the altar, if they are to be there for mass, or to the credence table, if they are to be there for mass. The proper vesture is house dress or choir dress, with the biretta. Alternatively, if they are the Sacred Ministers or other attendants wearing vestments for mass, they may be vested for mass with the biretta. The bishop, if wearing mass vestments, wears the mitre. The biretta is not removed while carrying the Sacred Vessels. See Fig. 2.18 for the manner of carrying the Sacred Vessels.

HOW TO SAY MASS IN THE ANGLICAN RITE

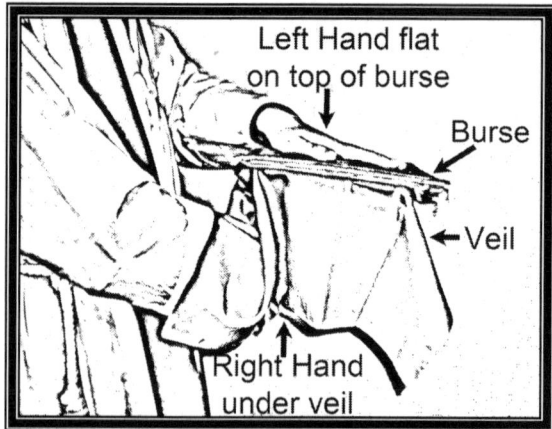

Fig. 2.18 – Method of carrying the Sacred Vessels.

The priest (or deacon or sub-deacon, hereafter simply referred to as the priest), takes the vessels in the manner of Fig. 2.18 and departs the sacristy. He may be alone or accompanied. He genuflects (if the blessed sacrament is reserved) or else bows upon entering the sanctuary (again, without removing the biretta), ascends the altar steps, and sets the Sacred Vessels on the altar steps to the epistle side. He then takes the burse off the top of the veil, opens it and removes the corporal. This he spreads on the center of the altar, unfolding it in the reverse order of the manner in which it is folded (see the section on mass linens above). The burse is placed standing up vertical on the Gospel side in a convenient location and becomes part of the altar decoration. See Fig. 2.19 below for placement, and Fig. 2.20.

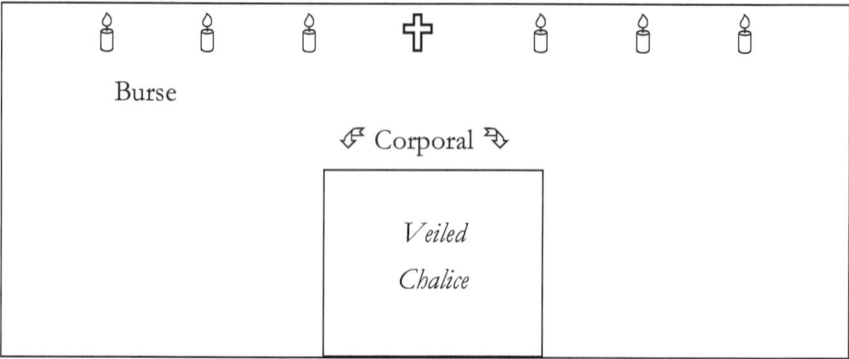

Fig. 2.19 – Placement of the Sacred Vessels on the altar.

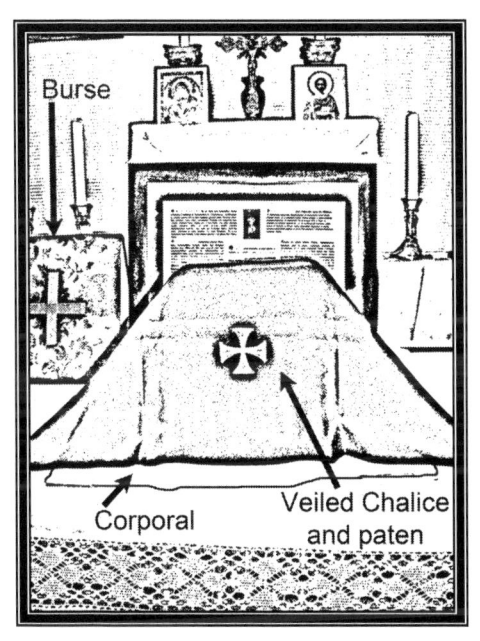

Fig. 2.20 – An example of the corporal, veiled chalice, and burse on the altar.

If the priest carrying the Sacred Vessels passes another altar at which mass is being said, and the elevations are being done at the consecration, then he genuflects, still holding the vessels and without removing the biretta, until the elevations have been completed.

If the Sacred Vessels are to be placed on the credence table, then all is as above, except that he goes to the credence table and places them there. He leaves the burse on top of the veiled chalice and does not spread the corporal. All items on the credence table are then covered by the humeral veil, if one is to be used in the mass.

After he has placed the Sacred Vessels, he genuflects or bows, removing the biretta, and then taking the biretta again, he returns to the sacristy.

OTHER OBJECTS FOR THE MASS

In addition to the Sacred Vessels, there are several other essential and useful items for the mass. These are outlined below.

Lavabo Pitcher and Bowl:

Fig. 2.21 – Lavabo pitcher and bowl

The lavabo pitcher and bowl are used in the mass to wash the priest's fingers. The lavabo towel (see mass linens above) is used to dry the fingers. The bishop uses a Ewer and Basin, which is a larger version of the pitcher and bowl. The pitcher should be quite small, approximately the size of a cruet. A water cruet may double as a lavabo pitcher if need be. The bowl should be the size that can be carried in the hand. The pitcher and bowl may be made out of metal, stone, or glass.

Cruets:

Fig. 2.22 – Cruets. The wine cruet is marked "V" and the water cruet is marked "A."

OBJECTS FOR SACRED USE IN THE MASS

Cruets are small bottles for holding the altar wine and water for the mass. They may made of class/crystal, metal, or stone. They sit on the credence table until needed, and are brought to the altar by the servers.

Flagon:

Fig. 2.23 – A flagon.

A flagon is an optional item. It is a large pitcher, usually of metal, for holding the altar wine. It may be used in lieu of a wine cruet during the mass for added solemnity, or may be used as a means of filling cruets in between masses.

Sanctus Bells:

Fig. 2.24 – A typical style of Sanctus bells.

Sanctus bells, or altar bells, are used during the mass as indicated in the rubrics. A typical style, as in Fig. 2.24 above, consists of four bells and is rung by being shaken by the hand. The altar bell need only be a single bell, however. The sanctus bells are also different from the bell that is rung once before the mass to indicate that the celebrant is entering the sanctuary from the sacristy.

Thurible:

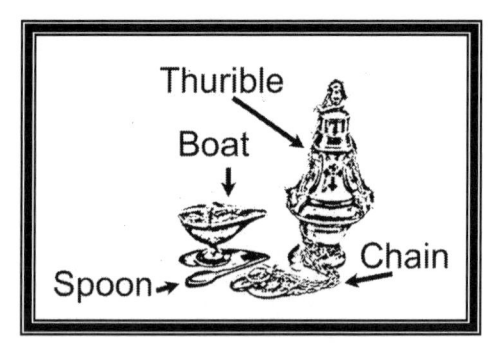

Fig. 2.25 – Thurible, Boat, and Spoon

The thurible is the pot for burning incense. It is on a chain so that it may be swung. The top of the thurible raises by means of another chain. The boat is a covered dish for containing the incense to be put into the thurible. The spoon is used to transfer incense from the boat to the thurible. Additionally, a pair of charcoal tongs is useful for manipulating the charcoal inside the thurible.

The thurifer should ensure that there is enough incense for the mass in the boat, as well as enough coals in the thurible to last through the mass. Extra charcoal may be kept nearby if needed. The thurifer may sit in the sanctuary with the servers, or may remain in the sacristy until needed.

Fig. 2.26 – Method of carrying the thurible.

The thurible is typically carried by the top of the chains in the right hand, as in Fig. 2.26. If there is no boat bearer, then the boat is carried in the left hand. Fig. 2.27 gives the method for holding the thurible when it is open, for example when it is presented to the celebrant to put incense in. In this case, the left hand is used to pull the chain to open the top of the thurible. The thurible should be held at an appropriate height for the celebrant putting incense into it. If necessary, the grip of the right hand may be changed to further down the chain.

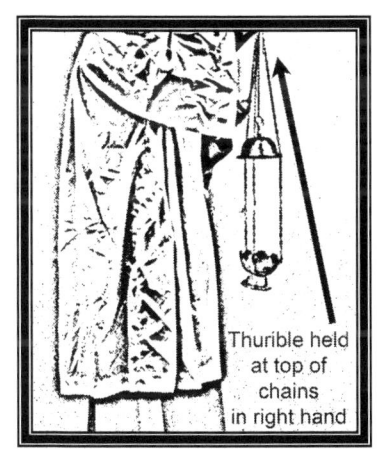

Fig. 2.27 – Thurible held in the open position.

Fig. 2.28 – Method of swinging a thurible.

To swing the thurible in a procession, the thurifer may use the holding position of Fig. 2.26, or the position of Fig. 2.28. The position of Fig. 2.28

is used when censing the altar, the sacrament, etc., as it gives much more control. The right hand holds the chain closer to the thurible, and the top part of the chain, now loose, is held by the left hand.

Processional Cross and Torches:

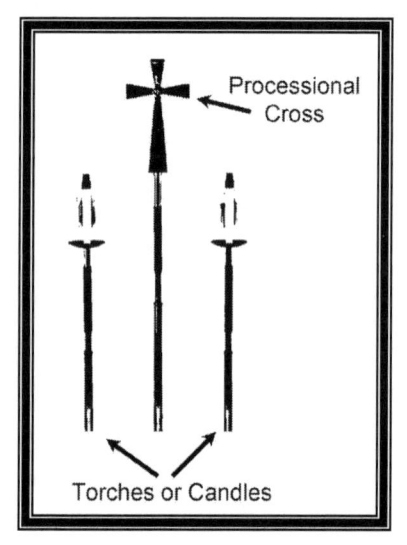

2.29 – Processional cross between two torches

The processional cross is used, as its name implies, in the procession of the mass. It is not used at a low mass. It may be wood or metal. It goes at the head of the procession and is carried by a crucifer. Most solemnly, it is flanked by two acolytes carrying torches or candles, and the cross is carried by the Sub-Deacon of the Cross (not the Sub-Deacon of the Mass) vested in choir dress or tunicle.

The cross of a Cathedral Chapter may be carried in front of the Chapter, and a second cross at the front of the procession is used only if the procession is particularly long. For a mass celebrated by an Archbishop, the cross is carried directly in front of the Archbishop with the front of the cross turned towards the Archbishop. In that case as well, a second cross at the front of the procession is used only if the procession is particularly long.

OBJECTS FOR SACRED USE IN THE MASS

Missal, Evangeliarium, and Epistolarium:

The Missal is the book from which the mass is said. For all masses except a pontifical high mass or pontifical sung mass, the missal is on the altar on the epistle side before the mass. A clergyman or acolyte places it on the altar, and it is carried in the manner of Fig. 2.30. For a pontifical high or sung mass, it is carried in the procession by the Book Bearer.

Fig. 2.30 – Father Francis shows the manner of carrying the missal. The top of the book rests against the chest.

The Evangeliarium is the book from which the Gospels are read or chanted, and the Epistolarium is the book from which the Epistles and Lessons are read or chanted. These are placed in accordance with the rubrics (see the sections for the various masses)

Communion Paten:

The communion paten is an optional but encouraged item (which may be required by local ordinance). See Fig. 2.31. It consists of a paten, usually larger than the one used on the altar, on a small handle. An acolyte often holds it under the chin of the person receiving communion, whether clergy or laity. It is not used for the celebrant. In some local uses, it is held in the right hand of the communicant under their own chin and passed down after they receive communion.

Its function is clear: to catch any falling crumbs from the host during communion. After the faithful have been communicated, it is taken by an acolyte to the altar to be purified with the other vessels. It is not, however, considered a sacred vessel.

Fig. 2.31 – Communion paten

Candles:

Candles used in the mass fall into two main categories: Those on or near the altar and those that are carried. Candles on the altar consist of the primary altar candles, benediction candles, and the Paschal candle (from Easter Vigil until the Gospel of the Ascension mass). Candles that are carried consist of torches or hand-carried candles.

Torches or hand-carry candles are used by acolytes in the procession and at the consecration, according to the rubrics. Both are appropriate for those uses. Carrying a torch is a simple matter of holding it before the breast with both hands, as a flag pole. Fig. 2.32 shows the manner of carrying a candle. The right hand holds the candlestick holder, and the left hand supports the base.

Candles on the altar are between 2 and 6 in number. Their position is given in the section for the altar. Two candles are for a low mass, four candles for a Bishop's low mass, and six for a sung or high mass. Additionally, at a pontifical high or sung mass, there may be a seventh candle placed in the center in front of or behind (depending on the physical constraints of the altar) the altar crucifix. For the Benediction with the Blessed Sacrament (Sacred Benediction), additional "benediction candles" may be added to the altar. These often consist of candelabras of

OBJECTS FOR SACRED USE IN THE MASS

6 candles each, with one candelabra placed on the Epistle side and one on the Gospel side.

Fig. 2.32 – Father Francis shows how to carry a candle

Holy Water Pot and Aspergillum:

The holy water post and aspergillum (sprinkler) are used any time there is a need to sprinkle holy water. This is most frequently done at the principal solemn mass on Sundays in the asperges.

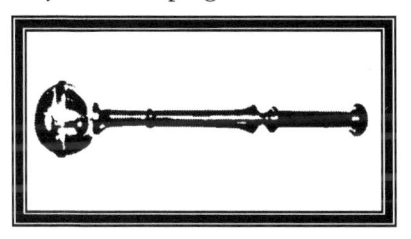

Fig. 2.33 – Aspergillum (Sprinkler)

Fig. 2.34 – Holy water pot

Tabernacle:

The tabernacle is what is used to reserve the consecrated hosts. It is most properly placed on the altar in the center back, but may be in other suitable locations if the physical constraints so require. The tabernacle may be made of wood or metal. It is usually lined with silk. When the host is reserved, it must have a corporal spread on the bottom. Also, when the host is reserved, the tabernacle must be veiled. It may optionally have an over-veil in the liturgical color to go over the primary tabernacle veil. The tabernacle must be secure, and if it does not itself have a lock, it must be housed within another container that can be locked, less the sacrament be profaned.

Fig. 2.35 – A style of tabernacle, shown without veil.

Host Box:

The host box is for storing hosts before the communion. It is usually present on the credence table, so that additional hosts may be added to the ciborium as needed according to the attendance. It may be made of metal, glass, or stone.

Fig. 2.36 – A style of host box.

OBJECTS FOR SACRED USE IN THE MASS

Bugia:

The bugia is an item particular to a pontifical sung or high mass. It is a candle on a handle, which may be a short stick, and is carried by the Candle Bearer. Outside of a pontifical solemn function, it is not used.

Fig. 2.37 – A style of bugia

Monstrance:

The monstrance is used for the Sacred Benediction. Additionally, mass may be celebrated in the presence of the exposed Blessed Sacrament displayed on a throne. Please see the Rituale. The monstrance has a stem and some form of decorated portion around a central chamber. The chamber has a glass front and some means, often a screw cap, of entry in the back for placing the sacrament during the Benediction or exposition.

Fig. 2.38 – A style of monstrance

BLESSINGS OF OBJECTS

All objects used in the mass should be blessed. However, if they are not blessed, but used anyway, they retain a sacred nature and should be treated as such.

The Chalice and Paten must be consecrated by a Bishop or a priest so empowered using the form in the Rituale and the Pontificale. They may be blessed by a priest until then using the form for blessing sacred ornaments or vessels in the Rituale.

Candles have a special blessing, found both in the Missale and the Rituale. Mass linens, icons and statues, the tabernacle, and many other objects also have their own special blessings. Crosses are blessed in a simple or solemn rite, both in the Rituale. All other items for which there is not a special blessing prescribed in the Rituale should be blessed with the form for blessing sacred ornaments or vessels.

PURIFYING AND CLEANING
MASS LINENS AND SACRED VESSELS

The chalice, paten, communion paten, and ciborium (if not being reserved) are purified by the priest during the ablutions in the mass. This process is explained in detail in the sections on the actions of the mass.

The corporal and purificator must be purified by a priest only before they may be laundered. They are purified by washing them three times in the sacrarium. The sacrarium is a sink, usually in the sacristy, with pipes that go to bare earth, not into the sewer system. This is used for disposing of particles of the consecrated hosts, holy oils, ashes from burned cleaning tissues and bread, etc.

Once the priest washes the corporal and purificator by hand in the sacrarium three times, they may be laundered. The priest should be certain within reason that the particles of consecrated elements have been removed as much as is humanly possible before they are commercially or privately laundered.

In the event that no sacrarium is available, the priest must purify the corporal and purificator in a large bowl set aside exclusively for this purpose. They are washed by hand in the water three times, and the water in this bowl is to be poured on bare earth. Then the linens may be washed commercially or privately.

The lavabo towel needs not to be purified first unless it came in contact with the consecrated elements or holy oils. Then it must be purified in the same manner as the corporal and purificator. The same applies to the pall.

PASCHAL CANDLE

Fig. 2.39 – Close-up of the center of a Paschal Candle

The Paschal candle is a large white candle for the Paschal season. It is lit from the new fire on the Easter Vigil (see the section on Rites of Holy Week). It remains lit at every mass from Easter Vigil until the appointed time in the Gospel on the Feast of the Ascension. From then on it is not lit again. During the time it is lit, it is on a floor stand on the Gospel side near the altar. After the Ascension, it is on a stand near the baptismal font. The standards for marking the candle are detailed in the rubrics for Holy Saturday in the Missale Anglicanum. Fig. 2.39 shows them in detail. A cross is inscribed (not visible), and five grains of incense, representing the five wounds of Christ, are inserted along the traced cross. Other markings are the year and the Greek letters alpha and omega.

DISPOSAL OF SACRED OBJECTS

Items coming in contact with the Precious Body and Blood should be purified as described above and elsewhere in this book. Items contacting sacred oils should also be cleaned with bread or paper tissues. If cloths are used for this purpose, then they should be purified in the sacrarium before being laundered. Paper tissues and bread used for cleaning holy oils should be burned. The ashes should be washed down the sacrarium (also called the piscina), buried (preferably in consecrated ground) or, if needed, scattered (preferably on consecrated ground).

For other items, the rubrics tend to be silent. The prevailing concept, though, is that all items with a sacred character, especially those that have been used in worship, must not simply be thrown into the trash. Candles, for example, could be burned reverently in lamps and then buried (or simply buried). Some items cannot be burned due to health and environmental concerns, and similarly some items should not be buried. Physical realities should be taken into account, and at the same time, all care must be exercised to ensure that, as much as is humanly possible within the constraints of these physical realities, that the objects be treated with due reverence.

Vestments

COLOR OF THE VESTMENTS

Vestments are in the color of the mass. This is given according to the liturgical calendar and the rubrics. In general, the following rules apply:

White:	Paschaltide, Maundy Thursday, Feasts of Our Lord, Feasts of Our Lady, Feasts of Confessors
Red:	Pentecost, Feasts of the Holy Spirit, Feasts of the Apostles, Feasts of Martyrs, Palm Sunday liturgy (but not the mass)
Purple:	Advent, Lent, Pre-Lent, Ember Days, most Vigils, Rogation Days, any other penitential occasion
Green:	Trinity Season, Christmas cycle
Black:	Masses of the Dead, Good Friday liturgy (but not the mass)
Rose:	Gaudete and Laetare Sundays and ferial masses during those weeks
Marian Blue:	Feasts of Our Lady

The following substitutions may be made:

White:	May be worn in lieu of red, green, or Marian blue.
Gold:	May be worn in lieu of white, red, green, or Marian blue.
Silver:	May be worn in lieu of white only
Purple:	May be worn in lieu of rose or black.

HOW TO SAY MASS IN THE ANGLICAN RITE

LOW MASS

In a low mass, there is only one minister, the Celebrant. Other clergy sit in choir. There are one or two altar servers, and for a bishop's low mass, there ideally should be two.

Celebrant:

The celebrant wears, in order of vesting:

1. Cassock
2. Fascia (or rope cincture over the cassock)
3. Amice
4. Alb
5. Cincture
6. Stole (with the ends crossed)
7. Chasuble (fiddleback or Gothic)
8. Maniple
9. Biretta

Fig. 3.1 – A priest wearing maniple and stole before putting on the chasuble.

VESTMENTS

Fig. 3.2 – A priest wearing a chasuble
The chasuble is a fiddleback style.

Altar Server:

The altar server(s) vests in black cassock and white surplice. The surplice may be made of lace. A full surplice is recommended over the short cotta. Servers do not as a general rule wear albs, but if they wear the alb in lieu of the cassock and surplice, it must be plain and without lace or adornment.

PONTIFICAL LOW MASS

All is as described for a low mass above, except that the bishop wears the pectoral cross under the chasuble. The maniple is placed on after the prayers at the foot of the altar. The pontifical dalmatic, mitre, gloves, etc., are not used, and the crosier is not carried, though the ring is, of course, still worn. In lieu of the mitre, the bishop wears the purple biretta. The exception to this rule is that the bishop may (and should) wear the pontifical dalmatic and mitre if at a low mass he is administering the sacrament of confirmation or ordination, consecration, benediction of an abbot/abbess, or consecration of a virgin, or otherwise carrying out a special pontifical function.

HIGH MASS

In a high mass, there are three ministers, the Celebrant, Deacon, and Sub-Deacon. There are a minimum of two altar servers, but more are highly desired. Other clergy assisting wear choir dress and, if appropriate, a cope.

Celebrant:

The celebrant vests as for low mass.

Deacon:

The Deacon vests as follows:

1. Cassock
2. Fascia (or rope cincture over the cassock)
3. Amice
4. Alb
5. Cincture
6. Stole (Diaconal stole, over the left shoulder)
7. Dalmatic
8. Maniple
9. Biretta

Fig. 3.3 – A Deacon wearing Diaconal stole and maniple before putting on the Dalmatic

VESTMENTS

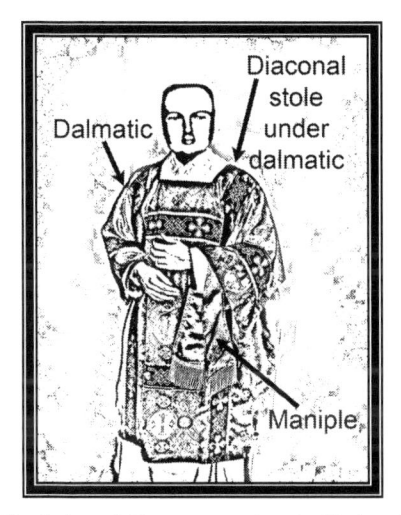

Fig. 3.4 – A Deacon wearing the Dalmatic.

Sub-Deacon:

The Deacon vests as follows:

1. Cassock
2. Fascia (or rope cincture over the cassock)
3. Amice
4. Alb
5. Cincture
6. Tunicle
7. Maniple
8. Biretta

The tunicle is the same garment in style as the dalmatic. Sometimes there may be only one bar instead of the two seen on the dalmatic, or other differences of decoration. Otherwise they are the same.

The Sub-Deacon does not wear a stole. The Sub-Deacon wears only the symbol of his office, the maniple.

Fig. 3.5 – A Sub-Deacon shown wearing the maniple before putting on the tunicle

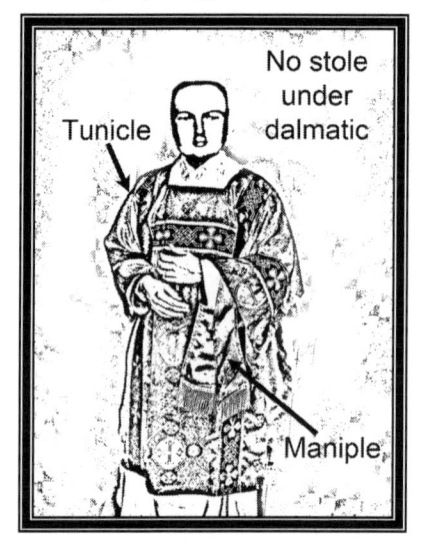

Fig. 3.6 – A Sub-Deacon shown in the tunicle. In this style, note the single bar on the tunicle, as compared to the double bar on the dalmatic of the deacon shown in Fig. 3.4.

Sub-Deacon of the Cross:

If there is a Sub-Deacon of the Cross, he optionally wears a tunicle over choir dress.

VESTMENTS

Master of Ceremonies and Assistant MC:

Cassock and surplice, with an optional cope and, for the MC, optional white gloves

Altar Servers:

Altar servers vest as for low mass.

SUNG MASS

In a sung mass, all is as High Mass, except that there is no Sub-Deacon. There may or may not be a Deacon. Some actions may optionally be changed in accordance with the rubrics, Canons, and Ceremonial.

PONTIFICAL HIGH MASS

In a pontifical high mass, the Celebrant (who is a bishop) wears full pontificals. He vests as below:

1. Cassock
2. Fascia
3. Amice
4. Alb
5. Cincture
6. Pectoral cross
7. Stole (with the ends straight)
8. Pontifical Dalmatic
9. Episcopal gloves
10. Episcopal ring (over the gloves)
11. Chasuble (fiddleback or Gothic)
12. Maniple (placed on after the prayers at the foot of the altar)
13. Pallium (if a jurisdictional Archbishop)
14. Mitre (with zucchetto underneath)
15. Crosier (in left hand as called for in the rubrics)

Fig. 3.7 – A bishop before placing on the dalmatic (at high mass or sung mass) or the chasuble at low mass. The maniple is shown in the drawing, but it is not placed on under after the prayers at the foot of the altar.

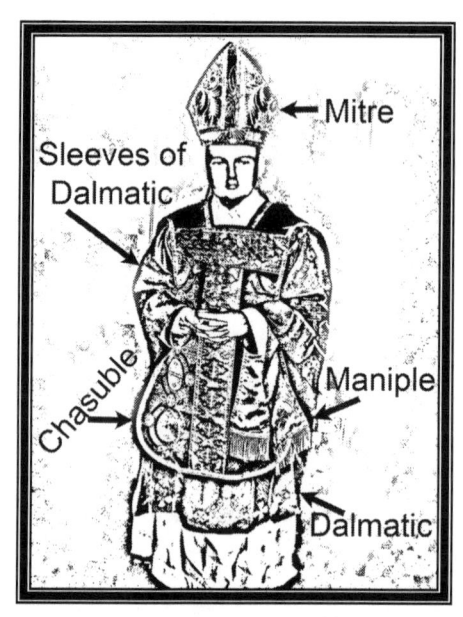

Fig. 3.8 – A bishop vested in full pontificals for high or sung mass. Note the pontifical dalmatic visible underneath the chasuble. With the fiddleback style of chasuble as in the drawing, the sleeves of the dalmatic are particularly visible as well.

VESTMENTS

Note on the Bishop's Mitre

The mitre comes in three types:

Precious: Typically jeweled, but otherwise richly embellished. It is worn only by jurisdictional bishops. It is not worn when their jurisdictional superior is present. It is also not worn when the liturgical color is purple, rose, or black. It may be optionally exchanged for the golden mitre in the mass from the Kyrie to the Offertory, when the Bishop again takes the mitre to go to the altar.

Golden: This mitre is gold in color. It may be embellished with an orphrey or a very simple symbol. Any more than this, and it becomes a precious mitre. A white mitre with an orphrey also falls in this category of mitre. It is worn by all bishops. In a pontifical mass, if the celebrant wears the precious mitre, then the other bishops in mitre must wear the golden mitre.

Simplex: This mitre is plain white with no embellishment, except that it may have red fringe on the ends of the lapits. It is the only mitre permitted to a mitred abbot. It is worn by all other bishops when the celebrant in the mass wears the golden mitre as his only mitre, unless invited to wear the golden mitre. It is also mandatory on Good Friday, Ash Wednesday, at the blessings at the Candlemass, and at Masses for the Dead.

Note on the Pontifical Gloves

The pontifical gloves are worn in accordance with the Canons and Ceremonial. They should be in the color of the mass. White gloves, however, may be used when the color is anything but purple, rose, or black. Purple gloves may be worn when the color is purple or rose. White gloves are used with Marian Blue vestments. Gloves are not worn when the color is black (Masses of the Dead and Good Friday). The pontifical ring goes over the right ring finger as usual, but over the glove. They are worn until the bishop washes his hands at the offertory, and they are taken again when he returns to the throne after the Ablutions. They may optionally be left off if the bishop will not be giving the Pontifical Blessing.

Note on the Pontifical Dalmatic

The pontifical dalmatic may be like any other dalmatic, or it may be made of a thinner material. Its purpose is to indicate the fullness of the bishop's Holy Orders. It is in the liturgical color of the day. A white or gold pontifical dalmatic may be worn under a gold, silver, white, red, green, or Marian Blue chasuble. A silver dalmatic may worn under a silver or white chasuble. A purple dalmatic may be worn under a purple, rose, or black chasuble. Dalmatics in red, green, rose, or black may only be worn under chasubles of matching color.

Note on the Gremial

The gremial is a cloth that goes in the lap of the bishop while he sits. It is in the liturgical color of the mass. A white or gold gremial may be used when the color is white, red, green, or Marian blue. A silver gremial may be used when the color is white. A purple gremial may be used when the color is purple or rose. A rose gremial is used only with rose vestments. The gremial is not used at masses of the dead.

Deacon:

As for any high mass.

Sub-Deacon:

As for any high mass.

VESTMENTS

Sub-Deacon of the Cross:
As for any high mass.

Master of Ceremonies and Assistant MC:
As for low mass.

Altar Servers:
As for any high mass.

Assistant Deacons:
Dalmatic over cassock and surplice.

Assistant Priest:
Cope over cassock and surplice.

Bishop's Chaplains:
The chaplains, i.e., the Mitre Bearer, Crosier Bearer, Book Bearer, and Candle Bearer, vest in choir dress and may wear the cope. All other attendants of the bishop vest in choir dress and may wear the cope.

PONTIFICAL SUNG MASS

All is as a pontifical mass, except that there is no Sub Deacon. Various elements may be omitted as necessary provided they are in accordance with the rubrics, Canons, and Ceremonial.

PUTTING ON THE AMICE

The amice is put on over the cassock before the alb. It must be worn when the alb is worn. Fig. 3.9 – 3.12 show the steps for putting it on.

Fig. 3.9 – First the amice is held in front by the top corners, with the ties on the top corners, hanging down. The cross on the amice is kissed before the next step.

Fig. 3.10 – The amice is taken over the head and set on the shoulders, with the ties in front.

VESTMENTS

Fig. 3.11 – The ends are crossed in front.

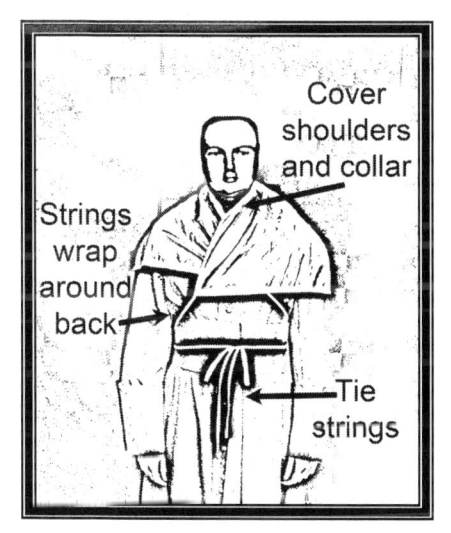

Fig. 3.12 – The ends are wrapped around behind, brought back to the front, and tied in a bow. The amice should completely cover the collar of the cassock.

TYING A CINCTURE OVER THE ALB

The cincture is tied according to the following method. It should hang on the left or center for Deacons, as their stole hangs on the right. It may be in the front, left, or center for all others. Additionally, there is a useful method detailed below for creating loops useful for holding the ends of the stole for priests and bishops.

Fig. 3.13 – First, find the middle of the cincture.

Fig. 3.14 – Take the middle of the cincture around your back. Hold it in one hand as shown, and hold the loose ends in the other hand.

VESTMENTS

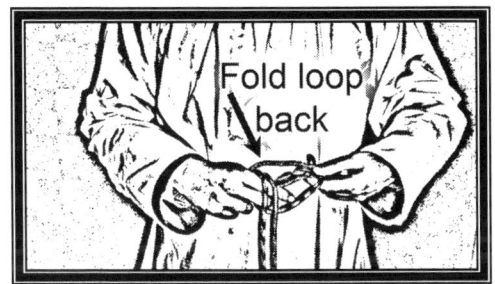

Fig. 3.15 – Fold the loop in the center of the cincture back on itself as shown.

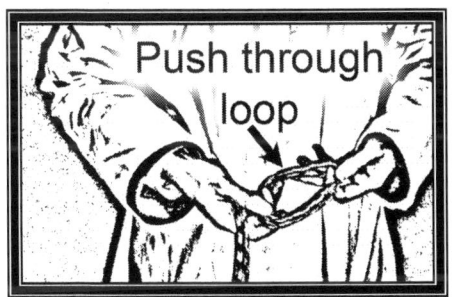

Fig. 3.16 – Push the two strands of the rope near the middle though the folded back loop. This is to make a Lark's head knot.

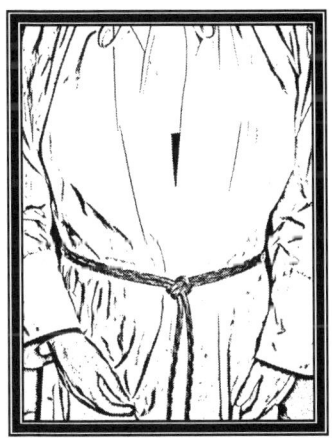

Fig. 3.17 – Tighten the cincture. The cincture is now tied and may be placed on either side of the body, or left in the center. For Celebrants, the following "loop" addition is recommended to keep the ends of the stole tidy and in place. For that addition, leave the knot in the center of the body as shown in this drawing.

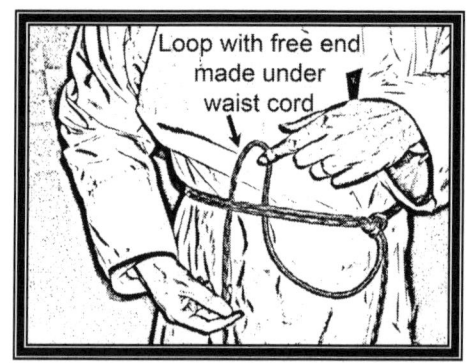

Fig. 3.18 – Take one of the free ends and push it up under the waist cord as shown, making a loop above the waist cord.

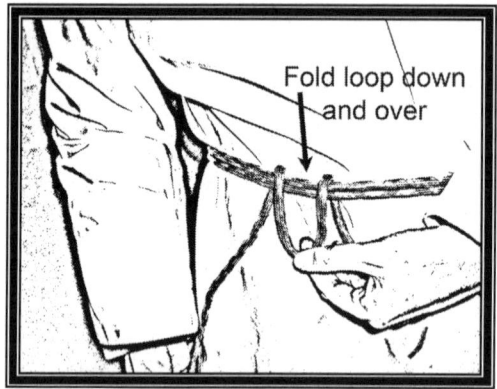

Fig. 3.19 – Fold this loop down over the waist cord.

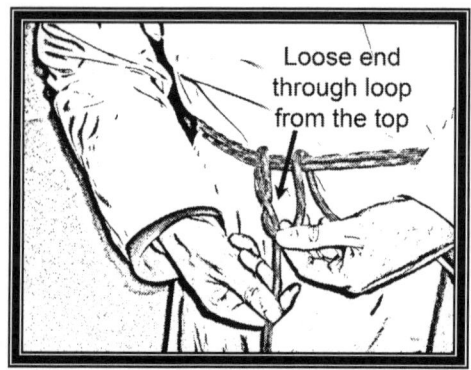

Fig. 3.20 – Take the loose end and put it through the loop from the top as shown. Then tighten it. This will be a type of slip-knot.

Fig. 3.12 – Repeat this for the other side, and the result should be as above. Then the ends of the stole are placed into the loops. The free ends are pulled to tighten the slip-knots, thereby tightening the loops that the stole ends are going through. Here the cincture is ready for a stole.

VESTING PRAYERS

The vesting prayers are found in the Rituale. They should be said by the Celebrant and, if applicable, the Deacon and Sub-Deacon. Each prayer may be said as its corresponding vestment is put on, or all prayers may be said at once prior to vesting.

Vesting begins with washing the hands, for which there is a prayer in the vesting prayers. A priest washes his hands three times: once in the sacristy before mass, one at the lavabo, and at the ablutions. A bishop does likewise, except at a high mass and, optionally, at a low mass. At a high mass, a bishop washes his hands four times: once before the mass in the sacristy, at the throne before going to the altar at the offertory, at the lavabo, and at the ablutions.

HOW TO SAY MASS IN THE ANGLICAN RITE

ALTAR SERVERS
ಬಂಡ

Altar servers are an essential part of the mass. They, as their name implies, serve at the altar. They make the work of the priest much easier, improve the flow of the mass, and contribute to the dignity and solemnity of worship. A priest can celebrate without servers (see the section on that subject under Special Occasions and Circumstances), but this is not ideal. This section details the various attendants at the mass.

Master of Ceremonies:

The Master of Ceremonies (MC) is only present in High or Sung masses. He is the chief of all attendants. His responsibility is to know the jobs of everyone from the Celebrant to the altar servers so that he can ensure that the actions and flow of the mass take place. He kneels only during the Prayers at the Foot of the Altar, the Confessional and Absolution, and the Consecration and Elevation. He assists at the missal in high mass or sung mass, as well as in pontifical high or sung mass if there is no Assistant Priest. His full duties are detailed, as with the servers, in the sections for the various masses.

Assistant Master of Ceremonies:

The AMC assists the MC as needed.

Acolytes (Altar Servers):

The acolytes, or simply called, the altar servers, assist the Ministers and others as needed. Their place is to take care of the credence table, and bring the ministers what they need. When they do so, they may follow one of the following two approaches:

1) Kiss the cruets only before handing them on at the Offertory and when taking them back.
2) Kiss all objects before handing them over.
3) Kiss no objects.

In all cases above, he kisses first the object and then the hand of the Celebrant (or whomever he is giving it to) before giving the item. When taking the item back, he kisses first the hand of the Celebrant and then the object. If he does not kiss the objects, then he does not kiss the hand. The kisses are completely omitted in Masses of the Dead. Whether or not the kisses are done, the server bows after handing the object (or after the kisses), and the person receiving it bows back (except for a jurisdictional bishop, who blesses the server with the sign of the cross).

Altar servers are also in charge of ringing the Sanctus bells. This is detailed in the sections for the various masses.

When servers present the cruets, it is done in one of two ways. In either case, they hold the cruet in a single hand with the handle facing the person to whom they are giving it. The tops are always taken off of the cruets at the credence table.

1) Two servers, each presenting a single cruet. In this case, they either place their left hand at the base of the cruet or hold it against their breast.

2) One server presenting both cruets. In this case, he holds the wine cruet in his right hand and the water cruet in the left. He first presents the wine cruet and then transfers the water cruet from the left hand to the right. He accepts the wine cruet back in his left hand and hands the wine cruet from his right.

After mass, the servers should wash, drain, and dry each cruet. Before mass, after they have been filled, they should be dried on the outside. Any time they become wet on the outside, the servers should wipe them off at the credence towel.

At the lavabo, the server brings the bowl, pitcher, and towel. Two servers accomplish this by one carrying the bowl (in the left hand) and pitcher (in the right hand) and the other the towel (held either with both hands before the breast or in the right hand, the left hand being held against the breast). A single server carries the pitcher in the right hand, the bowl in the left, and has the towel draped over the left arm. The water is poured over the priest's fingers from the pitcher into the bowl, which is held underneath the priest's fingers.

Thurifer:

The thurifer is in charge of the thurible. He swings the incense in the procession, and brings it to the celebrant when required in the mass. He also carries it in the Gospel procession and holds it when the Deacon is not incensing the Book of Gospels. If there is no Boat Bearer, he also presents the boat of incense. During the elevations at a high mass (and optionally at a low mass), he kneels and censes the sacrament (except at a Requiem, in which case this function is done by the Sub-Deacon).

When the thurifer brings the thurible and boat (if there is no boat bearer) to the Celebrant, he hold the boat in his left hand and gives it to the person to the Celebrant's right. He uses his left hand to pull the chain to raise the top of the thurible 3-4 inches (enough space to put the incense into the thurible). He then hold the thurible at a convenient height for the Celebrant to put the incense in. If necessary, his left hand is used to arrange the chains out of the way. Else, his left hand is on his breast. When the incense has been blessed, he lowers the top of the thurible.

To present the thurible, the manner of so doing depends on whether the person to whom he is handing it is going to use it or not (in the latter case, they take the thurible and give it to the person who will use it). If they are not using it themselves, then the thurifer holds the thurible at the top of the chains with one hand. If, however, the person is to use it himself, such as the Celebrant, then the thurifer hold the chains with two hands. The right hand holds the top of the chains, and the left hand holds the bottom of the chains. The lower portion of the chains are placed into the Celebrant's right hand, and the upper part into his left hand.

Boat Bearer:

The boat bearer is an optional server in charge of carrying the boat filled with incense. He accompanies the thurifer.

Crucifer or Sub-Deacon of the Cross:

This server is in charge of carrying the processional cross. Only if he is commissioned as a Sub-Deacon or otherwise licensed to act as such does he fill the role as Sub-Deacon of the Cross and wear the tunicle. Otherwise he vests in choir dress. In either case, the action of carrying the cross is the same. The figure is carried facing forward except in a pontifical mass celebrated by an archbishop. In this case, the cross is carried immediately before the archbishop with the figure (front of the cross) facing him. In this case, there is only another cross at the front of the procession if it is particularly long, and if so, then the figure on that cross faces forward.

AT A PONTIFICAL MASS

These attendants, known as the Bishop's Chaplains, appear only at a pontifical high or sung mass. They process behind the bishop, stand in front of the throne while he is at the throne, and follow behind him when he moves. At the altar, they stand on the pavement in front of and facing the altar, behind the Assistant Deacons. When the chaplains are carrying their special item, they do not genuflect, but only bow. Neither do they kneel when they are carrying their special item. To kneel at the consecration, they must first put their items they are holding away and then return to their place. Most properly, the crucifer is flanked by two acolytes, each carrying torches or candles.

Mitre Bearer:

The Mitre Bearer carries the bishop's mitre when it is not being worn. A vimpa, a white scarf similar to a humeral veil, is worn over the shoulders. He holds the mitre with both hands through the vimpa. The mitre is given to him flat with the point at the top towards him and the lapits on the top. He holds the mitre by the bottom, flat, with the top towards him. Alternatively, he holds it vertically, allowing the top to rest against his chest and the lapits to hang down. He presents the mitre to the bishop (or to the Assistant Deacon) flat, exactly as described above in the manner for holding it flat. If he holds the mitre, he should be standing in his appointed place. If he is to sit, then he must put the mitre down on a table.

Crosier Bearer:

The Crosier Bearer carries the Bishop's crosier when it is not being held by the Bishop. Like the mitre bearer, he has a vimpa and holds the crosier with both hands through the vimpa. The crosier is given to him with the crook at the top facing towards him. He holds the crosier with the crook still facing towards him. He takes it directly from the Bishop and gives it directly to the Bishop.

Book Bearer

The Book Bearer carries the Missal in procession. He stands holding it while the Bishop is at the throne when the bishop is not reading or singing from it. He holds the book for the Bishop to read from when he is reading. The Assistant Priest, however, takes the book and holds it when the Bishop is to sing. If the Bishop merely intones the beginning of a piece of service music to be picked up by the choir, then the Book Bearer holds the book. If the Bishop is standing, then the Book Bearer stands and holds the book by the bottom with both hands, allowing it to rest against his chest. If the Bishop is sitting while reading, then he kneels and holds the book by its bottom with both hands, allowing it to rest against the forehead.

Candle Bearer

The Candle Bearer carries the bugia, a ceremonial candlestick. The Candle Bearer stands in his appointed place next to the book when the Bishop is reading or singing from it.

Gremial Bearer

The Gremial Bearer's duty is to take off and put on the gremial when the Bishop stands and sits, or if there are Assistant Deacons, then to take and hold the gremial when it is not in use. This attendant is needed only if the gremial is in use, and may also easily be done by an altar server with other duties.

Train Bearer

The Train Bearer is needed only if the Bishop wears a vestment with a train, or that otherwise forms an effective train by its length. His duty is to carry the train behind the Bishop whenever the Bishop walks, and to arrange the train when the Bishop sits or stands upon arrival.

BOWS AND GENUFLECTIONS

The profound bow is made by bowing forward very low (so that it would be possible to touch the knees). This is never made by an altar server. It is always made standing and is by, for example, the clerics reading the *Confiteor*.

The medium bow is made by inclining the head and shoulders. This is the bow made during the *Confiteor* while kneeling. It is also the bow that is made when passing in front of the altar cross if the sacrament is not reserved, or if the server is carrying something.

The simple bow is made by inclining the head only. It is made to the cross in the sacristy, to the Celebrant or Deacon when handing anything to them, when bowing to the choir in clergy, or before and after incensing anyone.

A genuflection is made by bending the right knee so that it touches the ground. It is made when passing in front of the altar cross if the sacrament is reserved, during the proper locations in the Creed and Last Gospel, and other locations as required in the rubrics. Everyone approaching a bishop at the throne or faldstool genuflects upon arrival, except for a Prelate, who bows low. A genuflection is not done by anyone who is holding an object, unless specifically directed. The servers always genuflect when the Celebrant does, unless there is an except noted in the rubrics.

A double genuflection is sometimes referred to. This is simply kneeling.

Bows to the Clergy in Choir are done by servers when they pass the clergy seated in choir if they must pass them to get to the sanctuary. Else, they genuflect to the cross (or bow if the sacrament is not reserved) first and then bow to the clergy in choir. This is a simple bow as described above. This is done anytime the clergy in choir are passed. It is also done before and after any major function, such as the singing of the Epistle or Gospel, that takes the servers from the general vicinity of the altar. They first bow to the clergy on the Gospel side, then to the Epistle side, unless the greater dignitary is seated on the Epistle side, in which case that side is bowed to first. When returning, the server bows to the side they are facing first, then to the other side.

The thurifer also bows to the clergy in choir in the same manner as above if he is ever called upon to leave the sanctuary for a duty, such as the Gospel. He first genuflects to the sacrament and then bows to the choir.

POSTURES OF THE BODY FOR ALTAR SERVERS
(which apply to all participating in the mass except when otherwise noted)

The posture of the body of all participants in the mass is of utmost importance. The greatest respect must be shown for the Holy Mass as the highest form of prayer, and hence for Almighty God. Servers must be calm, restrained, and dignified in their movement. Absolutely no unessential action should be permitted, and no one should be allowed in the sanctuary without a purpose. Anything less disgraces the sacrament and disrupts the overall action of the mass.

The following are the general postures that altar servers must learn and practice. Through practice only can these be learned in a way that they are natural and contribute to the dignity of the mass.

Standing: Servers always stand facing the altar, unless required to do otherwise. The stance is erect, but natural, with the hands held in front of the breast and joined, with palms flat against each other. If he is holding something in one hand (usually the right), then the other hand goes against his breast with palm flat. The eyes are always directed to the altar or modestly and moderately cast downward in piety.

Kneeling: The server kneels facing the altar, with hands joined as described in "standing" above. He should kneel quietly. There should be no unessential or nervous movement. All focus should be directed to the action at the altar. He should not be looking around, even if to fix his cassock behind him.

Sitting: Servers sit erect, with hands resting on the knees and legs with the knees close together. The feet should be firmly on the floor and not moving about. Legs should never be crossed. When moving from a sitting to a kneeling position, he first stands and then kneels. He never moves from the sitting position directly to the kneeling position.

Eyes: The eyes should be directed either towards the altar or modestly and moderately cast downward. The eyes should not wander about. If necessary to perform a function, the eyes are directed towards that function. The position of the eyes is a matter of humble piety.

Walking: An altar server must walk in a calm and dignified manner, neither too slow nor too fast. It must not be a distraction. The body and head should be erect, with the eyes modestly and moderately downward-cast. No genuflections should be made while walking. He must stop fully and then genuflect. All walking must be forward, never sideways or backwards. When two servers (or any two participants in the mass) are walking side-by-side, they must leave enough space for ease of movement, but as little space as possible in between them. Servers usually walk side-by-side. If the pathway requires them to go single file, then the server to the left goes in front of the other. Then when possible they return to the side-by-side position.

Hands: The hands are held while standing or kneeling together with the palms flat and against each other. The elbows are held naturally in close to the body. The hands are at approximately a 45-degree angle. The thumbs are crossed over each other. The hands should never be against the breast when joined. When holding an object with both hands, it is held in the prescribed manner more that object (if any) in both hands in front of the chest. When holding an object in one hand, the other hand is flat against the breast. While sitting, the hands are placed flat, palms down, on the knees. The hands should never be allowed to dangle by the sides.

Also, the hands and arms should not be allowed to be raised over the shoulders or head unless absolutely necessary to perform an essential function. Hands and arms should be kept still unless movement is required, and then moved in a deliberate and dignified manner.

The right hand is used to strike the breast only at the *Confiteor* and people's *Domine non sum dignus*. The right hand is held half-closed, not in a tight fist. The right hand strikes the left breast. At the *Domine non sum dignus*, the breast is struck once per time that the *Domine non sum dignus* is said.

Feet: The feet and ankles are never crossed. This is the case whether sitting or kneeling. Feet should be kept close together, approximately at shoulder width. The server should stand in a natural stance. The feet should point forward or at a 45-degree angle. Feet and legs should be kept still unless necessary to move them.

Uniformity of Action of those Serving the Mass

All participants in the Sanctuary should be uniform in action. Servers working together for a certain purpose in the mass should move in unison. Few things look worse than two servers approaching the altar together, and then genuflecting at separate times. When the servers in general all genuflect, for example, at the same time as the priest, they should all do it in unison. The same is true at the genuflection in the middle of the Creed or any other similar time. It is also true for actions other than genuflections. This is the result of careful study and diligent drilling.

When several servers are together, they are guided by the timing of the server to their right. That is, the server bows, for example, when the server to their right bows. Particularly if there are a large number of servers, it is possible for one server to give a signal to the rest.

Chief Attendant

When there are more than two servers, there may be a Chief Attendant designated. This server is in charge of the rest. He may assist at the book if this function is not performed by the Master of Ceremonies or, in a pontifical mass, by the Assistant Priest.

At the Mention of Jesus and Mary

When the Holy Name of Jesus (not Christ, but specifically the name Jesus) is mentioned, all should slightly bow the head. Clerics wearing the biretta take of the biretta and place it on their knees and bow if they are sitting. Clerics wearing the biretta touch the front right of the biretta (without taking it off) with the forefinger and middle finger of the right hand at the mention of the name of Mary.

HOW TO SAY MASS IN THE ANGLICAN RITE

LOW MASS
☙❧

In a low mass, there is only a Celebrant. Any other clergy are in choir. There may be one or two servers (acolytes). Incense is not used. Only two candles are lit on the altar. There is no chant. The ordinary of the mass is not sung by the choir. However, hymns and anthems may be superimposed on the mass by the choir and congregation, provided they are not service music (*Sanctus*, *Agnus Dei*, etc.). There is also no procession in a low mass. The Celebrant simply enters the sanctuary from the sacristy, preceded by the altar servers, once the bell to announce the start of mass has been rung.

The usual place for the server is either at the credence table or kneeling on the lowest step of the altar on the side opposite the book (unless there is some action to perform). If there are two servers, they either are at the credence table or kneeling on both sides of the altar. If the option to kneel is used, then the altar servers kneel through the entire mass except for the Gospel or if there is some duty to perform. If at the credence table, then they stand, sit, and kneel as the congregation does (and as described below). Given that the option of kneeling needs no further explanation except for their specific actions, this section assumes that the servers will be at the credence table.

The servers must prepare everything needed for the mass, including the cruets and altar cards, but not including the Sacred Vessels. This is the duty of the priest.

GUIDE TO SYMBOLS

♼ CELEBRANT

1𝕬 First Server (Acolyte)

2𝕬 Second Server (Acolyte)

HOW TO SAY MASS IN THE ANGLICAN RITE

ARRIVAL AT THE ALTAR

The server precedes the Celebrant to the altar from the sacristy. If the missal is not on the altar already, he carries it with him. When he passes in front of the altar cross, he genuflects (when the priest genuflects, standing to the right of the priest) if the sacrament is reserved, or else bows if the sacrament is not reserved or he is carrying the missal. If he is carrying the missal, he takes it to the missal stand and then returns to the pavement and stands at the right side of the priest (a second server may stand on the left).

If on the way to the altar the Blessed Sacrament is passed, then the priest and server genuflect together (or the server bows if carrying the missal). This is also done if they pass another altar at which mass is being said and the consecration and elevations are taking place. In this case, they kneel until the elevations are over, and then continue.

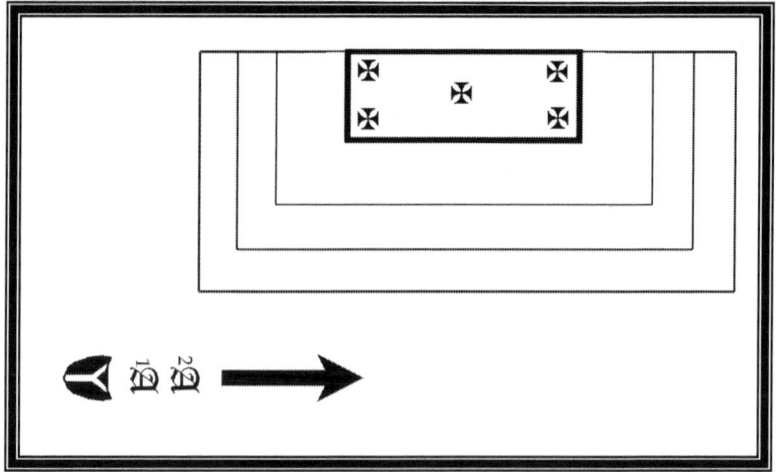

Fig. 5.1 – Entry from the sacristy

The server takes the priest's biretta when they arrive at the front of the altar and genuflect. The priest removes his biretta and hands it to the server. If the server is holding the missal, then he takes the biretta to the credence table first, and then places the missal on the stand. If there are two servers, then the second server, who goes first in the procession, carries the missal, and the first server follows. (See Fig. 5.2.) The first server stands to the right of the priest, while the second server stands to the left. See Fig. 5.1 for the procession order, Fig. 5.4 for the position

LOW MASS

before the altar. They genuflect all together with the priest only once the biretta has been placed on the credence table and the missal has been placed on the altar. The servers, though, when the pass in front of the cross, genuflect (or bow if the sacrament is not reserved or they are carrying the missal).

If the book is already on the altar, then the second server moves to the right to allow the other server and Celebrant to pass and then takes his position. (See Fig. 5.3.) The priest takes off his biretta and hands it to the first server, who takes it to the credence table. When he returns, all genuflect.

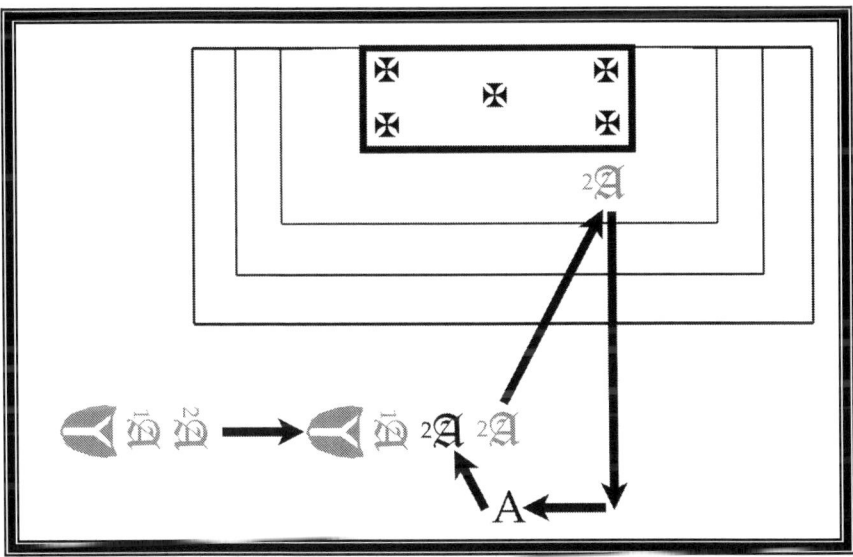

Fig. 5.2 – Pathway of the Second Server to take the missal to the stand. He bows in the center of the altar, then ascends the steps to place the missal on the stand. The Celebrant and First Server then move into their positions when the Second Server ascends the steps, the First Server genuflecting as he passes the cross (or bows if the sacrament is not reserved). After placing the missal, the Second Server comes back down the steps, genuflects at point A (or bows if the sacrament is not reserved), and goes to his place. Meanwhile, the First Server takes the biretta to the credence table.

HOW TO SAY MASS IN THE ANGLICAN RITE

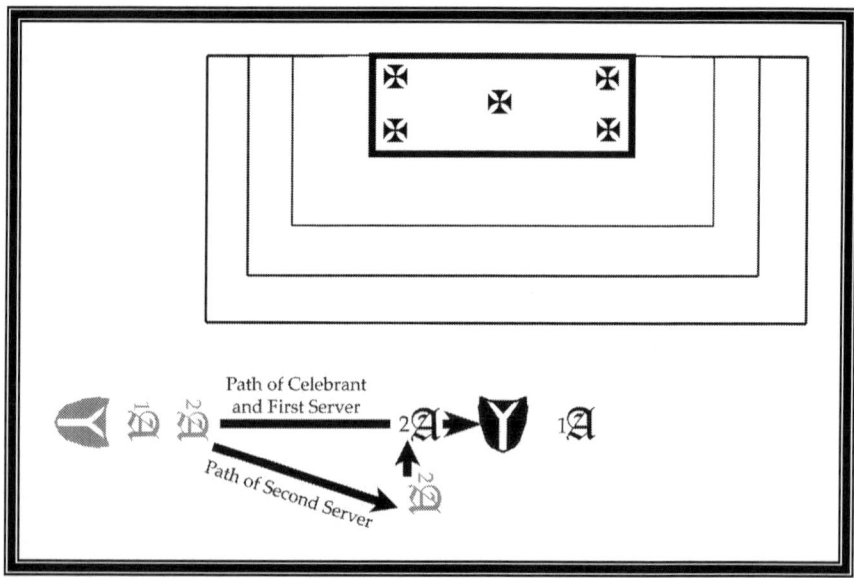

Fig. 5.3 – Path of two servers if the missal is already on the altar

PRAYERS AT THE FOOT OF THE ALTAR

The servers kneel on the pavement, and the Celebrant stands in the middle (See Fig. 5.4). Then the Prayers at the Foot of the Altar begin.

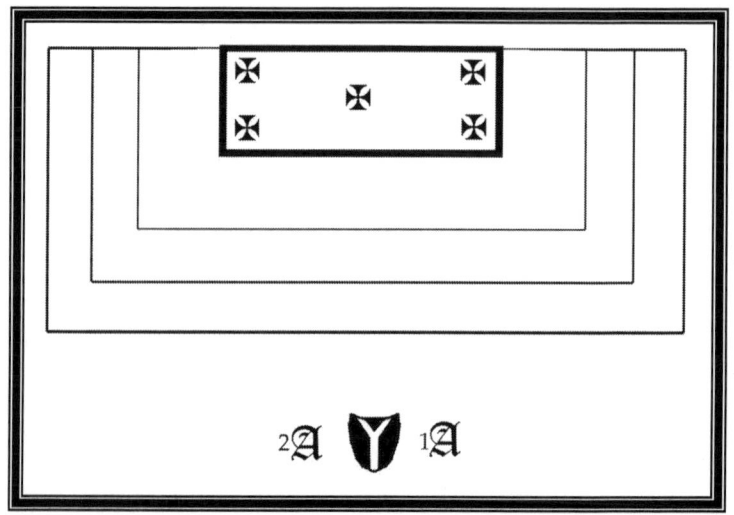

Fig. 5.4 – Position of the Celebrant and two altar servers for the Prayers at the Foot of the Altar. If there is only one server, he stands to the right of the priest.

LOW MASS

The priest makes a moderate bow as he says *In nomine Patris, et Filii, et Spiritus Sancti*. While saying this, he and all the servers may the sign of the cross on themselves. The server does not bow, but remains kneeling erect.

Sign of the Cross

The left hand is held with the palm open flat against the chest. The right hand right, with fingers joined and palm facing inward, makes the sign of the cross. First is the forehead, then the chest, then the left shoulder, then the right shoulder. The cross should be traced deliberately, not hurriedly. Also, the cross should be generous in size, not small. This is how the sign of the cross should be made by everyone, clergy and laity alike, unless otherwise specified for a specific purpose. See Fig. 5.5.

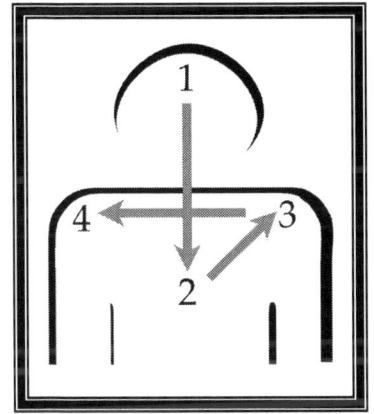

Fig. 5.5 – Order of making the Sign of the Cross

The priest, standing straight with hands joined, says the *Introibo ad altare Dei* and then recites the *Judica Me* with the servers, except on occasions when it is omitted (Masses of the Dead and from Passion Sunday until Easter).

Next the priest signs himself and says the *Adjutorum nostrum*, and the servers respond. Then the priest bows down to make his confession and says the *Confiteor* (see Fig. 5.6). When he gets to *Mea culpa*, etc., he strikes his breast three times with his half-closed right hand (not a clenched fist), once each as he says each *Mea culpa*, once as he says *Mea maxima culpa* (see Fig. 5.7).

HOW TO SAY MASS IN THE ANGLICAN RITE

Fig. 5.6 – Position of the priest during the Confiteor

Fig. 5.7 – Position of the priest during the Mea culpa. The left hand rests palm flat on the middle of the chest, and the right hand, held half-closed, strikes the upper left chest.

LOW MASS

The priest stands erect, the servers give their response, and the priest says "Amen."

Then the servers all bow to say their *Confiteor*, using the same hand positions and in the same manner as the priest (bearing in mind that the bow is not as low, as they are kneeling). Afterwards, they straighten up and the priest says the *Indulgentiam*, making the sign of the cross on himself. The servers all make the sign of the cross on themselves at the same time.

The Celebrant and servers bow moderately as they continue with the *Deus tu conversus*, etc.... They remain moderately bowing until the priest says the Collect for Purity, at which time they kneel erect. Before the Collect for Purity, the priest faces the altar and does not extend his hands at *Dominus vobiscum*, keeps them joined for *Oremus*, and then extends them for the Collect for Purity until *Through Christ our Lord*, at which time they are joined again.

Fig. 5.8 – The Priest in position for the Collect for Purity.

THE PRIEST ASCENDS THE ALTAR

The priest extends and then joins his arms in a single fluid motion while audibly saying *Oremus*. After this, he walks directly up the steps to the center of the altar. Once he begins to move towards the altar, the altar servers rise and go to their place without genuflecting (either kneeling on the lowest step or at the credence table). At their place they kneel through the Kyrie unless assisting at the missal.

Upon arrival at the altar, the priest says the *Aufer a nobis*, standing erect with hands joined. Then, he bows down at the altar with hands joined for the *Oramus te Domine*. When called for in the prayer, he places his hand on the altar (see Fig. 5.9) one on either side of the corporal, and kisses it in the center, and then continues with the prayer.

Fig. 5.9 – Bowing down with hands on the altar for the kiss in the Oramus te Domine

Having finished this prayer, the priest turns to the right, walks straight to the Epistle corner, turns to face the altar, opens the missal to the propers for the day, and prepares to read the Introit.

INTROIT

The priest makes the sign of the cross on himself (except when omitted according to the rubrics, such as Masses for the Dead, in which case the sign of the cross is made over the book). With hands joined, the priest reads the Introit. The customary form for reading the Introit is to read the Introit proper (the first part), then the Psalm (which immediately follows and is indicated by the letter "Ps." and the numbers of the Psalm), then say the *Gloria Patri*, and then repeat the Introit up until the Psalm, but not including the Psalm.

LOW MASS

When the *Gloria Patri* is said, the hands are joined and the priest bows moderately (similar to the *Confiteor*, but not so deeply). When the *Gloria Patri* is omitted according to the rubrics, the priest repeats the Introit after reading the Psalm up until, but not including the Psalm. See Fig. 5.10 for the body posture for reading the Introit and Fig. 5.11 for the position.

Fig. 5.10 – Reading the Introit

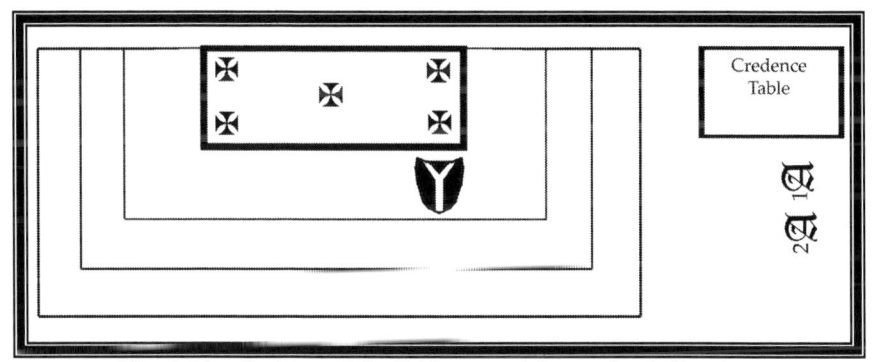

Fig. 5.11 – Positions of the Celebrant and Servers for the Introit

SUMMARY OF THE LAW

After he is finished with the Introit, the Celebrant turns to the left, walks to the center of the altar, turn to the right to face the altar and bows to the altar cross. He then turn to the people and says the Summary of the Law with his hands extended as at the *Dominus vobiscum* and eyes modestly and

HOW TO SAY MASS IN THE ANGLICAN RITE

moderately downward cast. He then turns to the left to face the altar again for the Kyrie Eleison. The altar servers remain kneeling.

KYRIE

The Celebrant says the Kyrie alternately with the servers as in the missal, with the people joining in if they wish. The priest's hands are joined. See Fig. 5.12 for the body posture at the Kyrie, and Fig. 5.13 for the position.

Fig. 5.12 – Reciting the Kyrie and Gloria

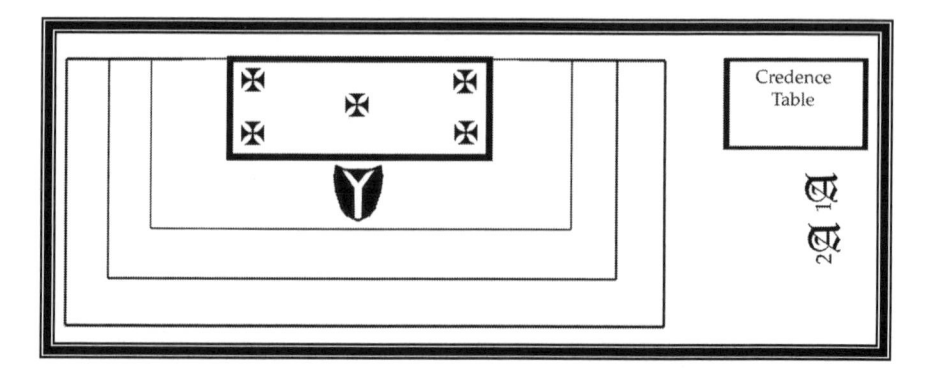

Fig. 5.13 – Positions at the Kyrie and Gloria

GLORIA

Then the priest begins the Gloria with *Gloria in excelsis Deo* or *Glory be to God on high*, depending on the language in which it will be recited. As he says these words, he extends, raises slightly, and then joins his hands again in one fluid motion as he did before ascending the altar. For the rest of the Gloria, he keeps his hands joined. See Figs. 5.12 and 5.13 for the positions. See Fig. 5.14 for the motions when saying *Gloria in excelsis Deo*. These left image shows the extension, the right image shows the arms being raised. This is done in one smooth motion, and the hands are brought back before the chest and joined.

Fig. 5.14 – At the beginning of the Gloria.

The Gloria is omitted when the color is purple, black, or rose. After the priest begins the Gloria with the words as above, the servers continue reciting it with him. The people may join in as well. The servers and all present stand.

When the following words are said: *We adore Thee, We give Thee thanks; Jesus Christ;* and *Receive our prayer,* the Celebrant, servers, and people all bow, and at the end they all sign themselves with the Sign of the Cross from forehead to breast.

SALUTATION

After the Gloria (or after the Kyrie is the Gloria is omitted according to the rubrics), the priest kisses the altar as at the arrival at the altar (see Fig. 5.9), and turns to the right all the way to face the people. He extends his hands and says *Dominus vobiscum*. The servers reply *Et cum spiritu tuo* whenever the priest says this. (It is good to note here, though it will be covered in the pontifical section, that a bishop celebrating mass say *Pax vobis* here if the Gloria is said. The response is the same.) See Fig. 5.15.

Fig. 5.15 – Dominus vobiscum

COLLECTS

After saying *Dominus vobiscum*, the Celebrant turns to the left and walks to the Epistle corner, turning left again to face the missal. Here, with hands joined, he says *Oremus*. See Fig. 5.16. After the salutation, the servers (if at the Credence table) sit. The people sit as well.

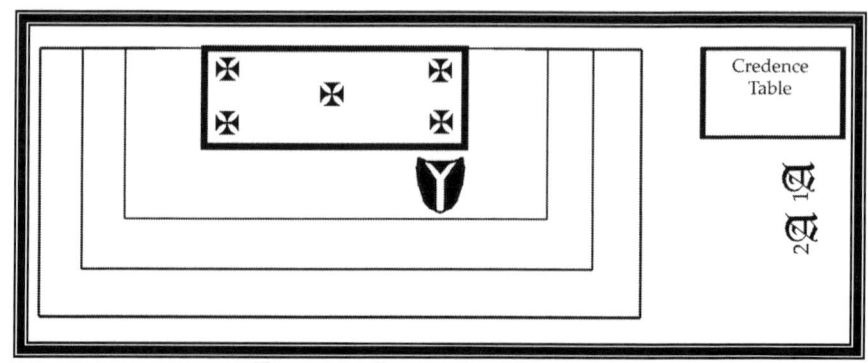

Fig. 5.16 – Position for the Collects

The Celebrant then extends his hands, facing the altar still, and reads the Collect for the mass he is saying. He then gives the Collect its own ending, joining his hands (he does this always at ending of Collects). The ending is usually abbreviated "Per Dominum." If this is what is written, then the full ending is given as usual in the General Rubrics of the missal. If there is a modification to be made, it will be indicated by the word to be inserted being written by the word in the usual ending before or after which it should be inserted. For example, "Per Dominum ejusdem Spiritus" would indicate that the ending is said as usual until before you get to the *Spiritus Sancti Deus*. Before Spiritus is added *ejusdem*. The Collect of the Day gets its own ending, except where the rubrics require it to be combined with another Collect under the same ending.

Seasonal Collects

The rubrics call for Seasonal Collects after the Collect of the Day. These are indicated at the beginning of each season in the Missale Anglicanum, as well as at the beginning of Octaves with their own Seasonal Prayers. Additionally, the same Collects are found in the Table of Prayers. These two Collects, and all that follow it, are given under one common ending. That is, the ending is not said at the end any of these Collects except the last one.

In most masses in the Octave of St. John the Baptist and the Octave of Saints Peter and Paul, there is an option in the Missale Anglicanum 2009 for the Seasonal Collect against the persecutors of the Church to be replaced with a Collect for the Holy Father. This is indicated by "vel pro Papa." This Collect is intended to be a commemoration of a Pope Saint, and the Collects from the mass for the Popes in the Common of the Saints are said. The Octave of Saints Peter and Paul is a particularly appropriate and special time to recall the canonized Popes, and the Octave of Saint John the Baptist, preceding that of Saints Peter and Paul, gives additional opportunity for this optional veneration. The living successor of Saint Peter, as first among equals of all Bishops, is remembered at every mass under the Missale Anglicanum 2009 in the Canon of the Mass.

Some masses do not permit Seasonal Collects or Commemorations. In these masses, only the Collect of the Day is said. This will be noted in the rubrics for the mass if this applies.

Collects ad Libitum

After the Seasonal Collects and before the Commemoration, the Celebrant may add any Collects from the Table of Prayers, Various Prayers, or Prayers for the Dead sections as he sees fit, provided the total number of Collects does not exceed seven.

Commemorations

After the Seasonal Collects and the Collects ad Libitum (if any), the Commemorations are said. Some masses have required commemorations in the rubrics. The priest may, when permitted according to the rubrics (which is during most masses) commemorate any mass he sees fit. On the last commemoration, he says the ending for that Collect. By so doing, he has joined all the Seasonal Prayers, Collects ad Libitum, and Commemorations under a single ending. If there are no commemorations, then the ending is said after the final Seasonal Collect or Collect ad Libitum as for that final Collect.

LESSON

The Celebrant has several options for reading the Lesson in a low mass. If he chooses to read it facing the altar, then he must read it from the missal. As he reads the lesson in this manner, he rests his hands apart either on the missal or on the altar. At the end of the lesson, the servers respond *Deo gratias*. The Celebrant may raise his left hand as a signal that the Lesson is over. On occasions like Ember days when there are multiple Lessons, the servers must pay particular attention to respond when required with *Deo gratias*.

Another option is for the Lesson to be read by the Celebrant from the predella from the Book of Epistles. If this is to be done, then the server takes the book from the credence table and moves to the second step to hold the book for the Celebrant. See Fig. 5.17. In the case of multiple lessons with Collects in between, if the option in Fig. 5.17 is used, then the server moves back to the credence table in between lessons.

LOW MASS

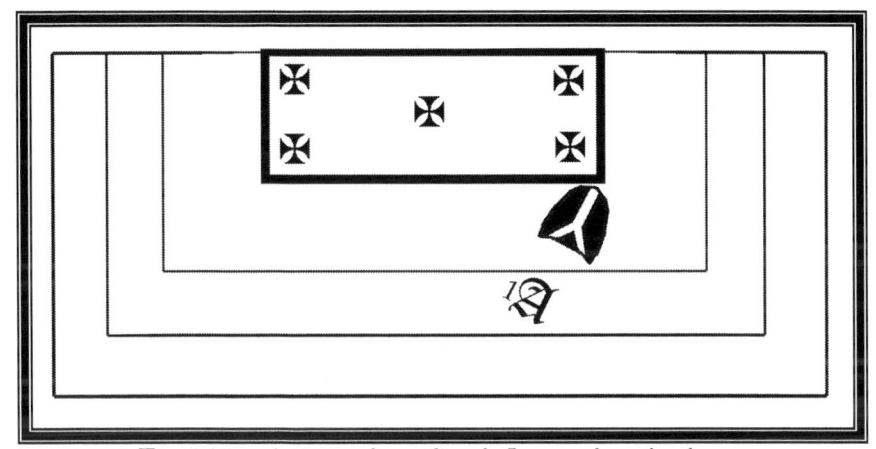

Fig. 5.17 – An option for reading the Lessons from the altar.

The third option is for the Celebrant or a Lector to read the lesson from the Lectern. If this is done, then the Celebrant takes the biretta from the server, moves to the Lectern, genuflecting in the center to the cross if he passes it (or bowing if the sacrament is not reserved, and removing the biretta while he does so), reads the Lesson, returns to the Epistle corner, genuflecting again in the center to the cross if he passes it as above (again removing the biretta while he does so), and giving up the biretta to the server upon arrival. Else, if a Lector is to read, the Lector goes to the Lectern and the Celebrant either stands as in Fig. 5.16 or goes to the sedilia. If he goes to the sedilia, then the server brings him his biretta, which he wears to the sedilia and while he sits. After the Lesson, he stands, goes back to the Epistle corner, and then gives the biretta to the server. (The biretta is always worn when travelling between the altar and the sedilia or the altar and the pulpit or lectern.)

GRADUAL

Standing at the Epistle corner with hands joined, the priest reads the Gradual and its Alleluia. If after Septuagesima, it is replaced with the Tract appointed in the missal. If during Paschaltide, there is instead an Alleluia that is read. This is read in a low voice, like everything in the mass that is not directed towards the people, or does not include the people joining in the recitation, or is otherwise appointed to be said in a louder voice.

The second altar server (or the altar server if there is only one) rises as the priest begins the Gradual and goes to the predella on the Epistle side of the altar to the right of the priest. He waits for the priest to finish the Gradual. When the priest has finished and moves to the middle of the altar for the *Munda Cor*, the second altar server takes the missal and transfers it to the Gospel side. (See Section 1, Fig. 1.6.) He then returns to the credence and sits until the priest announces the Gospel.

If the altar servers are using the option of kneeling before the altar in lieu of being at the credence table, then the transfer of the missal is similar, but not the same as above. In that case, the second server rises and follows the path in Fig. 5.18. Also, if there is only one server, the path is the same, as prior to the Gospel (and hence at the Gradual) he is kneeling on the Gospel side, which is also the position for the second altar server if there are two servers.

Fig. 5.18 – Pathway for the altar server to transfer the missal from the Epistle to the Gospel side if the servers are kneeling.

Observe Fig. 5.18. The server to move the missal, assuming the servers are using the kneeling option, will be at Point A. This is true whether there is one server or two. If there are two, this is the second server. The server rises, goes to the Epistle side on the pavement, genuflecting at Point B (or bowing if the sacrament is not reserved), ascends the steps on the Epistle side, takes the missal, follows the pathway back down to Point B, genuflects or bows again, goes back up the steps as shown to Point C

LOW MASS

and deposits the missal, then goes back to the pavement as shown down the steps on the Gospel side. He then follows the pathway on the pavement back to his original position, Point A, if there are two altar servers, or continues on along the path to Point D if he is the only server.

MUNDA COR

The priest, after reciting the Gospel, moves to the center of the altar and, bowing down with hands joined, recites the *Munda Cor, Iube Domine*, and *Dominus sit* (unless omitted according to the rubrics).

GOSPEL

After the Munda Cor, the Celebrant has three options for reading the Gospel. If he is to read it at the altar, then he then turns to the Gospel side, facing the missal. See Fig. 5.19.

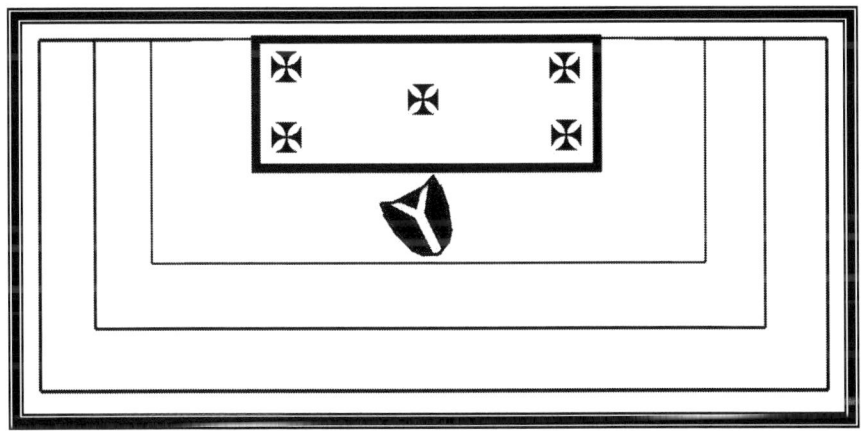

Fig. 5.19 – Celebrant's position for the reading of the Gospel from the missal at the altar.

In this first option, the Celebrant says *Dominus vobiscum* with hands joined and without turning to the people. He signs the book with his right hand as he announces the Gospel. See Fig. 5.20. He then makes the sign of the cross three times on himself in the usual manner for the Gospel. See Fig. 5.21. These small crosses are made with the tip of the thumb, the top of the thumb facing towards the individual signing themselves. The first cross is at the forehead. The second is on the lips. The third is over the heart. Some or all of these acts may occasionally be omitted when called to be omitted by the rubrics.

Fig. 5.20 – Blessing the Book of Gospels.

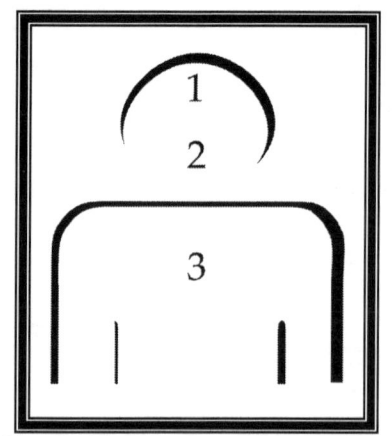

Fig. 5.21 – Positions for the small crosses when making the sign of the cross at the Gospel.

After the words of introduction, the servers respond *Gloria tibi Domine*. Then the Celebrant reads the Gospel with hands joined. See Fig. 5.22. When he is finished, he places both hands apart, flat on the Missal and kisses it, except when called for to be omitted, and says *Per evangelica*, etc. The servers respond, as they see the Celebrant kissing the missal, with *Laus tibi Christe*.

Fig. 5.22 – Reading the Gospel at the altar, facing the missal, with hands joined.

The second option is to read the Gospel from the Book of Gospels, standing on the predella facing the people. In this case, the altar server (if there are two, then the first altar server) goes to the credence table to get the Book of Gospels, goes to the center of the altar on the pavement and genuflects (or bows if the sacrament is not reserved), and ascends the steps to the Celebrant. The Celebrant remains on the predella, and the server stands on the second step. See Fig. 5.23. Even though he is facing the people, he keeps his hands joined for *Dominus vobiscum*.

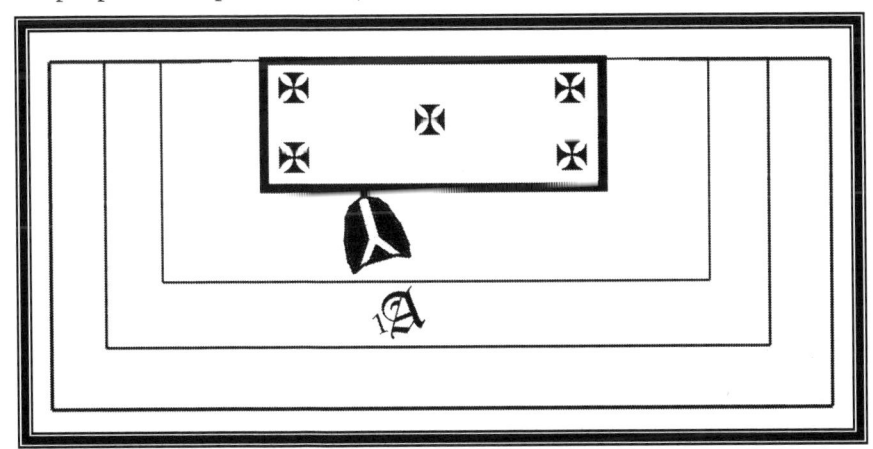

Fig. 5.23 – Positions for reading the Gospel at the predella from the Book of Gospels

The third option for reading the Gospel is to read it from the pulpit. In this case, the Celebrant returns to the Epistle corner after reading the Munda Cor, etc., the server brings him his biretta, and he goes to the pulpit, removing the biretta and genuflecting or bowing if he passes the altar cross. He removes the biretta before the salutation at the beginning of the Gospel. Even though he is facing the people, he keeps his hands joined for the Dominus vobiscum. All else is as usual. After he is finished and kisses the book, he takes his biretta and returns to the Epistle corner, genuflecting or bowing (as usual, according to whether or not the sacrament is reserved) and removing his biretta as he does so. When he reaches the Epistle corner, he gives the biretta to the server. He then proceeds back to the center of the altar, bowing upon arrival, for the Creed or Offertory. However, if there is to be a sermon, he remains in the pulpit.

SERMON

If at the primary mass on Sunday, there is little reason for a sermon to be omitted. However, the inclusion of a sermon is generally at the discretion of the Celebrant, subject to episcopal directives.

If the Celebrant used the third option for reading the Gospel, and hence is already in the pulpit, he remains there for the sermon. He may wear his biretta at his own discretion while preaching, but removes it for any prayers at the beginning and end. There is also a custom of removing the maniple to preach. This is, whoever, a matter of local use under episcopal directives. The maniple may just as well be left on. If it is removed, however, the cross is kissed as it is removed, and it is laid aside on the pulpit. After the sermon is over, the Celebrant again takes the maniple, kissing its cross as usual. He takes the biretta, and returns to the Epistle corner, genuflecting or bowing (as usual, according to whether or not the sacrament is reserved) and removing his biretta as he does so. When he reaches the Epistle corner, he gives the biretta to the server. He then proceeds back to the center of the altar, bowing upon arrival, for the Creed or Offertory.

If the Celebrant has used any other option for reading the Gospel, then he must go to the pulpit. He goes to the Epistle Corner, taking the biretta from the server, and he goes to the pulpit, removing the biretta and genuflecting or bowing if he passes the altar cross. Here he preaches the sermon and returns to the altar as above.

CREED

The Creed is said only on Sundays and on feast days for which the Creed has been specifically appointed. This is indicated in the missal by the presence of the word "Creed" or "Credo" after the Gospel. During some Octaves, the Creed is appointed throughout the Octave. This is indicated in the missal on days that always fall within such Octaves, but is at least mentioned on the principal feast.

The Creed is said, in Latin or English, in the center of the predella, facing the altar with hands joined. The Celebrant alone begins the Creed, and the servers and others join in. The beginning words said only by the Celebrant are *Credo in unum Deum* or *I believe in one God*. See Fig. 5.24 for the positions at the Creed.

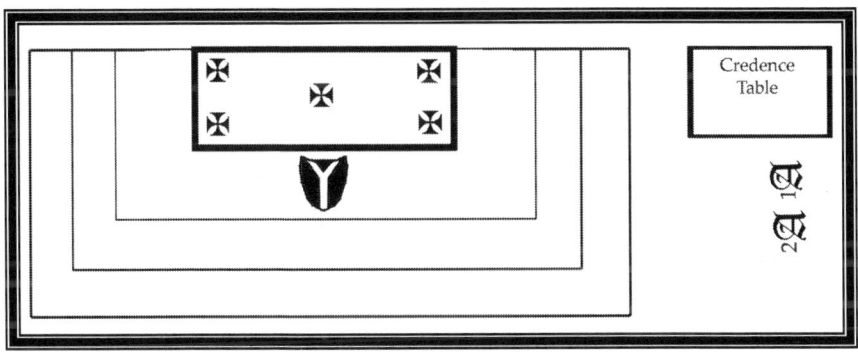

Fig. 5.24 – Positions at the Creed

If the servers are at the credence table, then they stand. If they use the kneeling option, then they remain kneeling.

When the Celebrant reaches the words *Et incarnatus est de Spiritu Sancto ex Maria Virgine: et homo factus est* or *And was incarnate by the Holy Ghost of the Virgin Mary: and was made man*, then all present genuflect or kneel. If the servers are at the credence table, they kneel as the rest. If they use the kneeling option on the lowest step, then they give a moderate bow. Then the Creed finishes as usual.

OFFERTORY

After the Creed (or immediately after the Sermon, if there is no Creed, or Gospel, if there is no Creed and no Sermon), the Celebrant, standing in the center of the altar, places both hands flat on the altar, one on either side of the corporal, and kisses it in the center. He turns to the people and says, with hands extended, *Dominus vobiscum* (see Fig. 5.15 above). Then, as the servers respond *Et cum spiritu tuo*, he turns back to the altar and says, with hands joined, *Oremus*. Then the Celebrant reads the appointed Offertory voice in a low voice for the mass being said.

As the priest is reading the Offertory, the servers rise and stand at the credence table. If they are kneeling in front of the altar, then they rise, genuflect or bow in the middle, and stand at the credence table.

Offering of the Host

First, the priest removes the chalice veil, holding the back corners of the veil and carefully bringing it forward. Then he folds it and sets it aside on the Epistle side of the altar. He removes the pall from the paten and sets it to the right of the corporal. Then he takes the paten (with the host on it) in both hands, and holding it above the corporal, says the *Suscipe Sancte Pater*. The altar server rings the Sanctus bells once as the priest offers the host. After the offering of the host, or on the last several words of it, he makes the sign of the cross over the corporal with the paten (this should extend over the entire length and width of the corporal). See Fig. 5.25.

Fig. 5.25 – Offering the host

LOW MASS

Next, the Celebrant takes the host off the paten with his left hand and places it on the corporal in front of the chalice. (If there are servers' hosts underneath, those are placed directly on the corporal to the right of the chalice.) The paten is then placed on the back right of the corporal. See Fig. 5.26.

Fig. 5.26 – Hosts and paten on the corporal after the Offering of the Host.

Offering of the Chalice

The priest removes the purificator from the chalice with his right hand. He takes the chalice in his left hand by the stem and wipes out the bowl of the chalice with the purificator (see Fig. 5.27). As he does this, the altar server, or servers, brings the cruets of wine and water to the Epistle corner. (See Section 4 for details on this procedure.) The priest takes the chalice in the left hand by the stem and moves to the Epistle corner (see Fig. 5.28).

Taking first the cruet of wine in the right hand, he pours some wine into the chalice and hands the cruet back to the altar server. Then the altar server holds the cruet of water up for him to bless. He then blesses the water with the *Deus qui* prayer, takes the cruet of water, and pours a little water into the chalice. The water cruet is then given back to the altar server. The typical method of blessing and pouring the water is to make the sign of the cross during the words *Deus,* ✠ *qui humanae substantiae,* and then to pour the water into the chalice at the words *da nobis per huius aquae et vini mysterium.* However, the water may just as well be poured in after the blessing is completed.

Fig. 5.27 – Wiping the bowl of the chalice with the purificator.

Fig. 5.28 – Positions for pouring the wine and water. The positions for two altar servers are given. As shown, the first server holds the wine cruet, the second server, standing on the second step, holds the water cruet. If there is only one altar server, then he stands in the position of the first altar server and carries both the wine and water cruets. Whenever the servers approach the epistle corner, they come straight up the steps from the credence table and return by the same path.

LOW MASS

Returning to the center of the altar, the priest takes the chalice in both hands and, holding it above the corporal, offers the wine with the prayer *Offerimus tibi Domine*. See Fig. 5.29. As with the paten, the priest makes the sign of the cross over the paten with the chalice, still holding it with both hands (either both on the stem, or the left hand supporting it under the base). Then he sets it in the center of the corporal and covers it with the pall. See Fig. 5.30. During this time the servers return to the credence table and stand.

Fig. 5.29 – Offering the chalice.

Fig. 5.30 – The chalice covered with the pall after the offering of the chalice.

The priest then says the *In spiritu humilitatis* while bowing with hands joined. Then he stands erect and makes the sign of the cross over the offerings with his right hand while saying the *Veni sanctificator*.

LAVABO

The priest then goes to the Epistle corner for the washing of the hands. He recites the *Lavabo* up until, but not including, the *Gloria Patri*. He may face the altar as he does this, particularly if he is reading it from the altar card. He may alternatively recite it while having the water poured over his fingers. Else, he has the water poured over his fingers after he says the *Lavabo*, but before the *Gloria Patri*.

The servers (or one server) approach the Epistle corner carrying the lavabo pitcher, bowl, and towel. The procedure for this is described in detail in Section 4 on Altar Servers. The position for this are the same as for the bringing of the wine and water cruets. See Fig. 5.28 above.

The priest places all his fingers over the lavabo bowl. The server pours the water from the pitcher over them. If there is only one server assisting at the lavabo, the priest takes the towel and dries his own fingers. Else, the second server, who is carrying the towel, dries the priest's fingers. Then the servers return to the credence table and sit. (Or, if they are using the kneeling option, then they go to their place before the altar and kneel.) The Celebrant stands at the Epistle corner facing the cross or in the center of the altar facing the cross and, bowing down with hands joined, says the *Gloria Patri* (except when it is omitted).

PRAYER TO THE MOST HOLY TRINITY
& ORATE FRATRES

Returning to the center of the altar, the Celebrant bows down over the altar with hands joined and says the *Suscipe Sancta Trinitas*. Then he places both hands flat on the altar on either side of the corporal as usual, and kisses the altar in the center. Turning to the people, he extends his hands as at the *Dominus vobiscum* and says *Orate, fratres*. He then turns back to the altar and says audibly, with hands joined, *ut meum ac vestrum*, etc.

SECRETS

Next the priest says the Secrets for the day, standing in the center of the predella and facing the altar with hands extended. These should match in number, subject, and order with the Collects said earlier. That is, it should be the Secret of the Day followed by the Secrets under the appointed Seasonal Prayers, followed by the Secrets associated with any Collects ad Libitum said earlier, followed by the Secrets for any commemorations. The first Secret gets its own ending. Each other Secret is combined under one single ending as described earlier for the Collects.

The Secrets are said in the "secret voice" rather than silently. That is, it should be clear to those nearby that the priest is saying something, but it should not be clear precisely what is being said. These are the priest's private intercessions on behalf of the people. At the end of the last Secret to be said, when the words *per omnia saecula saeculorum* are said, they are said audibly as a cue to the servers and people that the Secrets have ended. The priest joins his hands as usual when he says the ending to a Secret, just as earlier at the Collects. This is done at the end of the first Secret and at the end of all the other Secrets.

INVITATION TO COMMUNION

Here the priest, still with hands joined, bows to the cross and turns to the people. With hands extended as at the *Dominus vobiscum*, he says the Invitation to Communion. If he does not have this memorized, an altar server brings it to him on a card and stands on the second step towards the Epistle side.

CONFESSION

Turning back to the altar, the Celebrant bows low over the altar in the center. He says the General Confession audibly. The servers and people, kneeling, say this as well. The servers may come to the front of the altar and kneel on the lowest step for the confession if they are not there already (i.e., if they are using the option to remain at the credence table). Or, they may kneel at the Credence table, or on the lowest step of the altar on the Epistle side. They bow while during the Confession.

ABSOLUTION AND COMFORTABLE WORDS

The priest then turns to the people, standing on the predella in the center of the altar. He holds his hands extended over the people, palms facing the people, and pronounces the absolution. When he says the words *pardon and deliver*, he makes the sign of the cross with his right hand over the people (see the sub-section on the Benediction at the end of mass below for the procedure for making the sign of the cross over the people). While making the sign of the cross, his left hand is brought flat against his breast. The servers and people makes the sign of the cross over themselves as the priest makes the sign of the cross over them, as usual.

After making the sign of the cross, he again extends his hands over the people for the remainder of the absolution until the words *through Jesus Christ our Lord*. When he says those words, as it is a conclusion, he joins his hands. Then are read the Comfortable Words with hands joined. The Celebrant and servers bow when the name of Jesus is mentioned. When he is finished, he turns back to the altar.

If the Celebrant does not have the absolution and Comfortable Words memorized, then an altar server may hold a card containing them for him. The server stands or, if possible, kneels on the second step towards the Epistle side, holding the card so that the Celebrant may see it. A server fulfilling this duty is dispensed from making the sign of the cross.

SURSUM CORDA AND PREFACE

The Celebrant stands in the center of the altar, facing the cross, with hands joined over the offerings. He says *Dominus vobiscum* (see Fig. 5.31 below). The servers respond *Et cum spiritu tuo* as usual. As he says *Sursum corda*, he extends and raises his hands a little (see Fig. 5.32 below). The servers respond *Habemus ad Dominum*. Slowly rejoining his hands in a graceful and fluid motion, the Celebrant continues with *Gratias agamus Domino Deo nostro* (see Fig. 5.31 below). The Celebrant keeps his hands joined while the servers respond *Dignum et justum est*. It should be noted, in reference to the Missale Anglicanum 2009, that the Prefaces in text are shown to begin with *Per Omni Saecula Saeculorum*. This is included as a special case for priests celebrating alone, and hence the Confession, etc., is omitted. In such a case, the Sursum Corda follows immediately after the Secrets, and that *Per omnia* is the end of the last Secret. This is covered in the Section on Special Occasions and Circumstances under the Sub-Section "Celebrating Alone." Under usual circumstances, however, the

LOW MASS

Sursum Corda begins after the Absolution and Comfortable Words, and hence begins with *Dominus vobiscum*.

Then, extending his hands, he reads the Preface appointed for the mass. This is given in the missal for each mass.

Fig. 5.31 – Hand position for the Sursum Corda at the words Dominus vobiscum and Gratias agamus

Fig. 5.32 – Hand position for the Sursum Corda at the words Sursum corda.

At the beginning of the Sursum Corda, the server who is to ring the bell at the Sanctus must get into position. If the servers are using the option to kneel at the front of the altar on the first step, then they are already in position. The bell is on the first step ready. If the servers, though, are at the credence table, then one moves to the pavement on the Epistle side in front of the first step (he will kneel on the first step on the Epistle side during the Sanctus). The bell should be located there. He stands and waits, making the responses to the Sursum Corda.

SANCTUS

The Celebrant says the Sanctus while bowing down at the front of the altar with hands joined. When he reaches the *Benedictus*, he makes the sign of the cross on himself while still bowing. All others kneel. The altar server rings the altar bell three times. See Fig. 5.33.

Fig. 5.33 – Priest's position at the Sanctus

BEGINNING OF THE CANON OF THE MASS

The Celebrant, standing in the center of the altar and facing the cross, extends, raises, and then joins his hands, while raising his eyes to heaven, and then lowering them, all in one fluid motion. He bows at the altar, with his joined hands resting on it in the center. See Fig. 5.34. The servers and all present kneel throughout the Canon except otherwise directed.

Fig. 5.34 – Position at the beginning of the Canon. Bowing down with hands joined and resting on the altar.

When the Celebrant comes to the words *supplices rogamus ac petimus*, he places both hands flat on the altar, one hand on either side of the corporal as usual, and kisses the altar in the center. See Fig. 5.35. Then he continues with *uti accepta habeas* standing erect with hands joined.

He places his left hand flat against his breast and signs with his flat right hand (held with the palm facing to the left and the hand perpendicular to the altar, fingertips towards the altar cross) over the offerings at *haec* ✠ *dona, haec* ✠ *munera, haec* ✠ *sancta sacrificia illibata*. He extends his hands as usual at *in primis*. When he comes to *una cum famulo tuo Papa N., Metropolitano nostro, N., et Antistite nostro N.*, he inserts the name of the present Pope after "Papa," the Metropolitan after "Metropolitano nostro," and the name of the current Diocesan Bishop after "Antistite nostro." These names should all be in the ablative case if rendered in Latin. If the priest is directly under the Metropolitan, then the *Antistite nostro* is omitted.

Fig. 5.35 – Kissing the altar at the beginning of the Canon.

The Celebrant continues with the Commemoration of the Living, inserting the names of those for whom he specifically wishes to pray as for whom he especially offers the mass being said. He then joins his hands and, holding them in front of his face, prays silently for those whom he just mentioned, adding any other special prayers and intentions for the living he wishes. He then extends his hands and continues with the *et omnium circumstantium*.

COMMUNICANTES

The Celebrant says the Communicantes with extended hands. If a proper Communicantes is given in the propers for the day, then it is said instead. He rejoins his hands for the conclusion.

HANC IGITUR

Spreading his hands over the oblations, holding them flat with palms down (see Fig. 5.36), the Celebrant says the *Hanc Igitur*. For the occasions appointed in the missal, the proper Hanc Igitur is said instead. He rejoins his hands at the conclusion.

He then continues with the *Quam oblationem tu Deus, in omnibus quaesumus*, standing erect with hands joined. When he reaches *bene✠dictam, adscrip✠tam, ra✠tam*, he makes the sign of the cross over the oblations with the right hand in the manner previously described. For the words *rationabilem, acceptabilemque facere digneris*, he joins his hands. When he says *ut nobis Cor*✠*pus,* he signs with his right hand over the host only. At the *et San*✠*guis*, he signs over the chalice only. Then he rejoins his hands for *fiat dilectissimi Filii tui Domini nostri Iesu Christi.*

Fig. 5.36 – Hands over the oblations at the Hanc Igitur

WORDS OF CONSECRATION

The priest separates his hands and puts his index fingers on the corporal on either side of the host at the words *Qui pridie* (see Fig. 5.37). At *accepit panem*, he takes the host into his hands (see Fig. 5.38). At *et elevatis oculis*, the Celebrant raises his eyes to heaven (see Fig. 5.39). At *tibi gratias agens*, he bows his head slightly over the host in an act of thanks (see Fig. 5.40). At *benedixit*, he makes the sign of the cross over the host, holding it still in the left hand, and then takes hold of it with both hands again (see Fig. 5.41). He says *Hoc est enim corpus meum* audibly, so those around can hear clearly, but not in an elevated voice. The rest of the Canon, from the beginning to the end, is said in a low voice somewhat louder and more clear than the secret voice, except where otherwise indicated in the rubrics. The Canon, as a matter of dignity, solemnity, and respect, is not said in a loud voice. Every word should be said out loud, though, except where indicated. Also, after the consecration of the host, the thumb and forefinger of each hand are not disjoined, except to handle the host, until after the ablutions. This takes some practice to get used to.

HOW TO SAY MASS IN THE ANGLICAN RITE

Fig. 5.37 – Qui pridie...

Fig. 5.38 - ...accepit panem...

LOW MASS

Fig. 5.39 – Raising the eyes to heaven.

Fig. 5.40 - ...tibi gratias agens...

Fig. 5.41 – Blessing the host at the consecration.

ELEVATION OF THE HOST

Once the Celebrant has spoken the words of consecration, he places the host back in its place on the corporal. Placing his disjoined hands on the altar (with the thumb and forefingers of each hand still joined), he genuflects. (See Fig. 5.42.) The altar server rings the bell once.

Fig. 5.42 – Genuflection after consecrating the host

LOW MASS

Then the priest rises. Taking the host in both hands, he elevates it up so that the people may adore it (see Fig. 5.43). As he does this, the server rings the bell three times and bows.

Fig. 5.43 – Elevation of the Host

The Celebrant then places the host back on the corporal and genuflects again. As he genuflects, the server rings the bell once. The server, kneeling on the platform or top step to the right of the priest, holds the chasuble during the elevation (not during the genuflections). He holds it up slightly, but does not pull or tug on it. This is done for both the elevation of the host and chalice.

CONSECRATION OF THE WINE

The priest uncovers the chalice. As his thumbs and forefingers are joined, this means that all movements, such as removing the pall from the chalice, must be done holding the object between the forefinger and middle finger. The pall, for example, is removed by placing it between the forefinger and middle finger. This does take practice to get used to, and it should be practiced so that all motions are smooth and fluid.

After removing the pall from the chalice, the Celebrant places his hands on either side of the chalice, the fingers resting on the corporal for *Simili modo*. Then, at *accipiens et hunc*, he places his hands on the chalice, leaving it sitting on the corporal. His left hand he places on the stem, and his right hand he places on the underside of the bowl or just underneath the bowl on the stem. See Fig. 5.44.

Fig. 5.44 – Accipiens et hunc...

At the words *tibi gratias agens*, he bows his head slightly as before. At *benedixit*, he blesses the wine with the right hand. Then he switches his hand position so that now his right hand is holding the stem of the chalice, and the left hand is resting on the base. Because the thumb and forefinger are joined, the stem of the chalice is actually between the forefinger and the other three fingers. The chalice remains on the corporal until the words of consecration. At *Hic est enim*, etc., he holds the chalice slightly elevated off of the corporal, supporting the base with the left hand. The words of consecration are spoken somewhat louder so that those around can hear, but should not be said loudly. At the words *Haec quotiescumque*, etc., he places the chalice back on the corporal. Those words are spoken softly.

ELEVATION OF THE CHALICE

The priest then genuflects as at the elevation of the host, leaving the chalice uncovered. The server rings the bell once. The priest then elevates the chalice (see Fig. 5.45), and the server rings the bell three times and bows. After covering the chalice with the pall, the priest then genuflects again as the server rings the bell once.

Fig. 5.45 – Elevation of the chalice.

AFTER THE ELEVATIONS

The Celebrant extends his hands and continues with the *Unde et memores*. When he comes to the words *hostiam* ✠ *puram, hostiam* ✠ *sanctam, hostiam* ✠ *immaculatam*, he signs with his right hand over the oblations together three times as indicated. At the words *Panem* ✠ *sanctum*, he signs once over the host only. Then on the words *Calicem* ✠ *salutis perpetuae*, he signs once over the chalice only. Then he extends his hands and continues with the *Supra quae propitio*.

At the words *Supplices te rogamus*, he joins his hands and bows down, with his hands resting on the center of the altar. After the words *ut quotquot*, he places his hands on either side of the corporal (with the thumbs and forefingers still joined) and kisses the altar in the center. At *ex hac altaris*, he stands erect with hands joined. Then, at *Cor*✠*pus*, he signs once over the host (remembering that the thumb and forefingers are still joined). At *San*✠*guinem*, he signs once over the chalice. At *omni benedictione* ✠*coelesti*, he signs himself (see Fig. 5.46). Then he rejoins his hands as usual for the conclusion, *Per eumdem Christum Dominum nostrum. Amen.*

Fig. 5.46 – Omni benedictione...

COMMEMORATION OF THE DEAD

The Celebrant, with hands extended, begins with *Memento etiam*. He mentions where indicated the dead for which he especially intends to pray. After *somno pacis*, he joins his hands before his face as before and pray silently for the dead, especially those for whom he particularly wants to pray. These generally should include deceased relatives, friends, and benefactors of the priest, just as the prayers for the living should generally include the living relatives, friends, and benefactors of the priests, in addition to any others that he wishes to add. Then he extends his hands and continues with *Ipsis Domine*. He joins his hands at the conclusion, *Per eumdem*, etc.

INVOCATION OF THE SAINTS

The Celebrant strikes his breast once with his right hand (as at the Confiteor) at the words *Nobis quoque peccatoribus*, keeping his left hand flat on his breast as usual. He also says those three words in an elevated voice. He then extends his hands and continues with *famulis tuis*, etc., in the usual lower voice. He joins his hands as usual at the conclusion. See Fig. 5.47.

Fig. 5.47 – Nobis quoque peccatoribus

HOW TO SAY MASS IN THE ANGLICAN RITE

MINOR ELEVATION

The Celebrant keeps his hands joined for *per quem haec omnia*, and then signs in the usual manner over the oblations together three times at *sancti✠ficas, vivi✠ficas, bene✠dicis, et praestas nobis*. Then the priest uncovers the chalice, setting the pall to the right. He genuflects, and then takes the host in his right hand. He holds the stem of the chalice with his left hand. (Recall that he disjoins his thumb and forefinger to hold the host, but not to hold the chalice.) He makes the sign of the cross three times with the host over the chalice from rim to rim on the words *Per ip✠sum, et cum ip✠so, et in ip✠so*. See Figs. 5.48 and 5.49.

Fig. 5.48 – Position of holding the host over the chalice. Note the manner of holding the chalice with the left hand. The thumb and forefinger are still joined.

Fig. 5.49 – Order for making the sign of the cross with the host over the chalice from rim to rim. This is an aerial view of the chalice, with the ✠ indicating the direction of the altar cross.

Next he signs in precisely the same manner and size with the host over the corporal between the chalice and his breast at the words *est tibi Deo Patri* ✠ *omnipotenti, in unitate Spiritus* ✠ *Sancti.* He stills holds the chalice with his left hand. See Fig. 5.50.

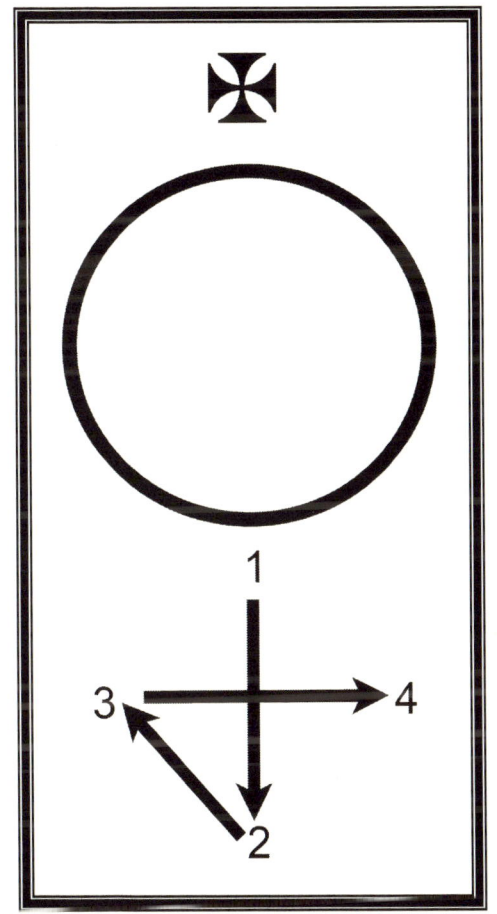

Fig. 5.50 – Manner of making the cross between the chalice and breast over the corporal. The right hand holds the host in the same manner as if it were held over the chalice. It is also held at approximately the same height.

Next, the Celebrant holds the host again over the chalice and elevates the chalice and host together a little bit (a few inches) off of the corporal as he says *omnis honor et gloria*. See Fig. 5.51.

HOW TO SAY MASS IN THE ANGLICAN RITE

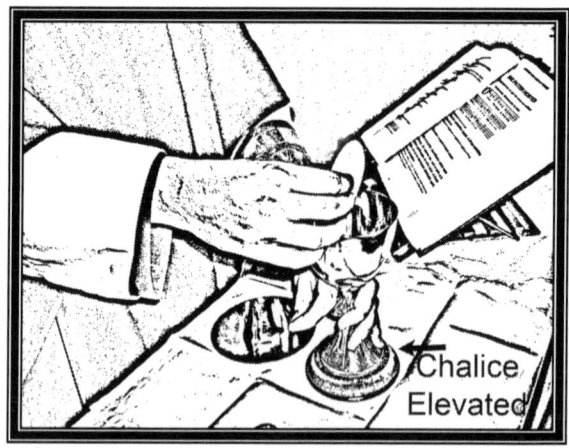

Fig. 5.51 – Omnis honor and gloria. The chalice and host are elevated a little bit above the corporal as those words are spoken.

Then the priest places the chalice back on the corporal. The host is also replaced in its usual position on the corporal. The priest covers the chalice with the pall and genuflects as usual (this manner of genuflecting after covering and uncovering the chalice when it contains the Precious Blood is the norm). Then he joins his hands over the chalice as usual and says audibly *Per omni saecula saeculorum*. The servers respond as usual with *Amen*. The words of the Minor Elevation before this are usually said in the typical lower voice, but may just as well be elevated slightly, but not as loud as the *Per omni saecula saeculorum* (with also should not be loud, but simply audible to those around who need to respond). See Fig. 5.52.

Fig. 5.52 – Manner of holding the hands joined after the Consecration of the Host.

PATER NOSTER

The Celebrant, still standing on the predella in the center of the altar facing the cross as usual in the Canon, continues with *Oremus. Praeceptis salutaribus*, etc., with his hands joined as in Fig. 5.52 above. When he begins the *Pater Noster*, he extends his hands. The priest alone says this. The servers and people do not join in saying the *Pater Noster*, except where indicated at the end. After the Celebrant says *Et ne nos inducas in tentationem*, he rejoins his hands, and the servers and people respond with *sed libera nos a malo*. The priest says *Amen* in a low voice. The servers stand, unless they use the option to kneel in front of the altar for the entire mass.

LIBERA NOS & DIVISION OF THE HOST

The priest takes the paten in his right hand. He holds it between his forefinger and middle finger, as the thumb and forefinger are joined. It is held flat over approximately where the host is resting on the corporal. The right forearm is approximately parallel to the altar top. The left hand, of course, is held "flat" against the breast (the middle, ring, and little fingers are flat, but the thumb and forefinger, of course, remained joined). The priest then says the *Libera nos*, etc., until and including the words *omnibus Sanctis*. See Fig. 5.53. The servers remain standing unless they are using the kneeling option.

Fig. 5.53 – Holding the paten at the Libera nos.

Then after *omnibus Sanctis*, the Celebrant signs himself with the paten (see Figs. 5.54-5.57 below), and then kisses the paten. (The kiss is made by bringing the top of the paten near the lips, bowing the head slightly, and kissing it in the center.) Then he continues with *da propitius*, etc. He places the paten underneath the host after he says *perturbatione securi*. (However, he may just as well place the paten under the host while the words *da propitius*, etc. are being said. The method of placing the paten on the host depends somewhat on the nature of the paten. If it is a "flat" paten, i.e., a paten without a lip around the edge, then it is usually easy enough to slide the paten underneath the host without having to pick up the host. An alternative method, which is equally acceptable, is to pick up the host with the left hand, place the paten on the corporal where the host was resting, and then place the host back on the paten in the center (see Fig. 5.58).

Fig. 5.54 – When signing with the paten, it is first brought to the top of the head, perpendicular to the ground, and with the top of the paten towards the priest.

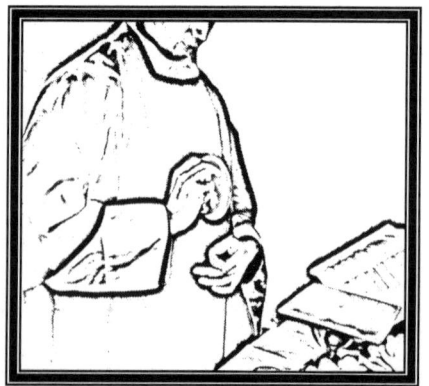

Fig. 5.55 – Next the priest continues tracing the lines of the cross by moving down to the lower chest, holding the paten in the same position. Note that the left hand is against the body, with thumb and forefinger joined.

LOW MASS

Fig. 5.56 – Then the priest moves the paten to the left shoulder.

Fig. 5.57 – The sign of the cross is finished by moving the paten to the right shoulder.

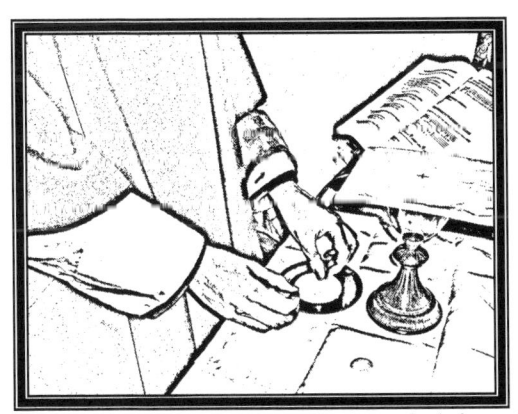

Fig. 5.58 – The paten is placed under the host. In the method shown in this figure, the priest picks up the host in the left hand, places the paten on the corporal where the host was with the right hand, and then places the host on the paten.

Having placed the host on the paten, the Celebrant uncovers the host, placing the pall to the right and genuflecting as usual. He then holds the host with both hands over the chalice. See Fig. 5.59.

Fig. 5.59 – Host being held over the chalice with both hands in preparation for the fracture.

The priest then breaks the host in half over the chalice as he says *Per eumdem Dominum nostrum*, etc. See Fig. 5.60.

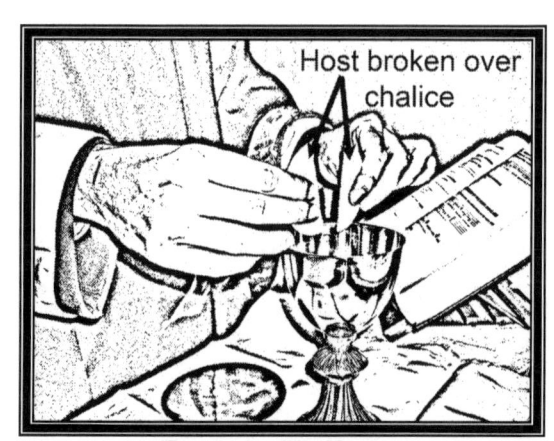

Fig. 5.60 – The Fracture

LOW MASS

The half in his right hand is replaced on the paten. The left half is held over the chalice. See Fig. 5.61. From the part in the left hand, be breaks a small piece off of the bottom with the right hand with the words *qui tecum vivit*, etc.. See Fig. 5.62. The left half is then placed on the paten and the small piece is held over the chalice in the right hand, and the stem of the chalice is held in the left hand (the chalice being left resting on the corporal) and says audibly *Per omnia saecula saeculorum*. The servers respond *Amen*. See Fig. 5.63.

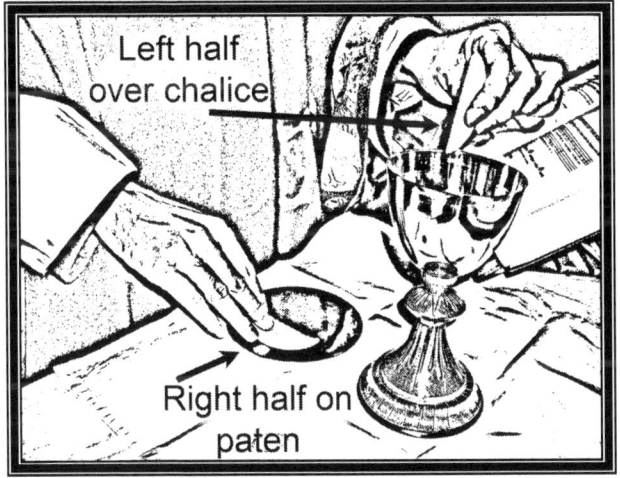

Fig. 5.61 – Right half of the host replaced on the paten, the left half held over the chalice.

Fig. 5.62 – The small piece is broken off of the bottom of the left piece using the right hand.

HOW TO SAY MASS IN THE ANGLICAN RITE

Fig. 5.63 – Holding the small piece over the chalice for the Pax Domini

PAX DOMINI

Next the Celebrant traces the sign of the cross with the small piece over the chalice (as in the Minor Elevation, see Fig. 5.49) at the words *Pax* ✠ *Domini sit* ✠ *semper vobis*✠*cum*. The servers respond, as usual, *et cum spiritu tuo*. As soon as he has made the three crosses, the Celebrant puts the particle into the chalice, saying *Haec commixtio*, etc. Having finished, he covers the chalice with the pall and genuflects. The servers remain standing for the Pax Domini unless they are using the option to kneel before the altar for the entire mass.

AGNUS DEI

The Celebrant bows at the altar with hands joined. He then says the *Agnus Dei* (there is another form of it for Requiem masses, and this is covered in that section). Each time he says the words *Agnus Dei*, he strikes his breast as at the *Confiteor* (see Fig. 5.64). The servers kneel if they are at the Credence table. If they use the option to kneel in front of the altar for the entire mass, then they bow while kneeling on front of the altar.

LOW MASS

Fig. 5.64 – Striking the breast at the Agnus Dei. The thumbs and forefingers of each hand of course remain joined.

PRAYERS FOR HOLY COMMUNION

Having finished the *Agnus Dei*, the priest stands inclined over the altar, with his hands joined and resting on the altar. He says *Domine Jesu Christe*, etc., the *Domine Jesu Christe Fili Dei*, etc., and the *Perceptio corporis tui*, etc. Or, in lieu of the last two, the Prayer of Humble Access. The first prayer is omitted in masses of the dead (see the Section on Requiem Masses). The servers and all present continue kneeling.

CELEBRANT'S DOMINE NON SUM DIGNUS

After the Prayers for Holy Communion are complete, the Celebrant genuflects, rises, and says *Panem coelestem*, etc. He stands inclined at the altar and takes both halves of the host into his left hand (see Fig. 5.65). These he holds between the left thumb and forefinger. Picking up the paten with his right hand (between the forefinger and middle finger), he places the paten in the left hand between the forefinger and middle finger, under the host. The left ring and little fingers may support the bottom of the paten. See Fig. 5.66.

Fig. 5.65 – Before the Domine non sum dignus, the priest takes both halves of the host in the left hand

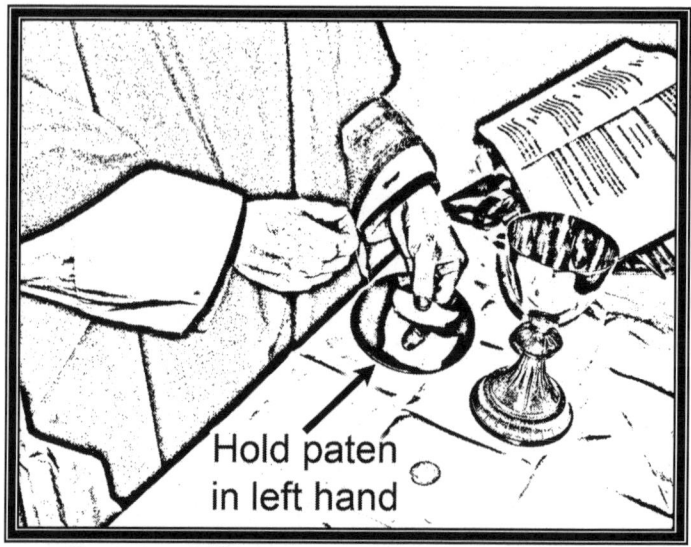

Fig. 5.66 – Hold the paten in the left hand under the host.

LOW MASS

Now the Celebrant strikes his breast with his right hand (as at the Confiteor, but still keeping his thumb and forefingers joined) each time he says the words *Domine non sum dignus*. These words he also says while raising his voice a little. This is not a shout or overly-loud voice, but raised to be definitely audible. He continues with *ut intres*, etc. The *Domine non sum dignus*, etc. is said three times. The server rings the bell three times: once each time the priest says *Domine non sum dignus*. See Fig. 5.67.

Fig. 5.67 – Domine non sum dignus

PRIEST'S COMMUNION OF THE HOST

Standing erect, the priest takes the two halves of the host in his right hand, holding them between his thumb and forefinger. The paten remains in his left hand where it was, and he rejoins the thumb and forefinger of the left hand. He makes the sign of the cross with the host over the paten from edge to edge while saying *Corpus Domini nostri*, etc. See Fig. 5.68. This sign is of the same nature as at the Minor Elevation or the Pax Domini.

Then the Celebrant, bowing down over the altar and holding the paten beneath his chin, reverently receives the host. See Fig. 5.69. It is important that the paten be there to catch any crumbs. The corporal remains a back-

HOW TO SAY MASS IN THE ANGLICAN RITE

up for this purpose, but the first line of defense is the paten. After receiving the host, the Celebrant places the paten back on the corporal in front of the chalice, joins his hands, and meditates silently a bit.

Fig. 5.68 – Signing with the host over the paten before Communion

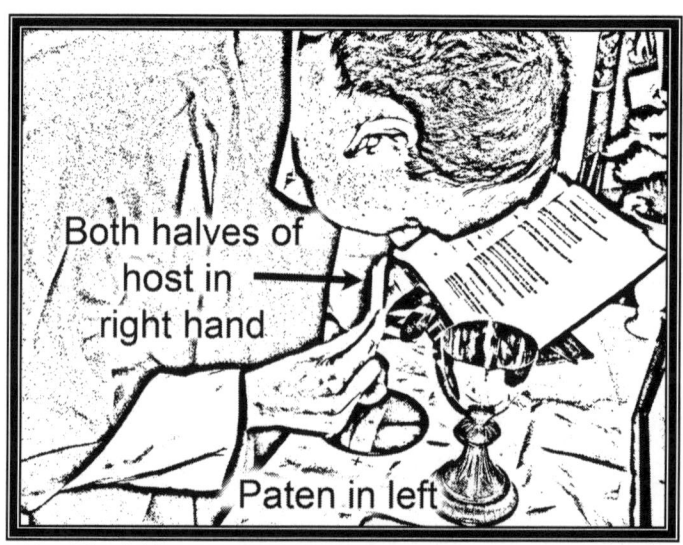

Fig. 5.69 – The Celebrant receives the host, bowing down over the altar and holding the paten underneath.

LOW MASS

COMMUNION OF THE BLOOD

The Celebrant, having finished his meditation after receiving the host, removes the pall from the chalice and genuflects. He picks up the paten in the left hand, holding it as at the communion of the host, but this time over the chalice, and uses his right forefinger to brush any crumbs on the paten into the chalice. At this time he says the *Quid retribuam*, etc. Having finished this, he places the paten back on the corporal in front of the chalice. He picks up the chalice by the stem with the right hand and signs over the corporal while saying *Sanguis Domini nostri*, etc. See Fig. 5.70 and 5.71.

Fig. 5.70 – Signing with the chalice over the corporal.

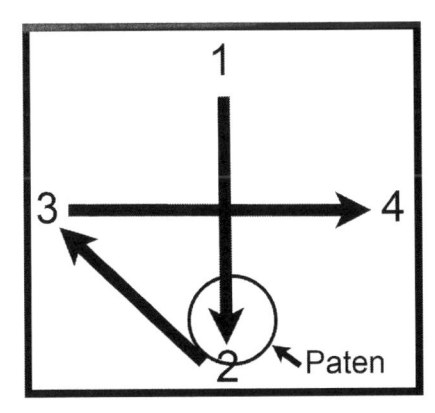

Fig. 5.71 – Method of making the sign of the cross over the corporal with the chalice.

Then, supporting the base of the chalice with the left hand, the Celebrant receives the entirety of the Precious Blood, including the small particle of the host that was put in the chalice at the co-mingling. See Fig. 5.72. After this, the Celebrant puts the chalice back on the corporal, but does not cover it with the pall.

Fig. 5.72 – Receiving the Precious Blood

COMMUNION OF THE PEOPLE

If the servers and/or people are to be communicated, then this is done now. Otherwise, the Celebrant proceeds immediately to the Ablutions.

Notes on the Ciboria and Reserved Sacrament

If the faithful are to be communicated from a ciborium expressly for the purpose of holding unconsecrated hosts to be consecrated and distributed, then this is on the altar before the mass. It sits on the corporal behind the chalice. If it has a lid, it is covered, but not veiled. The lid is removed before the consecration of the host, and replaced after. It may be veiled, but need not be. If the ciborium does not have a lid, then it simply rests open until after the consecration, at which time it may be veiled if physically practicable, but need not be. If there are any hosts remaining after communion, then the priests either consumes them or reserves them in the tabernacle. If he reserves them, and the tabernacle is already open, then he places the hosts in the ciborium for the reserved host. If the tabernacle is not open, then he opens the tabernacle, genuflecting if the sacrament is inside already, places

LOW MASS

the hosts in the tabernacle for the reserved sacrament, genuflects, and closes the door as usual before the ablutions.

If the Reserved Sacrament is to be used, then after saying the Agnus Dei, the Celebrant unveils the tabernacle (which must be veiled at all times when it is closed and the Blessed Sacrament is inside), opens it, and genuflects. He removes the ciborium for the reserved sacrament and places it on the corporal behind the chalice. It may be veiled, but need not be. However, the lid remains closed until the ciborium is put into use. If the reserved sacrament is used, then it is generally the practice to use the ciborium and a host there from for the *Ecce Agnus Dei*. The lid of the ciborium is placed back on after communion. It is placed back in the tabernacle before the ablutions, the priest genuflects, and the tabernacle is closed and veiled.

The priest holds a host over the paten or the ciborium and says the *Ecce Agnus Dei*. Then he and the servers and people who intend to receive communion say *Domine non sum dignus*, etc., or *Lord, I am not worthy*, etc. See Fig. 5.73.

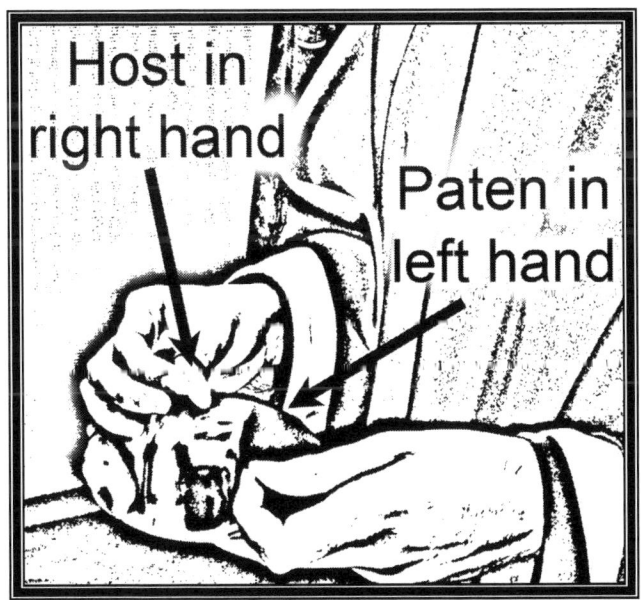

Fig. 5.73 – Displaying the host for the Ecce Agnus Dei. Here is shown held over the paten.

The priest first communicates the servers, then the clergy in choir, then the people. It is highly recommended that one server accompanies the Celebrant with the communion paten (see Section 2). The priest says *Corpus Domini nostri*, etc., while making the sign of the cross with the host over the face of the communicant, taking care that the host also remains over the ciborium or paten. He then places the host on the tongue of the communicant. All communicants kneel to receive communion. Only the Celebrant stands, bowing over the altar, to receive communion.

ABLUTIONS

Communion being given, the Celebrant returns to the center of the altar. If the reserved sacrament was used, then he replaces the ciborium in the tabernacle, genuflects, and closes and veils the tabernacle. If a ciborium was used for unconsecrated hosts to be consecrated during the mass, this vessel is placed on the corporal behind the chalice and will be purified later.

The Celebrant says *Quod ore sumpserimus*, etc. silently. Then he turns to the right, holding the chalice by its stem in his right hand, the left hand supporting the base. The server comes from the Credence table with the wine and water cruets (in the same manner as at the Offertory). The server takes the wine cruet (which is already open) and pours a little wine in the chalice. The Celebrant turns to face the cross, consumes the wine, swirling the chalice as needed to aid in purification and removal of all particles of the Body and Blood.

The Celebrant then says, either while still holding the chalice or placing it on the corporal and joining his hand, facing the cross, *Corpus tuum*, etc. This is also said silently. He turns again to the right for the second ablution. He picks up the chalice (if he was previously holding the chalice, then he must sit it down to change his grip) by the bowl. He cups both hands under the bowl and holds his joined forefingers and thumbs over the top of the bowl of the chalice. See Figs. 5.74 and 5.75. The server then pours a little bit of wine over the fingers of the priest and into the chalice; then a little bit of water so purify the priest's fingers. After this, the priest sets the chalice down on the corporal or on the Epistle side of the altar and dries his fingers on a purificator (not a lavabo towel). See Fig. 5.76.

LOW MASS

Fig. 5.74 – *Fingers held joined over the top of the chalice for the second ablution.*

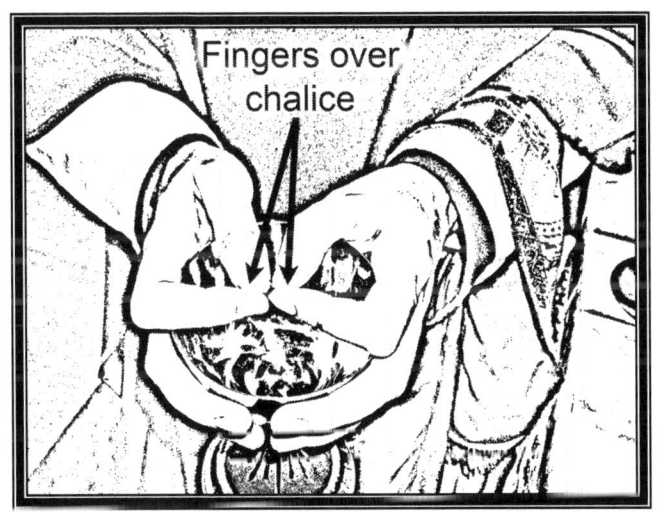

Fig. 5.75 – *Close-up of fingers held joined over the top of the chalice for the second ablution.*

From the Second Ablution on, the priest's thumbs and forefingers are no longer joined. He takes the chalice in his left hand and wipes out the bowl with the purificator. See Fig. 5.77. After, the chalice is set down in the center of the corporal.

HOW TO SAY MASS IN THE ANGLICAN RITE

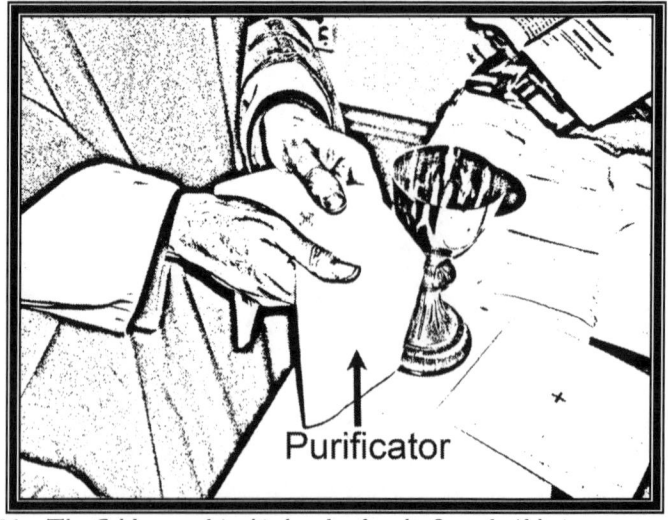

Fig. 5.76 – The Celebrants dries his hands after the Second Ablution on a purificator.

Fig. 5.77 – Purifying the chalice with the purificator.

Next the priest must purify the paten. He takes the paten in his left hand and wipes it over the corporal with the purificator. See Fig. 5.78. If it is a bowl paten, he may have the server pour some water (not wine) into it, which is then poured into the chalice and consumed, and the paten wiped dry with the purificator. It is important that this be done over the

LOW MASS

corporal, so that any particles of the Precious Body of our Lord would be caught by the corporal.

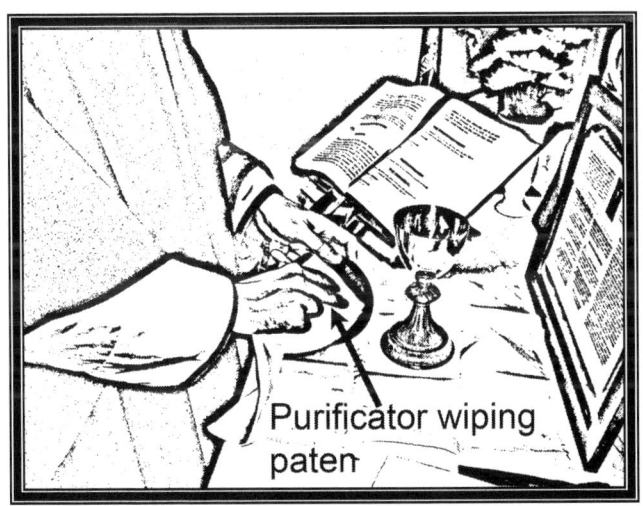

Fig. 5.78 – Purifying the paten with the purificator over the corporal.

If there is a ciborium that was used (not including the one for the reserved sacrament, which by now is safely back in the tabernacle), then it should be purified. It may be wiped with a purificator over the corporal as with the paten. Or, it may have water poured into it by the server. This is then poured into the chalice and consumed, and the ciborium is dried with the purificator. Now the Sacred Vessels are purified, and the chalice must again be stacked.

STACKING THE CHALICE AFTER THE ABLUTIONS

After the Ablutions are complete, the priest takes the purificator and places it on top of the chalice as before the mass. See Fig. 5.79. Then he places the paten on top of this. See Fig. 5.80. The pall goes on top. See Fig. 5.81.

Then the Celebrant must fold the corporal. To do this, he must move the stacked chalice off of the corporal. He picks up the chalice with the right hand on the step. His left hand goes flat on the top of the pall. The vessels are moved to the right and set down on the altar. See Fig. 5.82.

HOW TO SAY MASS IN THE ANGLICAN RITE

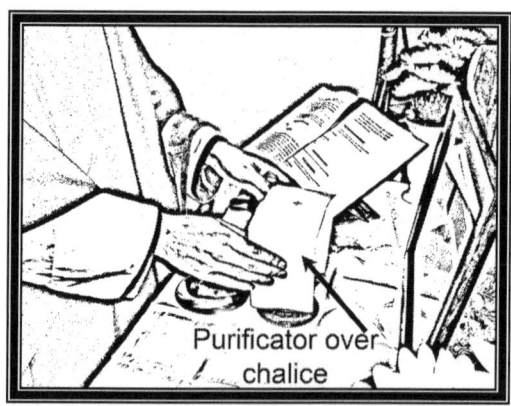

Fig. 5.79 – The purificator goes over the chalice first when stacking the chalice after the ablutions.

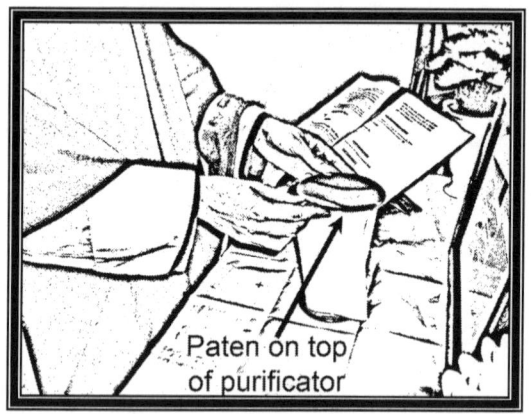

Fig. 5.80 – Next goes the paten...

Fig. 5.81 – And lastly is the pall.

LOW MASS

Fig. 5.82 – Moving the chalice off of the corporal.

Next the priest folds the corporal in the usual manner (see Section 2). He takes the burse, which should be on the altar on the Gospel side, opens it, and places the corporal inside (see Fig. 5.83). Closing the burse, he sets it to the right, or wherever is convenient. Then the stacked chalice is moved back to the center of the altar. See Fig. 5.84.

Fig. 5.83 – Placing the corporal back in the burse.

HOW TO SAY MASS IN THE ANGLICAN RITE

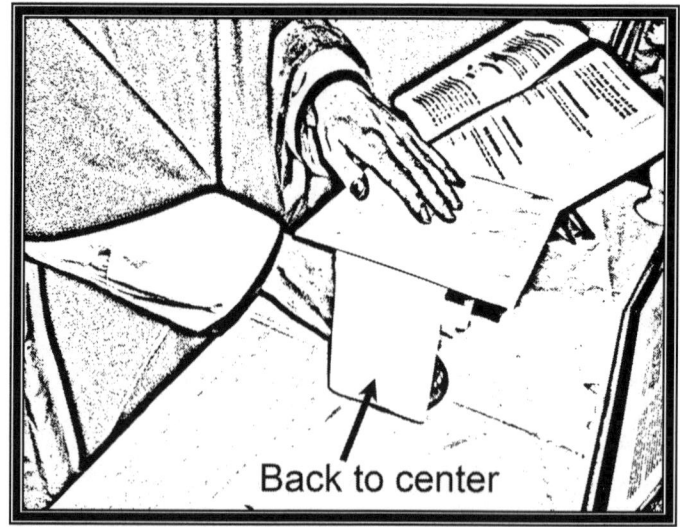

Fig. 5.84 – Moving the stacked chalice back to the center of the altar after folding the corporal and placing it in the burse.

Now the chalice must be veiled. The Celebrant takes the veil from the altar and veils the chalice from the front to the back as usual. He then places the burse on top. See Fig. 5.85.

Fig. 5.85 – Placing the burse on top of the veiled chalice.

After the ablutions are performed, and while the priest is stacking the chalice, the appointed server transfers the missal from the Gospel side to the Epistle side (in its original position). He follows exactly the same path as he did to transfer the missal the other way, only in reverse. During the ablutions, the servers remain kneeling at the credence table or in front of the altar until the General Thanksgiving when the priest says *Oremus*.

GENERAL THANKSGIVING

The Celebrant moves back to the Epistle corner in the same position as for the Collects. With hands joined, he says *Oremus*. The servers rise. Then, with hands extended, he recites the General Thanksgiving. He joins his hands as usual for the conclusion, *through Jesus Christ our Lord*, etc.

COMMUNION VERSE & POST-COMMUNION

With hands joined, standing at the missal on the Epistle corner, the Celebrant reads the Communion Verse appointed for the mass. Then, going to the center of the altar, he kisses the altar in the center in the usual manner, turns to the people, and says, with hands extended, *Dominus vobiscum*. The servers respond as usual, *et cum spiritu tuo*. The priest joins his hands and walks back to the missal. With hands joined, he says *Oremus*. He extends his hands and says the Postcommunions to match the Collects said earlier. These are said in exactly the same manner as the Collects.

DISMISSAL

Next the priest again returns to the center of the altar, kisses it in the center, and turns to the people (see Fig. 5.86). He extends his hands as usual and says *Dominus vobiscum*. The servers respond *et cum spiritu tuo*. Then, with hands still extended, he says *Ite Missa Est*, and the servers respond *Deo gratias*.

Whenever the *Gloria* is not sung (the color is purple or rose), *Ite missa est* is not used. After saying *Dominus vobiscum*, the priest turns back to face the altar and instead says, with hands joined, *Benedicamus Domino*. The response is *Deo gratias*. In masses of the dead, the dismissal is *Requiescant in pace*, said in the same position as for *Benedicamus Domino*. The response is simply *Amen*. During Easter week, the Dismissal is *Ite missa est, alleluia, alleluia*, and the response is *Deo gratias, alleluia, alleluia*.

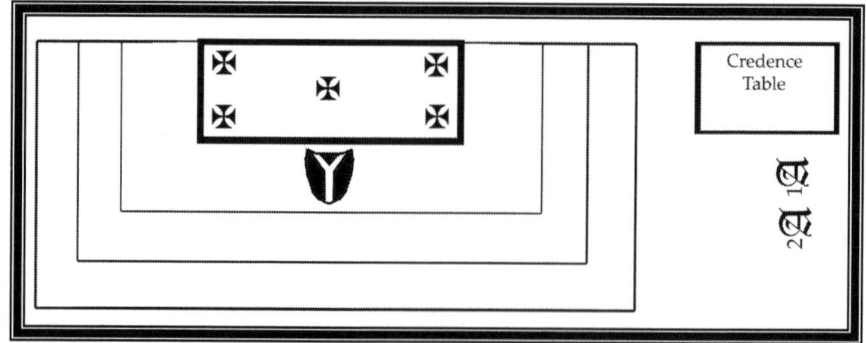

Fig. 5.86 – Position at the Dismissal and Blessing

BENEDICTION

The priest turns to face the also (or continues facing it if he used *Benedicamus Domino* or *Requiescant in pace*), bows down with hands joined upon the altar, and says the *Placeat tibi*. Then he kisses the altar in the center and turns to the people to give the Benediction. (In masses of the dead, there is no blessing. The altar is kissed, but the priest proceeds to the Last Gospel. See the section on Requiem masses.)

Facing the people in the center of the altar (see Fig. 5.86 above), the priest extends, raises, and joins his hands before his breast in one fluid motion as he says *Benedicat vos, omnipotens Deus*. See Figs. 5.87-5.90. Then as he says *Pater, et Filius, et Spiritus Sanctus*, he makes a single large cross with his right hand over the people while holding the left hand flat against the breast as usual (see Figs. 5.91-5.94). The servers and all present kneel for the Benediction and cross themselves as the priest makes the sign of the cross.

Fig. 5.87 – At the Benediction...first the hands are extended...

LOW MASS

Fig. 5.88 - ...and then raised...

Fig. 5.89 – The hands begin to be brought together...

Fig. 5.90 - ...and then brought down and joined before the breast.

HOW TO SAY MASS IN THE ANGLICAN RITE

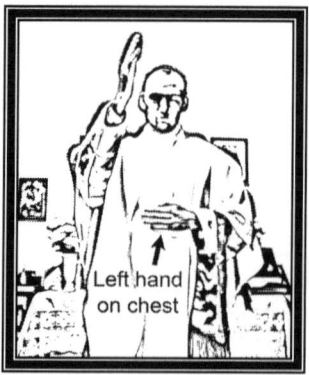

Fig. 5.91 – Making the sign of the cross at the Benediction. This is the first position, with the right hand raised as shown and the left hand flat on the chest as usual.

Fig. 5.92 – Then the priest continues tracing the cross by moving the right hand straight down.

Fig. 5.93 – And the to the priest's left...

Fig. 5.94 – Tracing the sign of the cross over the people at the benediction is completed by moving the hand to the right.

LAST GOSPEL

The priest then turns to the right to walk to the Gospel side, where is generally located with the most-used Last Gospel, the Beginning of the Gospel according to St. John. The priest may read the Last Gospel from an altar card or the missal, in which case the missal must be moved back to the Gospel side by the server in the usual manner. If the missal is moved, then it is placed further towards the Gospel side, and is placed straight, as it is on the Epistle corner, not as it is usually on the Gospel side during the Offertory and Canon.

Arriving at the Gospel side, standing in front of the altar card or missal, with hands joined and without turning to the people, the priest says *Dominus vobiscum*. The servers respond *et cum spiritu tuo*. As the priest announces the Gospel (for the usual one, it is Initium Sancti Evangeli secundum Ioannem), he makes the sign of the cross over the altar card (or the missal). See Fig. 5.95. The servers stand at the credence or, if using the kneeling option, they kneel before the altar. All is as at a regular reading of the Gospel.

The priest, after making the three signs of the cross on himself as usual (see Fig. 5.96) reads the Last Gospel with hands joined (see Fig. 5.97). He genuflects in the usual Last Gospel at the words *et verbum caro factum est*. The servers respond *Deo gratias* at the end.

HOW TO SAY MASS IN THE ANGLICAN RITE

Fig. 5.95 – Signing the altar card with the Last Gospel

Fig. 5.96 – The Celebrant signs himself thrice as usual at the Last Gospel.

LOW MASS

Fig. 5.97 – The Celebrant reads the Last Gospel with hands joined.

EXIT OF THE CELEBRANT AND SERVERS

The priest descends to the pavement from the Gospel side and stands in the center, facing the cross. The servers come to take their positions as at the Prayers at the Foot of the Altar (see Fig. 5.98).

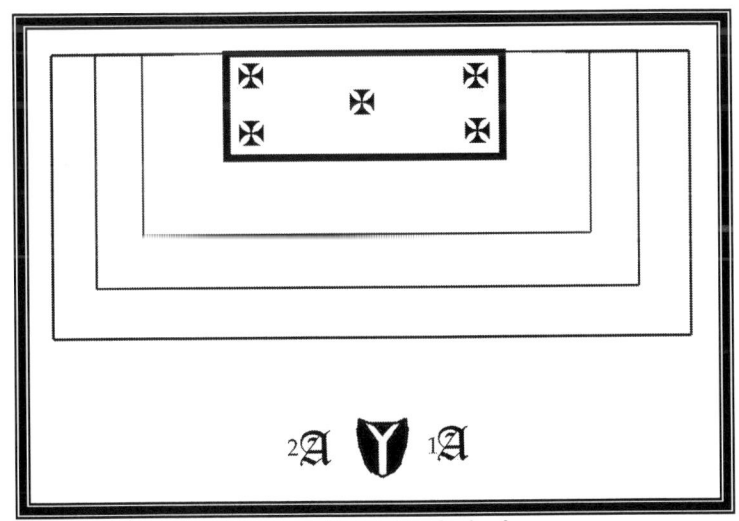

Fig. 5.98 – Positions before the final reverence.

If there are two servers, the server who goes to the left of the priest goes behind him, genuflecting as he passes the cross (or bowing, of course, if the sacrament is not reserved). The server to his right brings the biretta. He holds the biretta until after the reverence. The Celebrant genuflects (or bows as appropriate), and the servers genuflect (or bow) with him. Then the server to his right hands him the biretta.

After the reverence, the server to the left (second server) turns to his left and begins walking slowly towards the sacristy. The Celebrant also turns to the left, but waits for the first server to come in between him and the second server. See Fig. 5.99. As soon as the first server hands the biretta to the priest, he walks behind the server, genuflecting or bowing as appropriate, and then walks into the space made between the second server and the priest. This takes a bit of practice to time properly, but is not difficult. The object is to walk back to the sacristy in exactly the same manner as they walked from the sacristy.

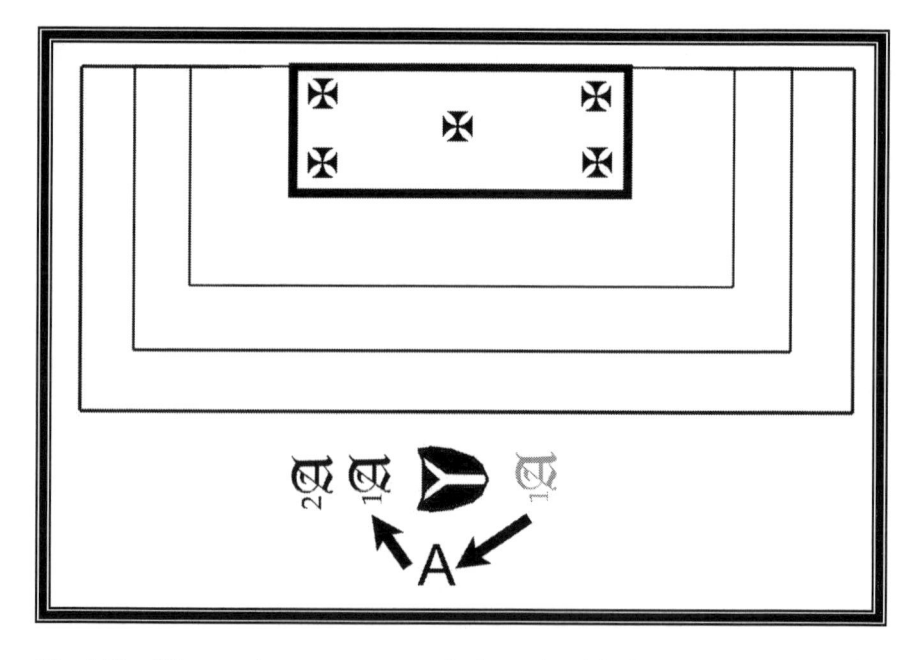

Fig. 5.99 – The second server moves towards the sacristy. The first server moves around behind the priest, genuflecting or bowing at "A", and going into position to walk to the sacristy as indicated. The priest turns to the left and prepares to walk out.

If the sacristy is on the Epistle side, then the second server does what is indicated for the first server in Fig. 5.99, and moves to stand in front of him. If there is only one server, then he stands to the right of the priest. After he hands the biretta to him, he does as is indicated in Fig. 5.99 for the first server, and then they walk to the sacristy.

IN THE SACRISTY

Upon returning to the sacristy, the Celebrant will lead the sacristy prayer(s). After this, the Celebrant should take the Sacred Vessels from the altar in the same manner as he placed them there (wearing the biretta). The servers extinguish the candles and take care of all that is on the altar.

A FINAL NOTE FOR PRELATES

Regarding genuflecting when crossing in front of the altar cross when the sacrament is reserved, bishop traditionally bow instead of genuflect (though, of course, they still do all genuflections called for in the missal). This privilege is also usually extended to the Prelates under the bishop, i.e., Canons, Deans, and Archdeacons. When they bow in lieu of genuflecting, though, the rest still genuflect.

HOW TO SAY MASS IN THE ANGLICAN RITE

High Mass

※☙

High mass is just as low mass in terms of the principal actions of the Celebrant. This section assumes familiarity with the low mass, and so here only the details for other participants are included, as well as differences between the high mass and the low mass.

BEFORE THE MASS

The Sacred Vessels are taken by the Celebrant, Deacon, or Sub-Deacon as at low mass, except they are not placed on the altar. They are taken in precisely the same manner, following the same protocol, but instead they are taken to the credence table. The burse remains on top of the veiled chalice, with the folded corporal inside. The other usual items are placed on the credence table, and the entire credence table should then be covered by the humeral veil to be used by the Sub-Deacon. It should be in the color of the mass. However, a white or gold humeral veil may acceptably be used when the color of the mass is white, red, green, or Marian blue; a purple humeral veil may be properly used when the color is purple or rose. At a Requiem mass, the humeral veil is not used.

The thurifer should have sufficient incense and extra charcoal, as well as other supplies, at his station near the credence table (or he may remain in the sacristy except when needed). The incense boat should be near the credence table, unless there is a boat bearer, who may carry it in the procession, but then takes it to the credence.

CHANT

All Collects are chanted in a high mass. The Canon is not chanted except where specifically indicated in the missal. All of these chants are also used. The ordinary music, i.e., the Kyrie, Gloria, Sanctus, Benedictus, and Agnus Dei, should be sung by the choir and/or congregation. The Creed may also be sung, and it is often a matter or tradition or rule to do so. The Gospel is sung by the Deacon, and the Epistle is sung by the Sub-Deacon. The propers of the mass, i.e., the Introit, Gradual, Offertory, and Communion, may be chanted by the choir. In addition to or in place of, it is often permitted by proper church authority to use hymns. However, if this is done, the Celebrant must still read the propers himself during the singing.

The Celebrant or Deacon dismisses the people with the dismissals in chant form given in the missal. However, the Benediction is recited, not sung. The Last Gospel also is not sung, including the *Dominus vobiscum* and introduction. However, all salutations in the mass are sung, as is the preface. The tone to be used is the solemn tone for feasts and Sundays and the ferial tone for ferial masses and masses of the dead. The ferial tone is either what is given as the tone "ad libitum" or recto tono (chanting everything on the principle tone).

SYMBOLS

Symbol	Role
♆	Celebrant
🧥	Celebrant vested in cope
▄	Deacon of the Mass
▄	Sub-Deacon of the Mass
𝔐𝔠	Master of Ceremonies
𝔄𝔐𝔠	Assistant Master of Ceremonies
1𝔄	First Acolyte
2𝔄	Second Acolyte
𝔗	Thurifer

ENTRANCE OR PROCESSION

If there is to be no procession, then everyone enters the Sanctuary from the sacristy as at low mass. The servers go to their positions for the beginning, if they are shown on Fig. 6.1, or they go to the credence or other appointed location. The Sub-Deacon, much like the second server at low mass, steps out of the way to the right so that the Deacon and Celebrant may pass to their place, and then he steps into his place as in Fig. 6.1. The crucifer, is a cross is carried from the sacristy, simply takes the cross to its location and goes to wherever is his appointed place.

If there is a procession, they process from the back of the nave to the sanctuary. The clergy in choir go to the choir. The crucifer takes the cross to its stand and then goes to his place, wherever the physical arrangement of the church dictate. Others go straight to their place as in Fig. 6.1. The Sub-Deacon peels to the left, the Deacon to the right, and the Celebrant comes in to the center between them. The thurifer in this case must stand out of the way until they pass. If there is to be an asperges, he should immediately deposit the thurible and take the holy water pot. Else, he has the option of kneeling for the prayers at the foot of the altar with the thurible or depositing it at the credence table and returning to the position in Fig. 6.1 for the prayers at the foot of the altar.

In either case of entry, the following is the order, from first to last:

Thurifer
Acolyte – Crucifer – Acolyte
Torchbearers (without torches)
Other Servers
Master of Ceremonies *(the Asst. MC may walk beside or in front of him)*
Clergy in Choir *(procession only)*
Sub-Deacon
Deacon
Celebrant

As the party arrives in the sanctuary, everyone genuflects (or bows, if the sacrament is not reserved), and goes to their place. The thurifer takes the thurible to the credence table and then comes to his place. The Sacred Ministers do not genuflect or bow until they are all in place. The MC takes the birettas of the Celebrant and Deacon from the Deacon. Then he passes to the left and takes that of the Sub-Deacon. The birettas are taken to the credence table or sedilia, and the MC returns. (The AMC may assist with this by, for example, taking the Sub-Deacon's biretta.) Then the Ministers and all the servers around them genuflect or bow together. A hymn or chant may be sung during the procession and before the asperges (if it is to take place). See Fig. 6.1. Additional servers, the crucifer, and the torchbearers take their positions at the credence or wherever else is physically convenient to locate them.

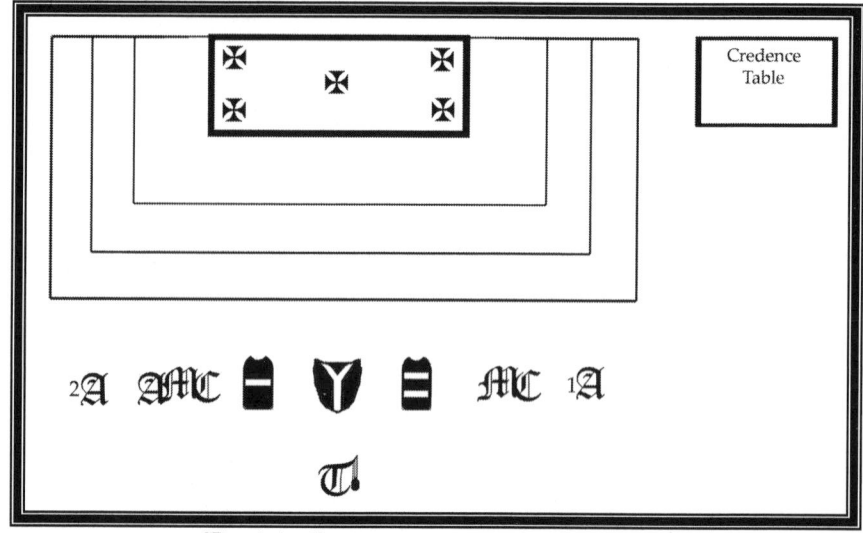

Fig. 6.1 – Positions upon arrival at the altar.

ASPERGES

If there is an asperges (that is, if this is the principal mass on Sundays), then the Celebrant will be vested in cope. The thurifer takes the pot of holy water and brings it to the Celebrant after the genuflection. All kneel as in Fig. 6.1 above for the Asperges.

The Celebrant intones *Asperges me* (or *Vidi Aquam* in Paschaltide), and the choir takes over the chant. The Celebrant, while kneeling, sprinkles the altar three times with the aspergillum. Then he sprinkles himself with holy water and rises. He sprinkles the Deacon and Sub-Deacon, who rise before being sprinkled. The Celebrant goes with the Deacon on his right and the Sub-Deacon on his left to sprinkle any clergy present in choir. The servers are sprinkled next, and they rise once they have been sprinkled. The people stand as soon as the Deacon and Sub-Deacon rise.

For the asperges of the people, the Celebrant walks between the Deacon (to his right) and the Sub-Deacon (to his left), who hold his cope open. See Fig. 6.2. He holds the aspergillum, and the thurifer walks to the right of the deacon holding the pot of holy water. The walk down the center aisle sprinkling both sides of the pews. When they reach the back, they turn around, maintaining they same relative position among the Celebrant, Deacon, and Sub-Deacon, and return to the sanctuary, genuflecting or bowing upon return. See Fig. 6.3. If the church is large enough, they may proceed similarly down other aisles sprinkling the people until all have been aspersed. When the choir sings the *Gloria Patri* in the Asperges or Vidi Aquam, the entire asperges party stops where they are and they all bow until the *Gloria Patri* is over. The people also, upon being sprinkled, should cross themselves.

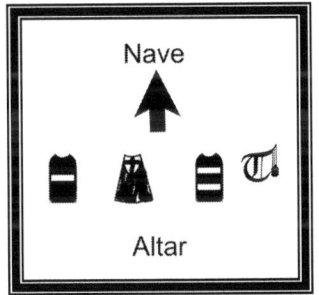

Fig. 6.2 – Positions for the Asperges when processing through the church.

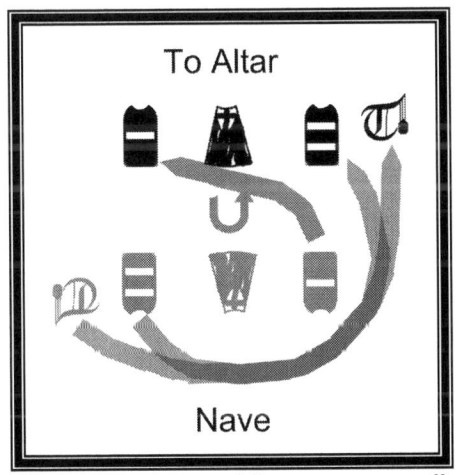

Fig. 6.3 – Turning around in the asperges. The asperges party effectively performs a left wheel maneuver so that they return to the altar in the same order and they left it.

Upon return to the sanctuary, the thurifer takes the aspergillum and holy water pot to the credence table. The Celebrant, Deacon, and Sub-Deacon go to the sedilia. The Celebrant exchanges his cope for a chasuble. First, the MC helps him remove the cope and lays it aside. Then the MC helps him on with the chasuble. The Celebrant typically kneels, and the chasuble is first laid over his head from the back and then down in front in a fluid and dignified motion. The best way to accomplish this is to fold the front of the chasuble back over the back of the chasuble. Then lay the back of the chasuble where it should go against the back of the Celebrant, positioning the hole for the head where it should go. Then it is a simple matter of taking the front of the chasuble and gently folding it over the head of the Celebrant. The Celebrant's head should typically go naturally right through the head-hole in the chasuble. This process should not look like an undignified struggle or quick clothes change.

After the chasuble has been placed on, the MC hands the Celebrant his maniple, and the Celebrant, first kissing its cross, puts it on (or the MC helps him put it on. The AMC may assist with this vesting. Meanwhile, the Deacon and Sub-Deacon put on their maniples. After this, all return to their positions as in Fig. 6.1.

If the asperges does not take place, the ministers all have their maniples on before the procession, and the Celebrant wears a chasuble instead of a cope (if he does the asperges, though, remember that he should process in the cope, not the chasuble). After their genuflection, they remain in position as in Fig. 6.1 and begin the Prayers at the Foot of the Altar.

PRAYERS AT THE FOOT OF THE ALTAR

All is precisely as at low mass, except that the Deacon and Sub-Deacon stand as the Celebrant. All others kneel. The Deacon and Sub-Deacon say their *Confiteor* with the servers, but remain standing, bowing low as the Celebrant did.

After they have said the Prayers at the Foot of the Altar, the acolytes go to their place at the credence. The MC and AMC go to the credence or wherever they are needed (they have less strictness with where they are located, due to their unique role). The Celebrant, Deacon, and Sub-Deacon ascend the altar side-by-side to the predella. The Celebrant says the *Aufer a nobis*, etc., and he alone kisses the altar in the center.

HIGH MASS

CENSING THE ALTAR

As the Ministers ascend the altar, the thurifer should prepare the thurible. He and the MC proceed up the side altar steps on the epistle side to the predella. See Fig. 6.4 for the positions at the blessing of the incense.

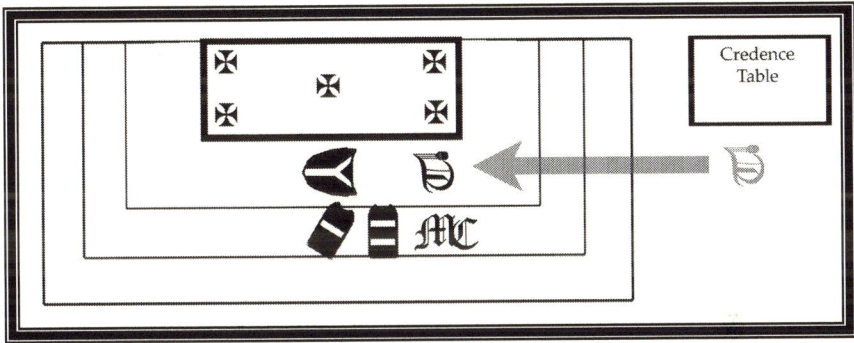

Fig. 6.4 – Positions at the blessing of the incense. If the predella is large enough to accommodate all shown in this diagram, then they all stand on the predella. Else, they stand as shown or as convenient according to the physical arrangements of the church. The boat bearer, if there is one, stands next to the Master of Ceremonies on the right.

The boat bearer, or the thurifer if there is no boat bearer, hands the incense boat to the MC or to the Deacon. The thurifer holds open the thurible (see the sections on physical property and altar severs for more details on this procedure and the ones following). The MC or Deacon holds the incense for the Celebrant to bless. Then the Celebrant puts incense into the thurible with the spoon. This is typically three spoon-fuls. The thurifer then closes the thurible, and the Deacon or MC hands the boat back to the boat bearer. (If there is no boat bearer, then the thurifer takes back the boat directly.)

The thurifer hands the thurible to the Deacon and then goes back to the credence table. The Deacon hands the censer to the Celebrant, and then the Deacon and the Sub-Deacon move to the right and left of the Celebrant respectively. The MC stands at the Epistle corner. After the Celebrant has censed the cross, the MC removes the missal (on its stand if possible) from the altar and stands out of the way until that side has been censed. Then he replaces it and remains at the Epistle corner. The Deacon and Sub-Deacon move in unison with the Celebrant, holding his chasuble out of the way. When the Celebrant bows to the cross, the Deacon and Sub-Deacon bow as well. See Fig. 6.5 for the positions at the censing. See Fig. 6.6 for the order of censing the altar (this is also in the rubrics in the missal.)

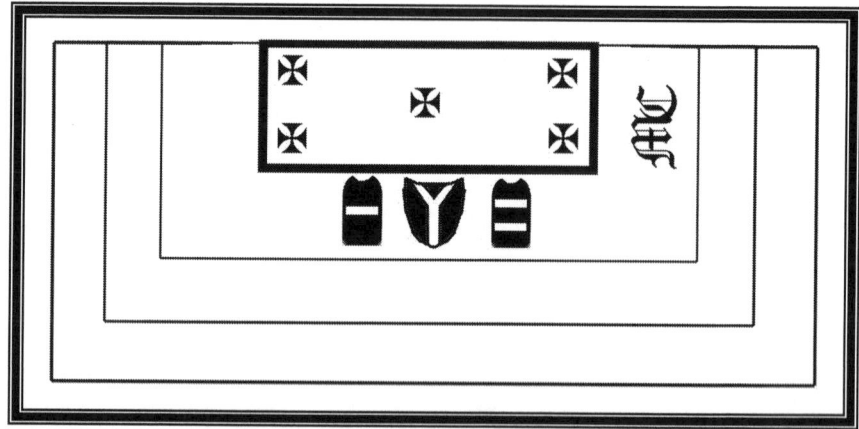

Fig. 6.5 – Positions at censing the altar

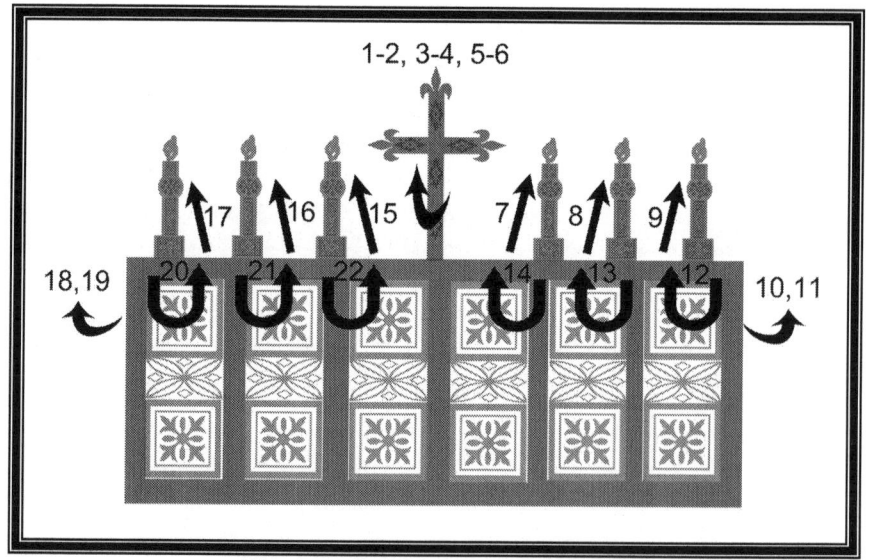

Fig. 6.6 – Order for censing the altar

If there is a low altar, then it will not be against the wall, as in Fig. 6.6. The details for censing a low altar are given in the General Rubrics in the missal. In short, the Celebrant censes the cross as in Fig. 6.6 above, and then walks slowly around the altar with the Deacon to his right holding the chasuble out of the way as needed, and the Sub-Deacon walking behind. The censing is done while walking, and the Celebrant swings the thurible in small circles. When they come to the back of the altar, they face the cross of the high altar and bow. Then they continue on around the altar in the same manner until they reach the front center, where they again bow.

If the low altar is to be censed, it should be censed before the high altar. There is also a tradition of censing the other small altars that may be within the church. The high altar should be the culmination of the censing process. The incense is blessed and put in the thurible on the predella of the high altar as described above. Then the Celebrant, Deacon, and Sub-Deacon, accompanied by the MC and others as needed, move to the first altar to cense. If they are censing small altars around the church, they should start with the one closest to the high altar on the Epistle side and move clockwise. Then the primary low altar is censed, and then the high altar.

When the censing of the altar is complete, the celebrant stands in the center of the altar facing the Epistle side (specifically, facing liturgical South). He hands the thurible to the Deacon, who bows upon receiving it, and the Celebrant bows back. This should be a slight, but definite bow. The Deacon censes the Celebrant with three double swings. The Deacon and Celebrant then bow to each other again. See Fig. 6.7 for the positions for censing the Celebrant.

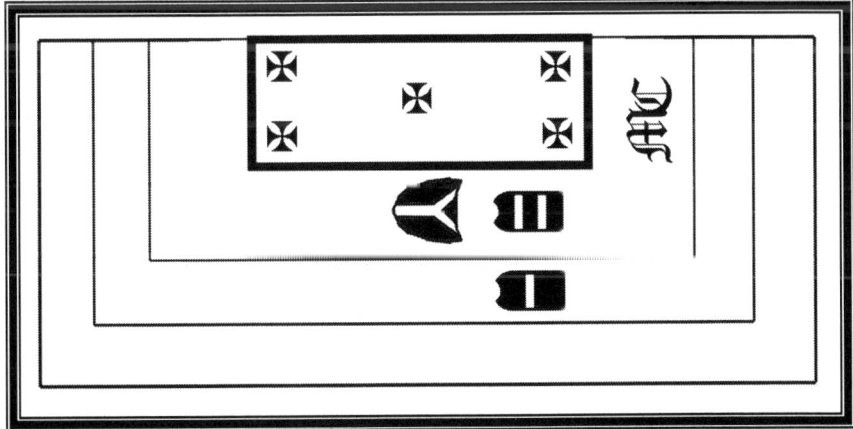

Fig. 6.7 – Censing the Celebrant

During the censing of the Celebrant, the thurifer approaches from the Epistle side. After he is censed, the Celebrant goes to his position for the

Introit and faces the altar (see Fig. 6.8). The Deacon and Sub-Deacon go to their own positions as well for the Introit. The MC remains at the Epistle corner, assisting at the missal as needed. The thurifer retires to the credence. If needed, he takes the thurible to the sacristy and replenishes the charcoal. He may, of course, always remain in the sacristy except when incense is called for in the mass.

INTROIT

The Celebrant reads the Introit as usual. During this time the choir is typically still singing the Introit. If they have sung the Introit (or are not doing so), then they may sing an anthem or hymn, or the congregation may sing a hymn. See Fig. 6.8 for the positions at the Introit. When the Celebrant finishes the Introit, the Ministers moves to the center of the altar on their own steps, genuflecting or bowing as appropriate upon arrival, and wait for the music to finish before continuing. See Fig. 6.9

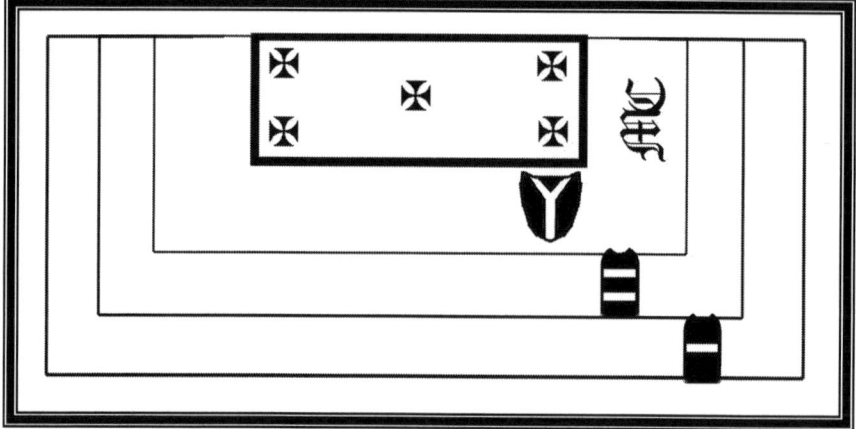

Fig. 6.8 – Position of the Sacred Ministers at the Introit

SUMMARY OF THE LAW AND KYRIE

The Sacred Ministers stand in the center of the altar as in Fig. 6.9 until the music has finished, if it has not already finished. When the music finishes (or immediately after their reverence, if the music has finished), the Deacon and Sub-Deacon move to the positions indicated in 6.10 as the Celebrant turns to face the people and say the Summary of the Law. They then return to their places as in Fig. 6.9 as the Celebrant turns to the altar for the Kyrie. The Celebrant says the Kyrie with the Deacon and Sub-Deacon giving the responses instead of the servers (as at low mass). The choir or congregation sings the Kyrie. If the Ministers finish the Kyrie before the choir and/or congregation (which is usually the case), the proceed to the sedilia and sit until the music is finished. The MC (and AMC and servers if needed) bring the ministers their birettas, which they wear from the steps to the sedilia, and while they are sitting. The congregation may sit when they are sitting. When the music is finished, they rise, go to the altar, and give up the biretta, and stand as in Fig. 6.9.

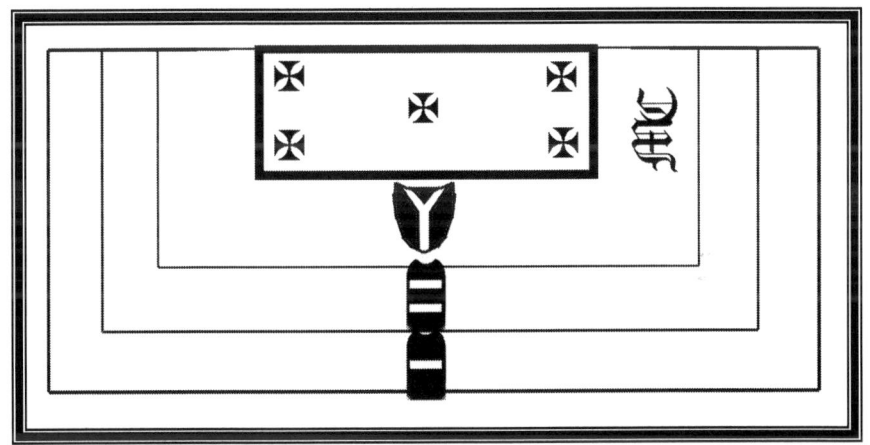

Fig. 6.9 – Positions before the Summary of the Law and at the Kyrie

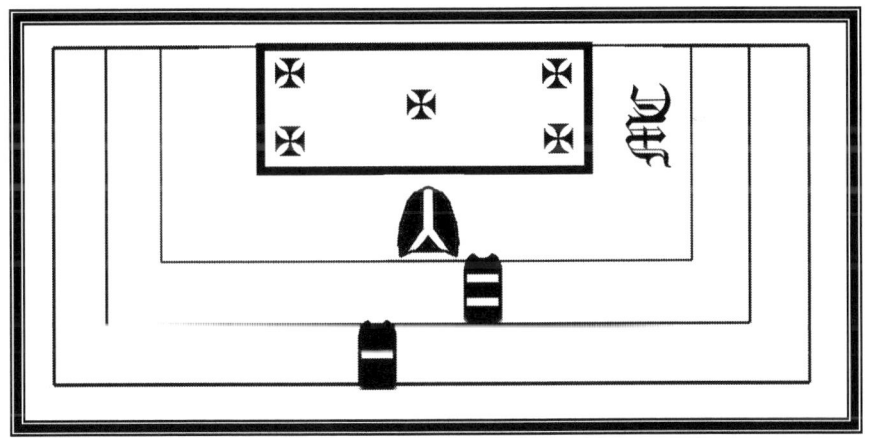

Fig. 6.10 – Positions at the Summary of the Law and also when the Celebrant turns to the people in the center of the altar and says "Dominus vobiscum"

GLORIA IN EXCELSIS

The Celebrant begins the Gloria as at low mass (with the same hand positions), but at high mass he intones the Gloria. The choir and/or congregation picks up the singing. The Celebrant says the rest of the Gloria himself in regular speaking tone. The Ministers begin as in Fig. 6.9, but once the Celebrant has intoned the beginning of the Gloria, they come up to the predella by him as in Fig. 6.11.

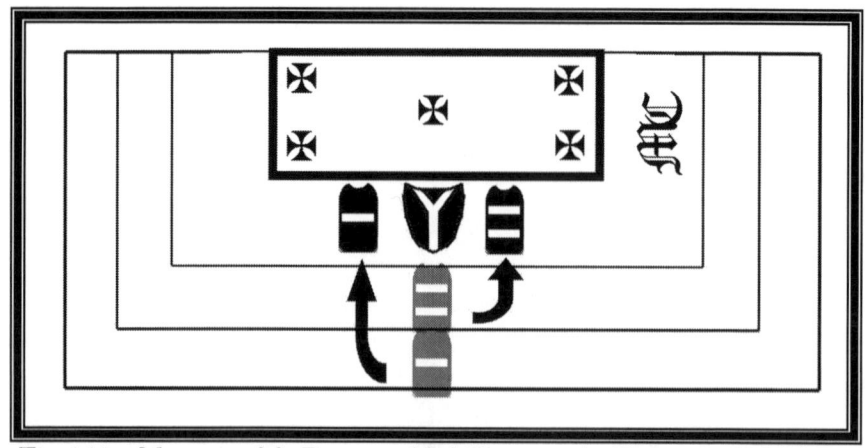

Fig. 6.11 – Movement of the Deacon and Sub-Deacon as the Gloria is intoned. They remain on the predella for the rest of the Gloria

The Deacon and Sub-Deacon bow and cross themselves when the Celebrant does. When the Celebrant is finished reading the Gloria, provided the music has not finished or is not about to finish, they return to the sedilia just as they did at the Kyrie and sit. When the music is finished or about to finish, they return. (It flows better as a general rule to return to the altar just as the music is finishing. It contributes more to the glory and solemnity of the mass to have music while the Ministers are walking. This requires practice with the choir and music staff.) When the Ministers return to the altar, they stand on their own step in the center of the altar as in Fig. 6.9. If they do not go to the sedilia (because the music is about to finish), then they simply go to their position as in Fig. 6.9 after the Gloria and wait.

SALUTATION AND COLLECTS

The Celebrant turns to the people and chants *Dominus vobiscum* in the appropriate tone (festal or ferial) as usual, and the Deacon and Sub-Deacon move to the side as in Fig. 6.10. The Deacon and Sub-Deacon (and the choir, servers, etc.) respond *Et cum spiritu tuo*. When the Celebrant goes back to the missal, the Deacon and Sub-Deacon follow and stand as at the Introit in Fig. 6.8.

HIGH MASS

On Sundays and feasts, the salutation may be intoned as follows:

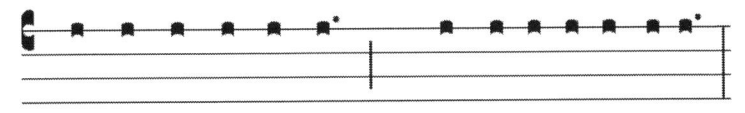

Do – mi– nus vo- bis- cum.   Et cum spi-ri- tu tu- o.

The above tone, as it is recto tono, is also used on ferias. For chanting the salutation in English, the tone is the same as above.

The following tone ad libitum may be used any time.

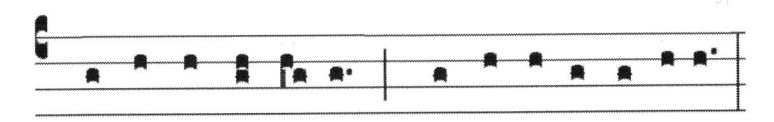

Do - mi– nus vo- bis- cum.   Et cum spi- ri - tu tu- o.

In English, the ad libitum tone is:

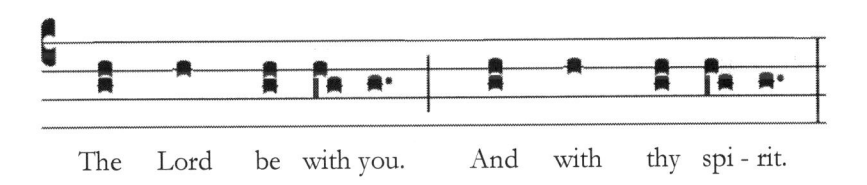

The   Lord   be with you.   And   with   thy spi - rit.

The Celebrant chants the Collects, following the same rules as at low mass. Remember that at high mass, virtually everything is sung. All the Collects and Post-communions are sung, but not the Secrets (as they are said in the secret voice).

The word Oremus, or the words Let us pray are chanted recto tono. Then the Celebrant chants the collects. For a ferial mass, the tone should be recto tono (everything sung on the principal tone) or the tone ad libitum as given below. For Sundays and feasts, the tones for chanting are also given below. They are given in Latin, but the metrical principals apply the same to English as well.

Festal Tone *(Sundays and Feasts)*

The collect is chanted on the principal tone from the beginning of the sentence until just before the end of the sentence or phrase. The three options for ending each sentence/phrase are to continue on the principal tone, a flex, or a metrum.

Flex:

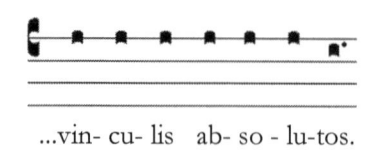

...vin- cu- lis ab- so - lu-tos.

In the flex, the last syllable is sung one tone down from the principal tone, i.e., a half step down. It should also be lengthened a bit.

Metrum:

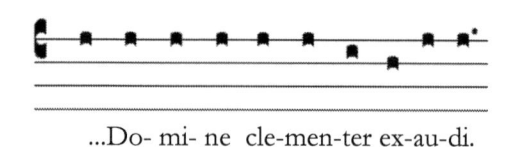

...Do- mi- ne cle-men-ter ex-au-di.

In the metrum, the last stressed syllable (*-au-* of *exaudi* above) and all syllables remaining in the sentence or phrase are sung on the principal tone. The two syllables preceding the last stressed syllable are sung as indicated above.

Conclusion:

The conclusion is sung on the principal tone, with a metrum for *Spiritus Sancti Deus* (with *Deus* back on the principal tone). Then the remainder, including *Amen*, is sung on the principal tone.

Tone ad Libitum

The tone ad libitum begins with a different *Oremus*, as given below (the same apply for the English *Let us pray*).

Oremus for the Tone ad Libitum:

O-re-mus.
Let us pray.

Beginning of Sentences and Phrases:

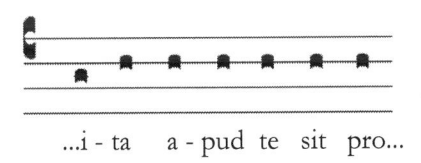

...i - ta a - pud te sit pro...

Sentences and phrases begin on the note three positions down on the staff from the principal tone for the first syllable of the phrase or sentence. Then the rest of the sentence is sung on the tone two positions on the staff down from the principal tone until the ending of the sentence or phrase.

Flex:

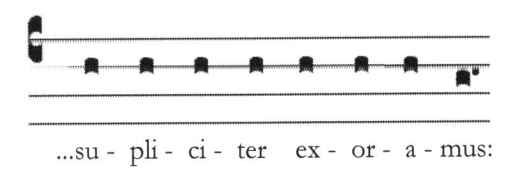

...su - pli - ci - ter ex - or - a - mus:

At ends of phrases (usually marked in the prayers with the colon as indicated above), the flex is used. The final syllable of the phrase is sung on the tone three positions down from the principal tone.

Full Stop:

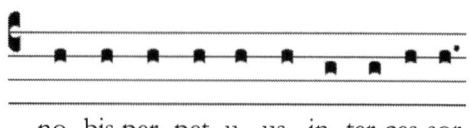

...no- bis per- pet- u - us in- ter-ces-sor.

The full stop (end of a sentence) is sung with the last syllable of the sentence and all syllables after it on the tone two positions down on the staff from the principal tone. The two tones before are sung one position down from that.

Conclusion:

The conclusion begins as any other phrase.

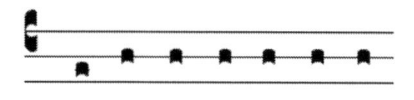

Per Do- mi-num nos-trum Je-sum...

The ending of the first phrase is then:

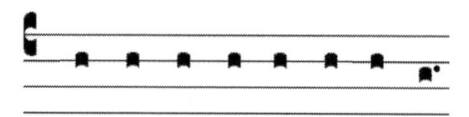

...Chris-tum fi - li - um tu- um:

And then...

qui te- cum vi - vit et re-gnat...

Followed by...

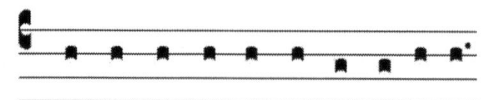

...in un - i - ta - te Spi- ri- tus Sanc-ti De-us,

And then...

Per om-ni - a sae-cu- la sae-cu- lo - rum.

And finally...

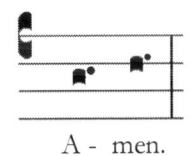

A - men.

For chanting in English, the above sentence, phrase, and collect endings are precisely the same metrically. The English words are simply fit to the chant tones as given above.

When the Celebrant has begun the last collect to be said, the MC bows and moves to the credence table and takes the Book of Epistles. The AMC moves to the Epistle corner to assist with the missal (or, if absolutely needed, the Deacon may move up to do this...though it is preferable that he remain where his usual place is).

When the Celebrant begins the conclusion/ending for the last collect, the MC precedes the Sub-Deacon to the center of the altar. They make the proper reverence (genuflect or bow) and go to the chancel gate facing the people. The Sub-Deacon stands in the center, and the MC stands to the Epistle side and slightly behind the Sub-Deacon. See Fig. Fig. 6.12.

EPISTLE

After the Collects, the Celebrant and Deacon move to the sedilia, first taking their birettas, and sit for the Epistle. Servers may accompany the Sub-Deacon if needed, standing on either side of him or slightly behind. Provided this is not done to excess, it can add to the solemnity.

HOW TO SAY MASS IN THE ANGLICAN RITE

Fig. 6.12 – Positions at the Chancel Gate for the Epistle

The Sub-Deacon may alternatively stand by the chancel rail on the Epistle side and face the altar to chant the Epistle. Regardless of position, the Sub-Deacon chants the Epistle in the tones as given in the Epistolarium. All who are not attending him sit.

When the chanting of the Epistle is over, the Celebrant and Deacon rise, go to the altar, giving up their birettas upon arrival, and stand as in Fig. 6.13. The Sub-Deacon and MC come to the altar as well. The Sub-Deacon holds the Book of Epistles. Kneeling before the Celebrant, he presents the Book of Epistles closed. The Celebrant places his right hand on it, and the Sub-Deacon kisses it. The Celebrant then makes the sign of the cross over the Sub-Deacon. Having finished this, he turns to face the altar at the Epistle corner. The Sub-Deacon rises and gives the Book of Epistles to the MC, who takes it to the credence table. The Sub-Deacon goes back to his own step at at the Introit (see Fig. 6.8).

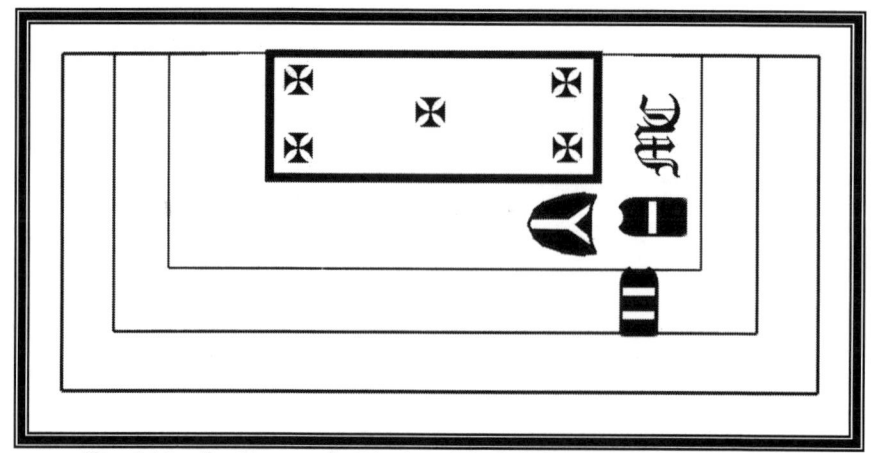

Fig. 6.13 – Positions at the Blessing of the Sub-Deacon after the Epistle

GRADUAL

The Celebrant reads the Gradual for the day from the Epistle corner. He should remember in certain masses that may happen in different seasons that the Alleluia may be replaced by a Tract, etc., and he should pay close attention to this in the missal. During this time the MC takes the Book of Gospels from the Credence table to the Deacon, who comes straight down to the pavement from his own step, and receives the Book of Gospels. He goes to the center of the altar on the pavement, bows, and ascends the steps. He places the Book of Gospels in a reverent position in the center of the altar. He then returns to the pavement, kneels on the lowest step, and says the *Munda Cor*.

Once the Celebrant has finished reading the Gradual, the Sub-Deacon ascends to the predella directly and transfers the missal to the Gospel side exactly as a server would, taking care to walk around the Deacon and make his reverence behind the Deacon. When he has done this, if there is time, he goes to the pavement and stands to the left and behind the Deacon. Meanwhile, the Celebrant moves to the center of the altar and stands, facing the Epistle side. The thurifer approach on the predella as at the Introit, with the MC, who holds the incense boat to be blessed (instead of the Deacon). See Fig. 6.14. Once the incense has been put into the thurible, the thurifer and MC go to the pavement. As they do, the Celebrant turns to face the Deacon, who rises and kneels on the second step or on the predella, if it is large enough, before the Celebrant. The Sub-Deacon goes with him, standing behind and to the left. The Deacon says *Jube Domne*, etc. See Fig. 6.15. The Celebrant blesses the Deacon with the *Dominus sit*, the Deacon rises, and takes the Book of Gospels from the Celebrant. They then go to the positions as in Fig. 6.16.

In Fig. 6.16, the Deacon and Sub-Deacon come to the pavement. The thurifer and First Server change positions, making the proper reverence, and the crucifer moves into position as indicated. They then process during the singing of the Gradual or Gradual hymn (the latter being an appropriate hymn, rather than a sung version of the appointed Gradual for the day from the propers of the mass) to the place where they are to chant the Gospel. This is generally just outside the chancel gate, but may just as well be in the central aisle within the nave or in some suitable location within the sanctuary. The acolytes, if they are holding candles as usually appointed, bow, but do not genuflect.

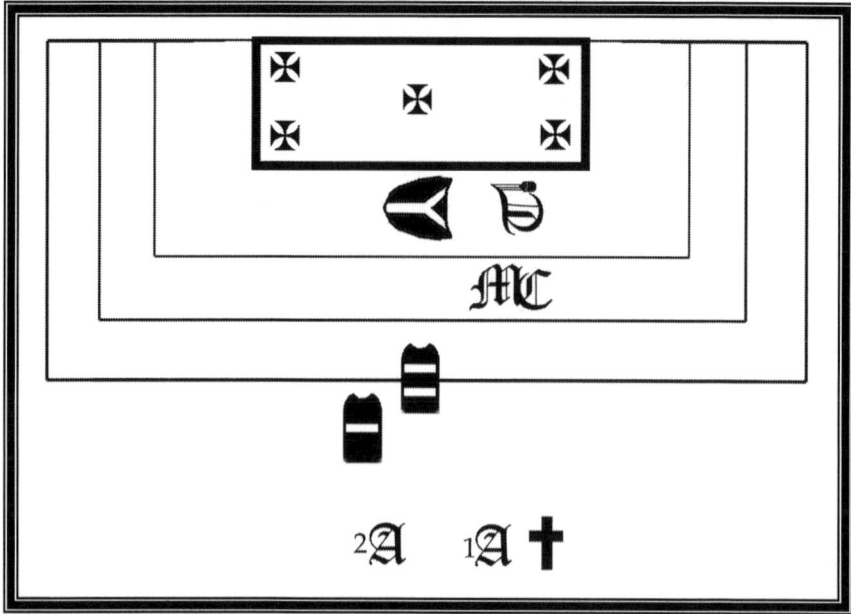

Fig. 6.14 – As the Deacon says the Munda Cor and the incensed is blessed. The crucifer, if one is used, stands out of the way on either side.

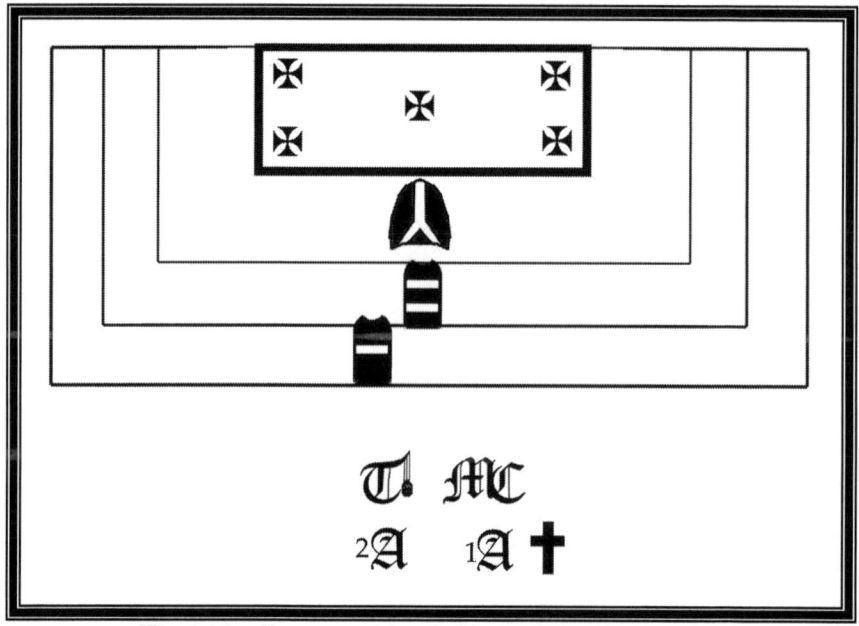

Fig. 6.15 – Deacon receiving the blessing before the Gospel

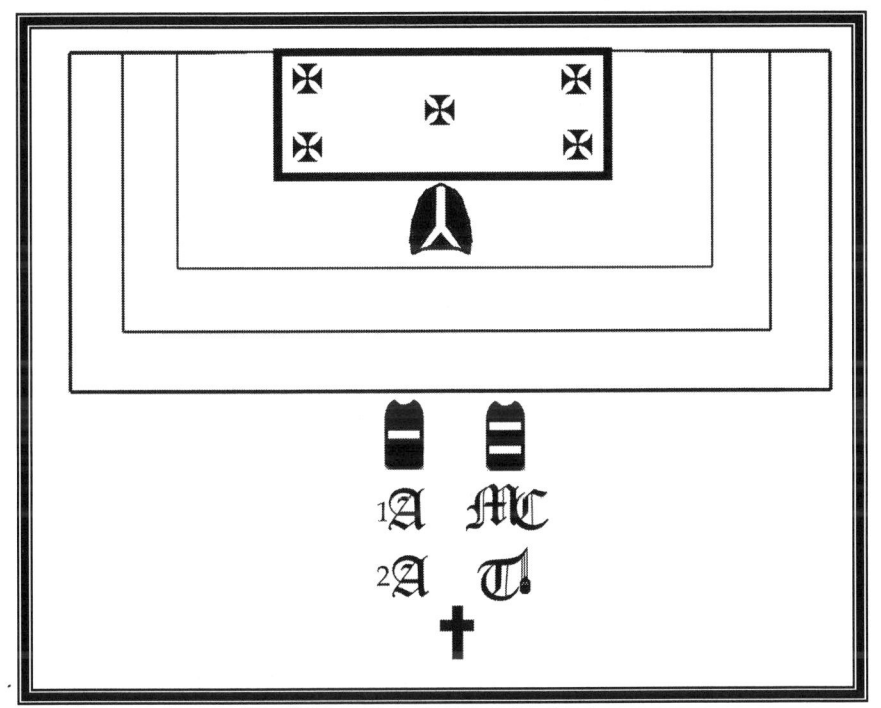

Fig. 6.16 – Gospel party before leaving.

When the Gospel party arrives, the second server steps out of the way and lets the first acolyte and Sub-Deacon pass. The thurifer continues to his position. The MC steps out of the way to let the Deacon pass, and then goes to his position. The positions for chanting the Gospel are given in Fig. 6.17.

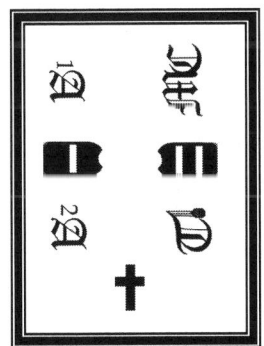

Fig. 6.17 – Positions at the Gospel

The Deacon should be facing liturgical North. The Celebrant remains standing on the predella in the center of the altar, facing liturgical West.

The Deacon hands the Book of Gospels to the Sub-Deacon, bowing with him as usual. The Sub-Deacon or the MC opens the Book of Gospels to the appropriate page, and the MC points out the Gospel to the Deacon. The Deacon announces the Gospel as usual, making the sign of the cross.

During this time, the MC takes the thurible from the thurifer. This is done behind the Deacon. The Deacon, turning to the right, accepts the thurible from the MC, bowing to each other as usual. The Deacon censes the Book of Gospels and hands the thurible back to the MC, who passes it behind the Deacon back to the thurifer. (During the Gospel, the thurifer keeps the thurible swinging.) Then the Deacon chants the Gospel in the appropriate tone with hands joined.

After the Gospel has been chanted, the Deacon points out the first words of the Gospel to the Sub-Deacon. The Sub-Deacon moves individually and directly to the Celebrant and, standing on the second step, presents the Book of Gospels to the Celebrant to kiss. See Fig. 6.18. Afterwards, he hands the Book of Gospels to the MC, who places it back on the credence table. If, as a matter of timing, the Sub-Deacon must wait for the MC, he moves to the Epistle corner on the second step and waits, facing the credence table. Alternatively, the AMC may assist by taking the Book of Gospels.

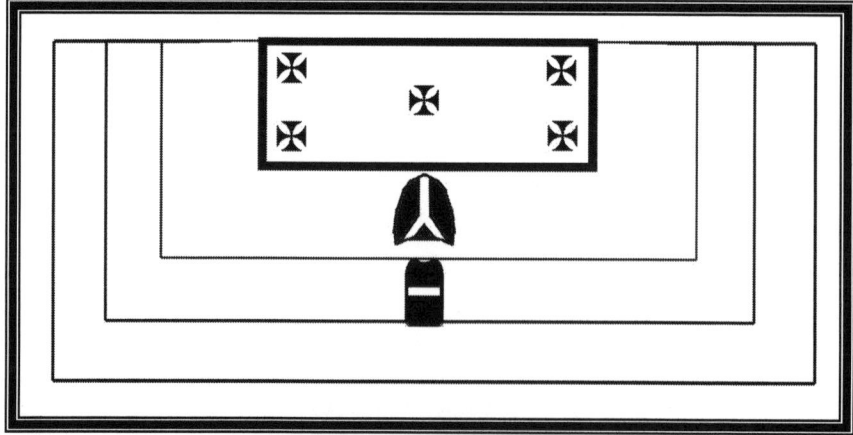

Fig. 6.18 – The Sub-Deacon takes the Book of Gospels to the Celebrant to kiss.

HIGH MASS

The remainder of the Gospel procession forms exactly as before, only this time moving towards the altar (and the Sub-Deacon is absent). The acolytes are already in proper order. The thurifer comes behind the Deacon and in front of the MC. The Crucifer moves to the front of the procession. The Deacon moves to the center rear. See Fig. 6.19.

Fig. 6.19 – Positions of the Gospel party for procession back to the sanctuary/altar. The crucifer is closest to the altar, and all are facing the altar.

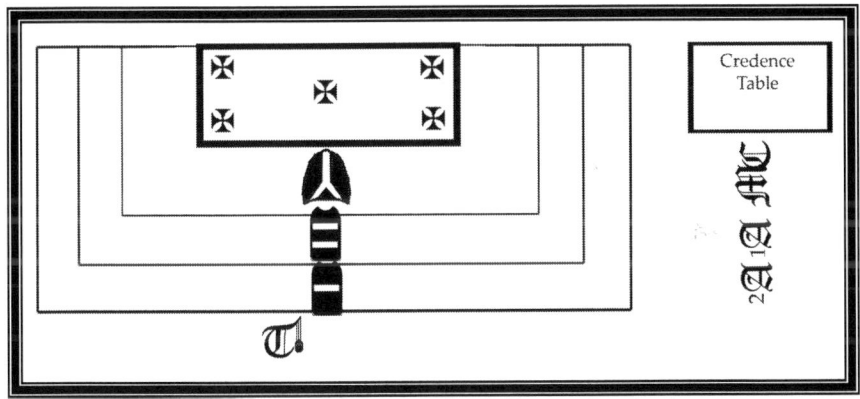

Fig. 6.20 – Positions for censing the Celebrant after the Gospel

Upon arrival in the sanctuary before the altar steps, the acolytes stand aside to let the Deacon pass and then return to their places at the credence table, as does the MC. The thurifer stands aside as the Deacon passes and hands the thurible to the Deacon. Ascending the steps, the Deacon, standing on the predella or second step as dictated by the physical arrangement of the altar steps, censes the Celebrant as at the Introit (with three double swings), bowing to each other as usual. The Deacon faces the altar and the Celebrant faces west. The thurifer approach the Deacon on the side (by ascending the steps) and takes the thurible from him, returning it to the credence table or the sacristy. The

Sub-Deacon during this time stand on his own step in the center of the altar facing the altar (right behind the Deacon), and the thurifer stands to the left of him on the pavement. See Fig. 6.20.

SERMON

After he has been censed, the Celebrant turns to face the altar if there will be no sermon. However, if there will be a sermon, then the Ministers receive their birettas from the servers and go to the sedilia and sit. The preacher goes to the pulpit. If the preacher is one of the ministers, then after receiving his biretta, he goes straight to the pulpit. There is an optional custom that the maniple may be removed by a Sacred Minister for the sermon. The biretta also may be worn for the sermon itself, but is removed for any prayers before and after the sermon. The chasuble, if the Celebrant is preaching and must go a long distance to the pulpit, may optionally be removed, but need not be. Even if the chasuble is removed, the biretta is worn.

During the sermon time, but before the sermon itself, the preacher may read the Epistle and Gospel in English if they were chanted in Latin earlier. During this time the biretta may also be worn.

CREED

If the Creed is appointed to be said (it is a Sunday or at a feast on another day for which the Creed is especially appointed), then it is said at this time. If there is no sermon, then the Celebrant, Deacon, and Sub-Deacon are already in position after the Gospel. The Celebrant simply turns to face the altar. See Fig. 6.9. If there was a sermon, then the Sacred Ministers go to the altar, give up their birettas, and take the position as in Fig. 6.9. (If the preacher was one of the Ministers, then he returns first to the sedilia, and then all of the Ministers return to the altar together, processing as usual, with the Sub-Deacon first, then the Deacon, and then the Celebrant.)

The Celebrant intones *Credo in unum Deum* or *I believe in one God*. After this, he reads is as the congregation and/or choir sing the rest. Once he has intoned the beginning, the Deacon and Sub-Deacon move up to the predella and stand as in Fig. 6.11 for the remainder of the Creed. They bow and genuflect when the Celebrant does. The servers and all present stand for the Creed. The MC moves to the Epistle horn on the predella as well.

After they have recited the Creed, the Sacred Ministers take their birettas from the servers and go to the sedilia and sit while the singing finishes. When the congregation/choir sings *Et incarnatus est de Spiritu Sancto ex Maria Virgine:et homo factus est* or *And was incarnate by the Holy Ghost of the Virgin Mary: and was made man*, they rise, giving up the biretta, and genuflect. Just before these words, the MC, still at the Epistle corner, turns to face the Ministers as a signal. At the actual words, he and all present kneel. There is also a custom that, on the Feast of the Nativity and the Feast of the Annunciation, the Sacred Ministers move to kneel on the lowest step of the altar for these words while they are saying them, returning to the predella to finish the Creed (and they kneel as usual at the sedilia).

After the words have been sung, the MC rises, goes to the credence table, uncovers the table and lays the humeral veil aside, and takes the burse with the corporal in it to the Deacon at the sedilia. The Deacon rises if he was sitting, bows to the Celebrant, and ascends the altar steps to the center, making, as usual, the proper reverence. He opens the burse and spreads the corporal in its proper place in the center of the altar, placing the burse as usual open and on the Gospel side in an attractive manner. (Remember that the burse forms part of the decoration of the altar during this time to the greater glory of God and should not be neglected.) The Deacon then returns to the sedilia. Even if the singing has not finished, he returns to the sedilia and all Sacred Ministers will return to the altar together.

If there is no Creed, then there are several options the Deacon may follow. First, if there is a sermon, and he is not preaching, then he may spread the corporal as above towards the end of the sermon. If there is no sermon, then it becomes more complex. A hymn may be sung by the choir and/or congregation (and this could also be done if there is no Creed, but there is a sermon) with the Sacred Ministers at the sedilia, and towards the end of that hymn, the Deacon goes to the altar to spread the corporal. If there is no hymn, then the Ministers may process to the sedilia and sit while the Deacon spreads the corporal, though without music, this is a bit tedious. So, if there is no creed, no sermon, and no hymn, the practical option left is for the Celebrant, after the Gospel, to move a little to the Gospel side and face the altar. Then the Deacon, taking the burse from the MC, ascends to the predella, spreads the corporal, places the burse, and he and the Celebrant return to their places to continue with the Offertory.

OFFERTORY

The Sacred Ministers stand facing the altar on their own steps, as in Fig. 6.9. The Celebrant kisses the altar and turns to the people, the Deacon and Sub-Deacon moving out of the way as in Fig. 6.10. The Celebrant sings *Dominus vobiscum* as given in the missal, turns to the altar, and after the people respond, sings *Oremus*. The Celebrant reads the proper Offertory verse for the day while the choir chants the Offertory, the choir and/or congregation sings a hymn, or some combination of the two.

Once the Celebrant has finished singing *Dominus vobiscum*, the Deacon makes a slight bow and moves up to the predella on the Celebrant's right. Also at this same time, the Sub-Deacon makes the proper reverence and goes to the credence table, where the MC places the humeral veil over his shoulders. See Fig. 6.21.

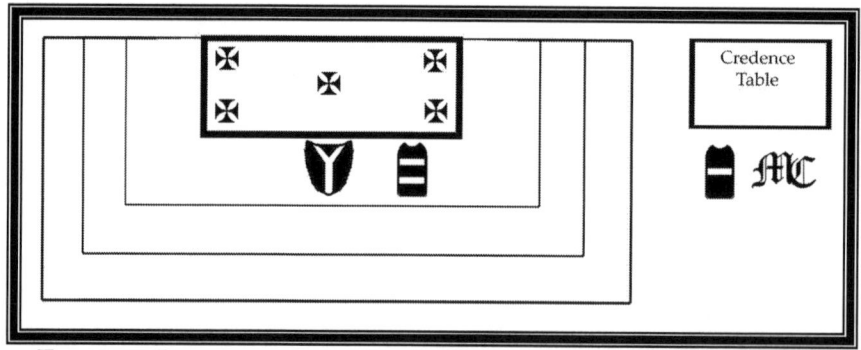

Fig. 6.21 – Positions at the beginning of the Offertory after the Celebrant intones Dominus vobiscum. The Sub-Deacon goes to the credence table, where he receives the humeral veil. The Deacon stands on the predella next to the Celebrant.

Next the Sub-Deacon removes the chalice veil from the sacred vessels and hands it to the MC, who places it appropriately on the credence table. The Sub-Deacon picks up the chalice and paten with both hands through the humeral veil. (The hands go inside the humeral veil, and the outside of the veil touches the vessels.) See the Section on physical property for a description on carrying the vessels (though note that here, the vessels are not carried veiled). The right hand takes the chalice by the stem, and the left hand at first may be used to cover the chalice with the humeral veil

HIGH MASS

before taking it with the right hand. Then the left hand, through the humeral veil, lays flat on top of the pall.

Holding it before his breast, the Sub-Deacon carries the chalice and paten up the altar steps on the Epistle side to the predella. He hands them to the Deacon and then to the Deacon's right on the predella. See Fig. 6.22. If needed, he may set them on the altar and then the Deacon may take them.

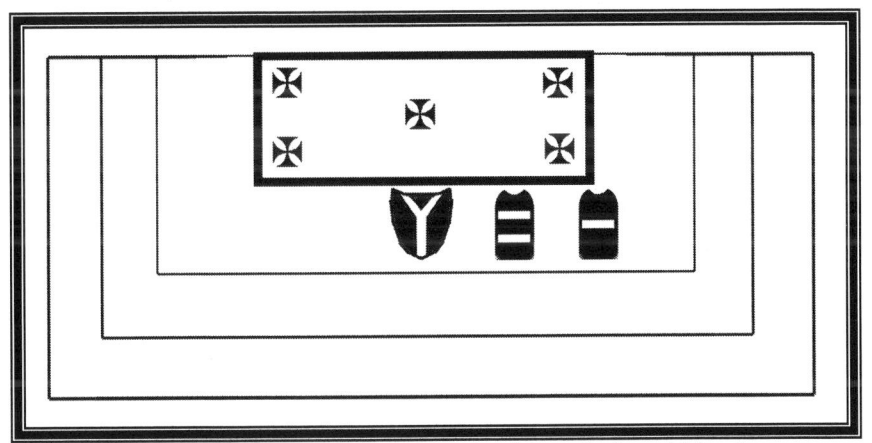

Fig. 6.22 – Positions after the Sub-Deacon brings the Sacred Vessels.

The Deacon sets the vessels on the altar on the Epistle corner. If there is a ciborium to be used (not containing, of course, reserved consecrated sacrament), then the MC brings it to the altar at this time and hands it to the Deacon directly. The Deacon places it on the corporal behind the chalice. The MC throws the right side of the humeral veil over the shoulder of the Sub-Deacon so it will be out of the way, and then stands at the Epistle corner.

The Deacon removes the pall and hands the paten to the Celebrant, who proceeds with the Offering of the Host, the *Suscipe Sancte Pater*, etc., and the acolyte rings the bell once, as at low mass. If there is a ciborium, then the Deacon raises it slightly off of the corporal during the offering of the host, placing it again on the corporal in time to be out of the way so the Celebrant can place the paten on the corporal (as at low mass).

During the Offering of the Host, the Sub-Deacon takes the chalice and holds it supporting it by the base and/or stem on the altar through the humeral veil with the left hand, and then wipes out the bowl with the purificator. During this time, the Acolytes approach the predella by ascending the steps on the Epistle side with the cruets of wine and water (see the Section on Physical Property and the Section on Altar Servers).

After the Sub-Deacon has wiped out the bowl of the chalice, he takes the wine cruet in his right hand from the server. The server, unlike at low mass, should hold the cruets by the handles. The Sub-Deacon takes the cruet in the right hand by its body, and then the Deacon can take it by the handle.

The Sub-Deacon hands the wine cruet to the Deacon, who, taking the chalice in his left hand, pours in a suitable amount of wine. Meanwhile, the Sub-Deacon takes the water cruet from the server and holds it up for the Celebrant to bless (with the *Deus qui*, etc., as at low mass). After the water has been blessed, the Sub-Deacon pours a little water into the chalice (which is held by the Deacon by the left hand). The Sub-Deacon then hands the water cruet back to the server. Taking the wine cruet from the Deacon, the Sub-Deacon hands that back to the server. Again, all of this is done with the Sub-Deacon's right hand.

The Deacon then presents the chalice (with the wine in it) to the Celebrant. If physically necessary, the Deacon may set the chalice in the center of the corporal first, and then the Celebrant may pick it up. However, it is preferable for the Deacon to hand it to the Celebrant directly. Then the Celebrant offers the Chalice with the *Offerimus tibi*, etc., as at low mass. The Deacon either supports the base of the chalice or the Celebrant's right arm. After the offering of the chalice, the Deacon covers the chalice with the pall.

As the Celebrant begins the *In spiritu humilitatis*, the MC replaces the right side of the humeral veil over the Sub-Deacon's shoulder. The Deacon places the paten in the right hand of the Sub-Deacon. The Sub-Deacon goes straight down to his own step, holding the paten with the right hand at eye level. The paten is held such that the top of the paten (where the host rests) is towards the Sub-Deacon. The left hand is flat on the chest. Upon arrival at the center of the altar, the Sub-Deacon bows or genuflects as appropriate. See Fig. 6.23.

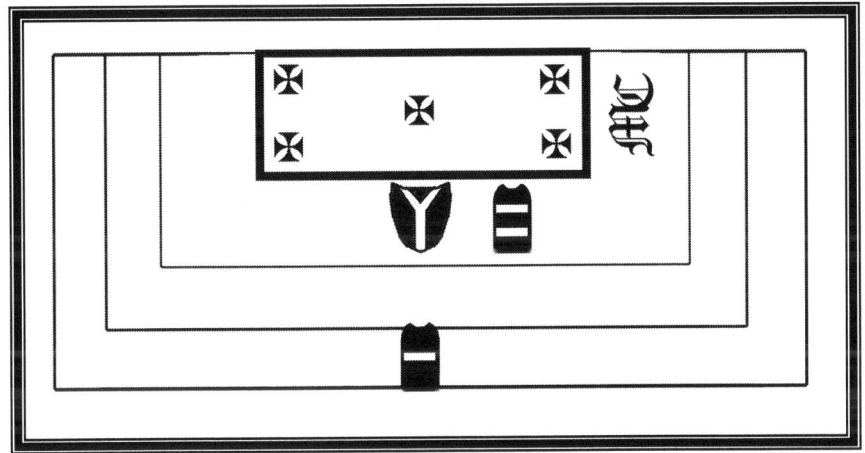

Fig. 6.23 – Position for the Sub-Deacon holding the empty paten at eye level during the Offertory.

CENSING AT THE OFFERTORY

The blessing of the incense is done in exactly the same positions as at the Introit, except that the Sub-Deacon is in his position, holding the paten, as in Fig. 6.23. The proper prayers for blessing the incense at the Offertory are used. Once the incense has been blessed, the MC goes to the pavement, makes the proper reverence, and crosses to the Gospel side, ascending the steps again to the left of the Celebrant. See Fig. 6.24.

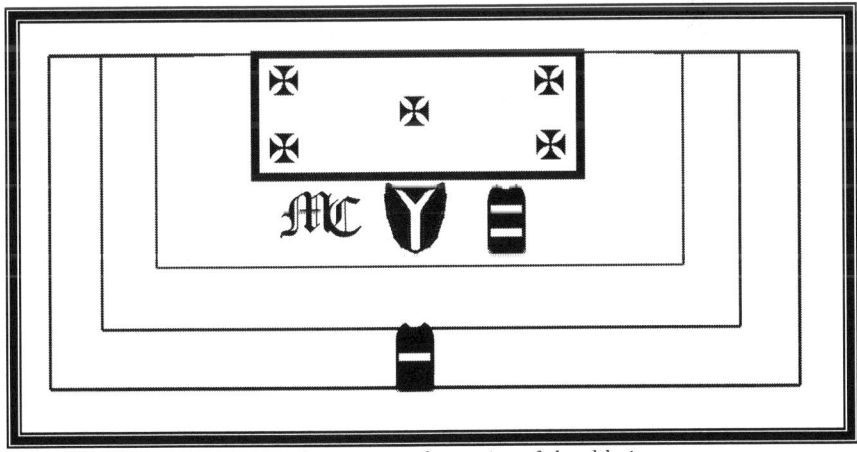

Fig. 6.24 – Positions at the censing of the oblations

As the offerings are censed, the host should be covered by folding the front left corner of the corporal over it. The Deacon places his hand firmly on the base of the chalice while the oblations are censed. The offerings are censed according to the pattern given in Fig. 6.25. The Celebrant says the proper prayers as the offerings and altar are censed, as given in the missal.

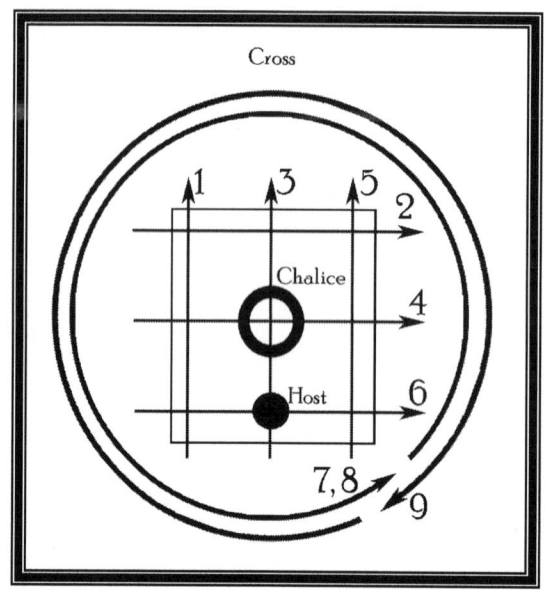

Fig. 6.25 – Pattern for censing the offerings

The details for this are also given in the Missale Anglicanum 2009 rubrics. The Celebrant, Deacon, and MC bow to the cross before the offerings are censed. Then they bow again before censing the altar. The censing of the altar is exactly as at the Introit. The thurifer moves to the Gospel side to remove the missal (and stand, if possible) while that side is being censed.

CENSING OF THE MINISTERS

The Celebrant is censed by the Deacon as at the Introit. Next, the Deacon, retaining the thurible, goes to the right of the Sub-Deacon on the lowest step. The Sub-Deacon turns to the right to face the Deacon, lowering the paten. The Deacon incenses the Sub-Deacon with one double swing. The thurifer stands at the Epistle corner during this.

After the Sub-Deacon has been incensed, the Deacon hands the thurible to the thurifer and stands on his own step, facing liturgical South. The thurifer censes the Deacon with two double swings. The thurifer then censes the clergy in choir with three single swings, the servers collectively with three single swings, and then the congregation collectively with three single swings.

LAVABO

As soon as the Celebrant has been incensed and the Deacon has moved to cense the Sub-Deacon, the Celebrant moves to the Epistle corner for the lavabo. This he may read from the center of the altar out of the missal or from an altar card on the Epistle horn. The servers set to perform the lavabo should time their actions to be present on the predella at the same time the Celebrant arrives. The lavabo is precisely as at low mass. Finishing the lavabo, the Celebrant returns to the center of the altar.

ORATE FRATRES

The Celebrant, having returned to the center of the altar, and the Deacon and Sub-Deacon in their places on their own steps behind him, facing the altar, says the *Suscipe Sancta Trinitas*. He then kisses the altar and turns to the people to say *Orate Fratres*. The Deacon and Sub-Deacon move out of the way, as at the *Dominus vobiscum* (see Fig. 6.10). As the Celebrant turns back to the altar, the Deacon and Sub-Deacon again move back into line.

SECRETS

The Celebrant says the Secrets as usual as at low mass. The Deacon and Sub-Deacon remain as in Fig. 6.9. When concluding the final Secret, he sings *Per omnia saecula saeculorum*, as given in the missal.

INVITATION TO COMMUNION & CONFESSION

The Deacon and Sub-Deacon again move out of the way as in Fig. 6.10. The Celebrant turns to the people to give the Invitation to Communion. For the Confession, the Deacon and Sub-Deacon move back to their line as in Fig. 6.9. During the Confession, the Deacon and Sub-Deacon kneel and bow. All servers and people present kneel and bow as well.

When the Celebrant turns to give the General Confession, all remain in position and kneeling. The exception is if a server will hold a card with the absolution on it. The MC kneels until the Comfortable Words, at which time he goes to the Epistle corner.

SURSUM CORDA AND PREFACE

The Deacon and Sub-Deacon rise after the Comfortable Words and remain in position as in Fig. 6.9. They remain there for the Sursum Corda and Preface.

SANCTUS

Just before the Sanctus begins, the Deacon and Sub-Deacon move to the predella as in Fig. 6.26, and the MC goes to the Gospel corner.

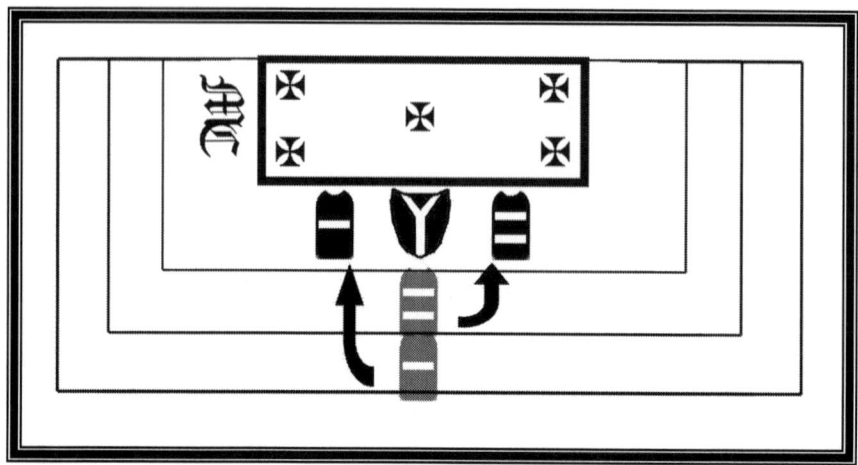

Fig. 6.26 – The Deacon and Sub-Deacon move up to the predella just before the Sanctus.

The Celebrant says the Sanctus while the choirs and/or congregation sings it. The server rings the bell three times. All kneel, except the MC, Deacon, and Sub-Deacon. However, they bow as the Celebrant does. The servers move to the pavement at the front of the altar and kneel in a line before it. If there are torchbearers, they come out when the Deacon and Sub-Deacon go up to the predella and stand as in Fig. 6.27. When the Sanctus begins, the servers and torchbearers all kneel and remain kneeling through the Consecration.

After the Sanctus and Benedictus, the Sub-Deacon returns to his position in the center of the altar, still holding the paten, as given in Fig. 6.28. The MC move to the Celebrant's left on the predella to assist at the missal. The Deacon, remaining at the right of the Celebrant, will assist on that side at the beginning of the Canon.

HIGH MASS

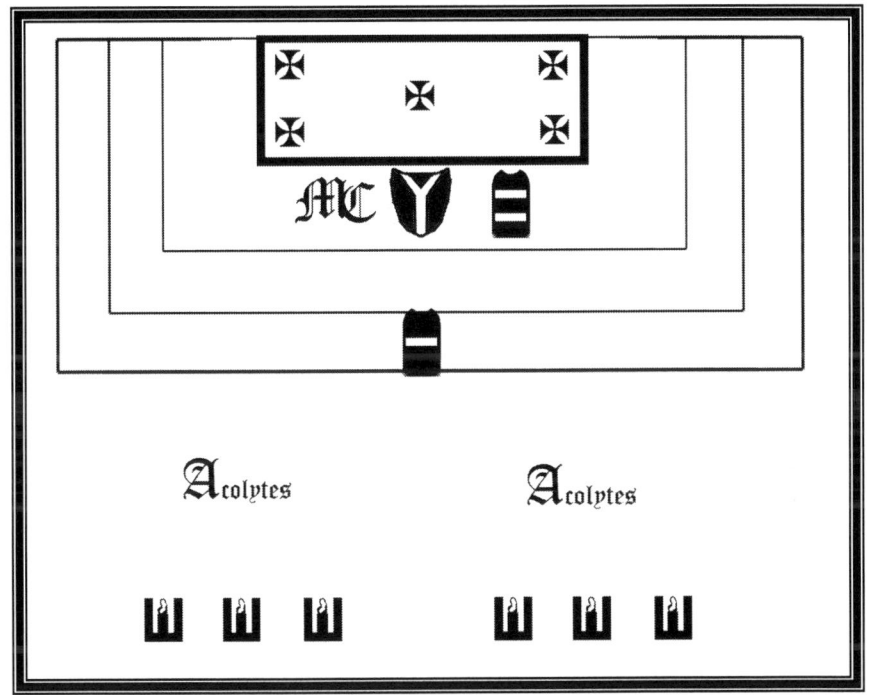

Fig. 6.27 – Position of torchbearers. They should be in even numbers and no more than six for a solemn high mass, or eight for a pontifical high mass. The altar servers not needed elsewhere are in front of them.

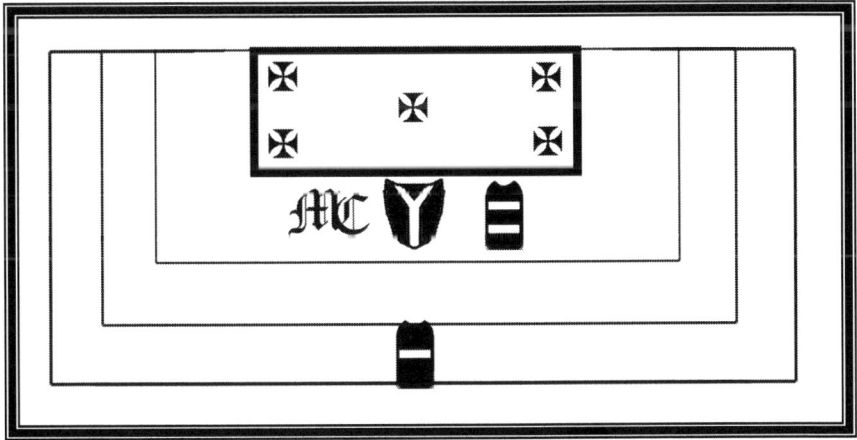

Fig. 6.28 – Positions at the beginning of the canon.

BEGINNING OF THE CANON OF THE MASS

The thurifer should come to high place to cense the sacrament (see Fig. 6.29 below) and kneel when the servers come to kneel, during the Sanctus, or just before the words *Qui pridie* (*who the knight before...*). He remains there until after the elevations, at which time he retires to the credence table or sacristy.

The Celebrant says the Canon of the mass as at low mass, except he sings those parts appointed to be sung at a high mass in the missal. Everyone kneels during the beginning of the Canon except for the Celebrant, Deacon, Sub-Deacon, and MC. At the *Hanc Igitur*, the acolyte rings the bells once as at low mass. When he comes to the words *Qui pridie* (*who the knight before...*), the MC kneels on the predella, the Sub-Deacon kneels on the second step (still holding the paten), and the Deacon kneels on the predella. Before kneeling, the Deacon removes the lid from the ciborium, if any. Everyone kneels during the Consecration through the elevations, except that the Deacon temporarily rises during this time to perform some essential duties.

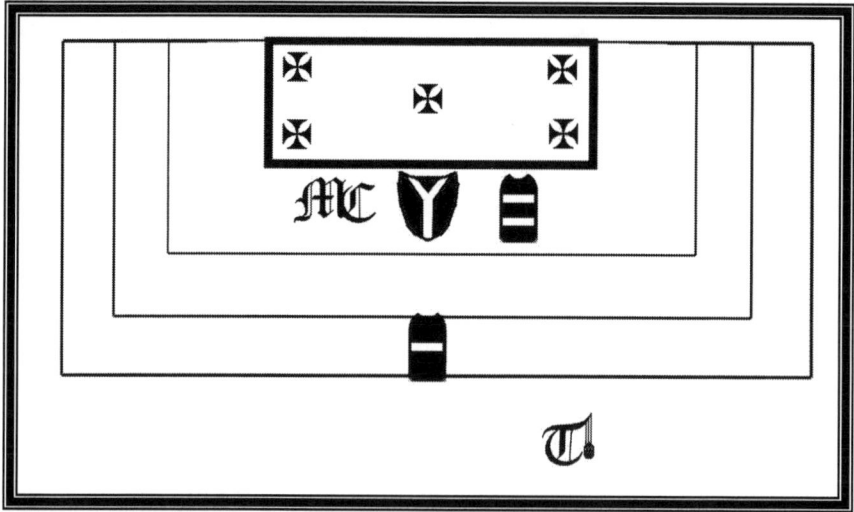

Fig. 6.29 – Positions at the consecration and elevations

As the Celebrant genuflects before he elevates the host, the thurifer censes the sacrament from his position on the pavement (see Fig. 6.29 above) with one set of triple swings (though some traditions use double swings). When the Celebrant elevates the host, the Deacon holds the chasuble up (as the server does at low mass), and the thurifer again censes

HIGH MASS

the sacrament with a set of triple swings. Then the Celebrant genuflects again, and the thurifer censes the sacrament one last time with a set of triple swings. During this time, the sacrament has been censed with a total of three sets triple swings. The acolytes also ring the bells exactly as at low mass.

As the Celebrant rises after the last genuflection, the Deacon rises as well. He covers the ciborium, if any, and if it has a lid. He also veils it. Then he removes the pall from the chalice and immediately kneels again.

The Celebrant continues with the consecration of the wine. The acolytes also ring the bells exactly as at low mass. The actions of the Deacon and thurifer are almost exactly the same for the genuflections and elevation of the chalice as for the elevation of the host. That is, the Deacon holds the chasuble during the elevation, and the thurifer censes the chalice with a total of three triple swings. However, the Deacon rises after the elevation, covers the chalice with the pall, and genuflects with the Celebrant. After this, he remains standing.

After the Celebrant and Deacon genuflect, the torchbearers rise and take their torches back to the sacristy. The acolytes and other servers rise and go back to the credence and sit. The MC rises and remains at the missal. The Sub-Deacon rises and stands on his own step, still holding the paten. The faithful remain kneeling until the Lord's prayer.

THE LORD'S PRAYER/PATER NOSTER

For the minor elevation, the Deacon uncovers the chalice and genuflects with the Celebrant. He stands to the Celebrant's right, supporting his right arm if needed. Then when appointed in the missal, he covers the chalice, genuflects with the Celebrant, and goes to stand behind him on his own step. (See Fig. 6.30.) After the minor elevation, the Celebrant sings *per omnia saecula saeculorum*, and the choir and all present respond by singing *Amen*, as given in the missal. This is the cue to the faithful to rise. The Celebrant then continues with chanting the introduction to the Lord's Prayer and the Lord's Prayer in the appropriate tone for the mass, either festal or ferial, as given in the missal. Shortly before the prayer ends, the Deacon and Sub-Deacon genuflect together and then go to stand on the predella. The Deacon stands to the right of the Celebrant, and the Sub-Deacon to the left of him. The MC remains at the missal. See Fig. 6.31.

HOW TO SAY MASS IN THE ANGLICAN RITE

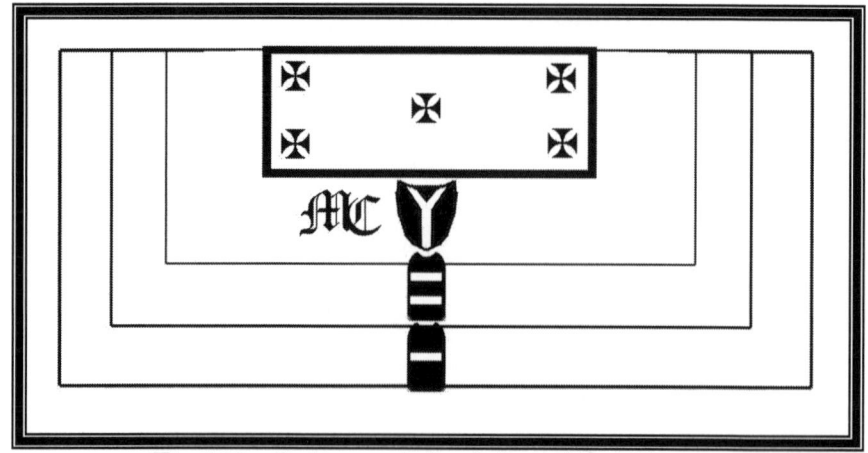

Fig. 6.30 – Positions at the Lord's Prayer/Pater Noster

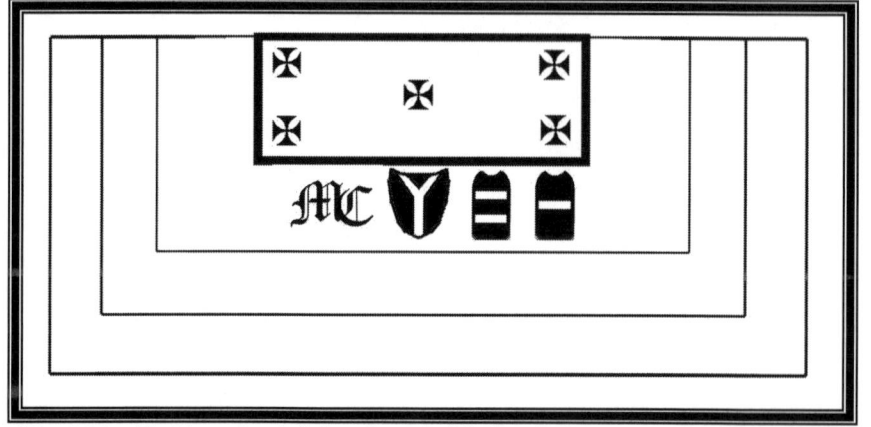

Fig. 6.31 – Positions shortly before the end of the Lord's Prayer. As the Deacon and Sub-Deacon reach the predella, the MC remains at the missal.

LIBERA NOS

When the Sub-Deacon arrives at the predella, he at once hands the paten to the Deacon. The Deacon takes the paten with his right hand, transfers it to his left, and then wipes it off with a purificator. The Lord's Prayer being finished the Deacon hands the paten to the Celebrant, holding it with both hands though the purificator. When the Celebrant signs himself with the paten, the Deacon, Sub-Deacon, and MC all sign themselves.

HIGH MASS

FRACTURE

The Deacon uncovers the chalice as given in the missal before the fracture. The Deacon and Sub-Deacon genuflect with the Celebrant. After the particle has been placed in the chalice (the *Pax Domini*), the Sub-Deacon goes on the second step, genuflecting in the middle, and stands to the left of the Celebrant in time to genuflect with the Celebrant and Deacon. See Fig. 6.32. The MC signals this move by himself retiring to the pavement as shown in Fig. 6.32. The Deacon covers the chalice with the pall after the particle has been placed in, and he and the Sub-Deacon genuflect with the Celebrant after the Celebrant says the prayer appointed in the missal. The servers remain standing from the Lord's Prayer to the Agnus Dei.

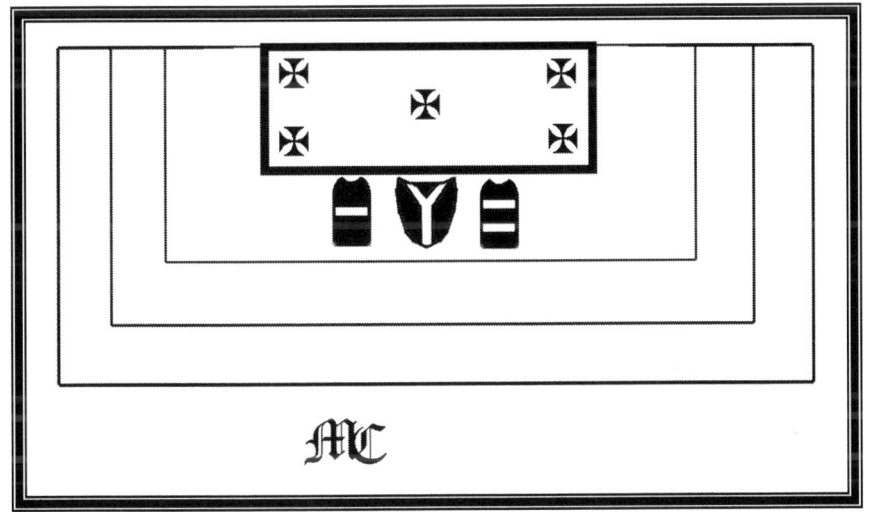

Fig. 6.32 – Positions after the Pax Domini for the Agnus Dei

AGNUS DEI

All kneel for the *Agnus Dei*, except for the Celebrant, Deacon, Sub-Deacon, and MC. The Celebrant recites the *Agnus Dei* as at low mass, and the choir and/or congregation sings the *Agnus Dei*. The Celebrant, Deacon, Sub-Deacon, and MC all bow towards the Blessed Sacrament during the *Agnus Dei*. After the *Agnus Dei*, the Sub-Deacon genuflects and goes to his own step, not genuflecting on arrival, right behind the Celebrant.

THE PEACE

The Celebrant say the prayer before the peace, as appointed in the missal, and the Deacon bows. The prayers continue even if the singing of the *Agnus Dei* is continuing. Then, kissing the altar, the Celebrant turns to the right and gives the peace to the Deacon. This is done by the Celebrant and Deacon taking each other by the shoulder and giving one kiss on each cheek, first the right, then the left. The Celebrant says *Pax tecum*, and the Deacon responds *Et cum spiritu tuo*. Next, the Deacon goes down the steps to the Sub-Deacon and then returns to the predella on the Celebrant's left. See Fig. 6.33. The Sub-Deacon turns to the right, and the Deacon gives the peace to the Sub-Deacon. The Sub-Deacon, descending to the pavement, gives the peace to the MC and then goes to the predella on the Celebrant's right. See Fig. 6.33. The MC then gives the peace to the senior cleric in choir, who passes the peace to the other clergy in choir. The MC then goes to the thurifer, gives him the peace, and returns to the Epistle side of the altar. The thurifer passes the peace to the first acolyte, who passes it to the second acolyte, and then to the other servers and torchbearers. The Celebrant then continues with the other appointed prayers before communion.

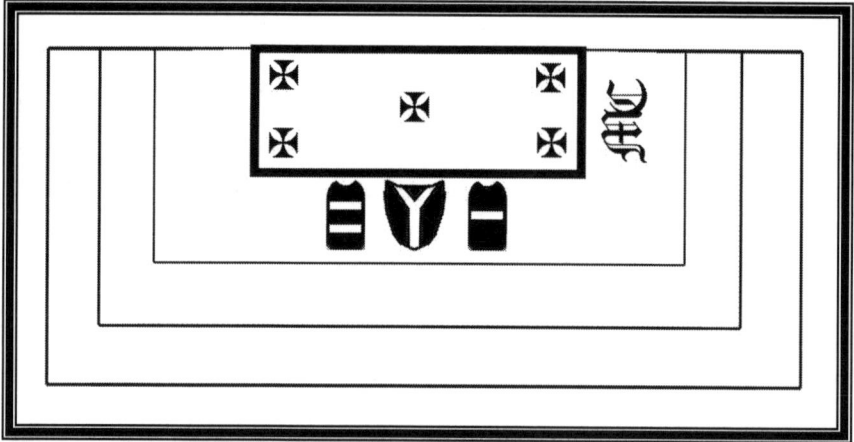

Fig. 6.33 – Positions after giving the peace.

COMMUNION OF THE PRIEST

When the priest genuflects before receiving communion, the Deacon and Sub-Deacon genuflect with him. All is as at low mass, except that before the communion of the Precious Blood, the Sub-Deacon removes the pall from the chalice instead of the Deacon. The Deacon and Sub-Deacon do not bow at the priest's *Domine non sum dignus*. However, as the Celebrant receives the host and blood, the Deacon and Sub-Deacon bow

HIGH MASS

profoundly. (The MC does this as well.) During this time, the acolytes remain kneeling at the credence table.

COMMUNION OF THE FAITHFUL

After the communion of the priest, the Deacon and Sub-Deacon genuflect and switch sides, standing on the second step. They genuflect again upon arrival. See Fig. 6.34. The Deacon, Sub-Deacon, and MC then kneel.

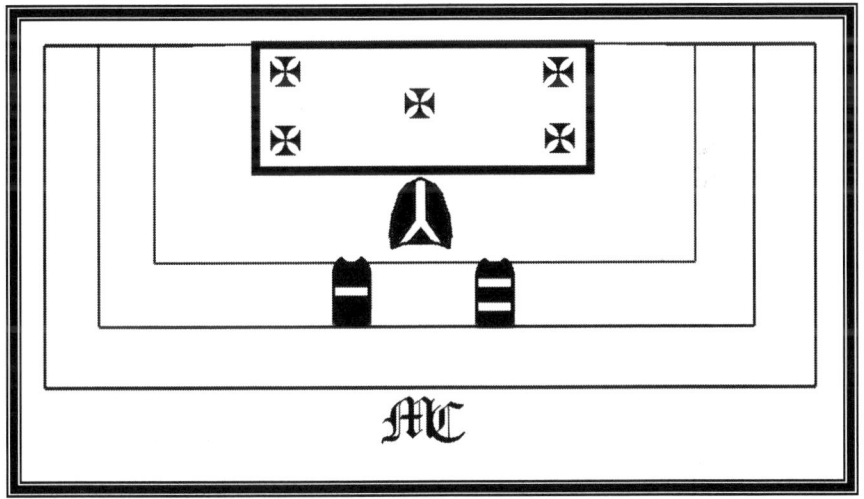

Fig. 6.34 – Positions at the Ecce Agnus Dei and for the Communion of the Sacred Ministers

The Celebrant says the *Ecce Agnus Dei* as usual. The Ministers and people respond as at low mass. The server who will hold the communion paten approaches the predella or second step. (He may also come before the *Ecce Agnus Dei* and kneel with the paten on the lowest step with the MC. The Celebrant then communicates the Deacon with the host, then the Sub-Deacon. Both rise when they have received communion. The Celebrant then proceeds with the acolyte holding the communion paten to communicate the clergy in choir. The Deacon goes on the right of the Celebrant, and the Sub-Deacon on the left. After communicating clergy in choir they return to the altar steps, where the servers are now kneeling on the lowest step. They communicate the MC, AMC, thurifer, first and second servers, and then the other servers. Then they move to the chancel rail to communicate the people. Regarding the acolyte holding the communion paten, he is communicated last of the servers, and the Deacon holds the communion paten. For the communion of the faithful either the Deacon holds the paten and the acolyte remains at the credence, or the acolyte accompanies them to hold the paten, walking slightly in front of the Deacon. At the rail, in that case, the Deacon must stand back a bit to make room.

ABLUTIONS

For the Ablutions, all is essentially as at low mass in terms of the basic actions. The reserved sacrament, if any is out, is replaced to the tabernacle as usual before the ablutions are carried out. After the communion of the faithful, the Celebrant, Deacon, and Sub-Deacon return to the predella and stand as in Fig. 6.35. The Sub-Deacon handles both cruets, which he gets from the altar servers, who bring them as at the Offertory. The Deacon assists at the missal, and the MC stands at the Epistle corner, assisting as needed.

Fig. 6.35 – Position for the Ablutions.

The Celebrant says the first Prayer at the Ablutions silently, standing in the center of the altar, either with hands joined, or taking the chalice in both hands. Then, taking the chalice if he has not already done so, he turns to the right, and the Sub-Deacon pours in a little wine. Turning back to the altar, the Celebrant consumes the first ablution as at low mass. Then, he says the second prayer silently. Changing his hand positions for the second ablution as at low mass, he turns to the right, and the Sub-Deacon pours the wine and water over his fingers as the server does at low mass. Turning again to the altar, the Celebrant sits the chalice on the altar. The Sub-Deacon places the purificator over the Celebrant's hands and the Celebrant dries his fingers. Then the Celebrant picks up the chalice and consumes the second ablution as at low mass. Taking the purificator from the Sub-Deacon, he wipes out the center of the bowl of the chalice, the paten, etc., all as at low mass. He gives the purificator to the Sub-Deacon.

Next, the Sub-Deacon reassembles the Sacred Vessels as is done at low mass, standing to the right of the Celebrant (who remains in the center of the altar). The second altar server brings the chalice veil and burse to the Sub-Deacon. When the veil has been placed on top and the burse (with the corporal in it) placed on top of that, the Sub-Deacon takes the vessels to the credence table. During this time an altar server transfers the missal back to the Epistle corner as at low mass. As the Sub-Deacon goes to the Credence table, the Deacon goes to stand behind the Celebrant on his own step. When the missal has been transferred, the Celebrant and Deacon move to their positions as in Fig. 6.36. After returning the Sacred Vessels, the Sub-Deacon returns and stands in his position as in Fig. 6.36.

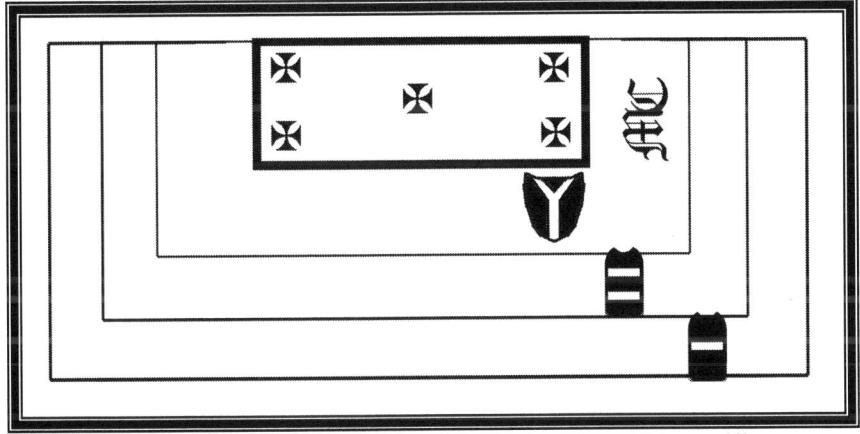

Fig. 6.36 – Positions for the General Thanksgiving, Communion, and Post-Communion

GENERAL THANKSGIVING AND COMMUNION VERSE

Standing in the position indicated in Fig. 6.36, the Celebrant chants *Oremus*, and then chants the General Thanksgiving with hands extended. The solemn or ad libitum tone is used for feasts, and the ferial or ad libitum tone is used for feriae. He joins his hands as usual for the conclusion. The servers and all present stand.

This having been finished, he recites the Communion Verse with hands joined. During this time, the choir may chant the Communion Verse or sing a hymn, or the congregation may sing a hymn. Once the Celebrant has finished reading the verse, the Sacred Ministers go to the sedilia and sit as described before. Shortly before the singing is finished, the Ministers rise and go back to the altar, standing as in Fig. 6.37.

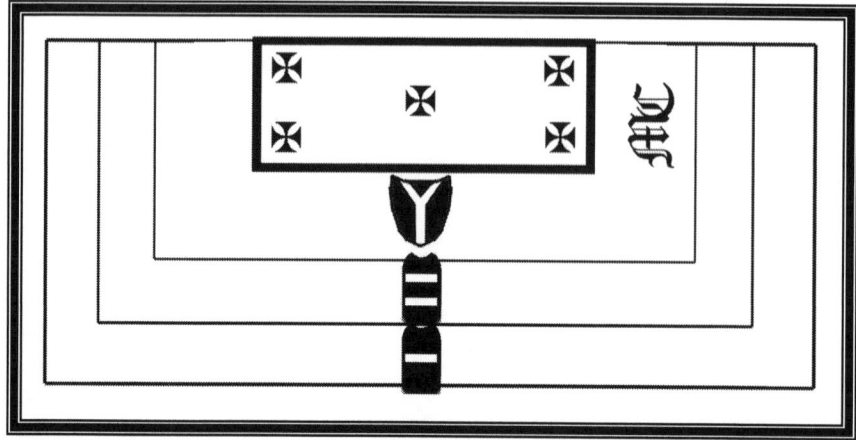

Fig. 6.37 – Positions as the singing finishes after the Communion Verse

POSTCOMMUNION

When the singing has finished, the Celebrant kisses the altar as usual and turns to the people to chant *Dominus vobiscum*. The Deacon and Sub-Deacon move as before and shown in Fig. 6.38.

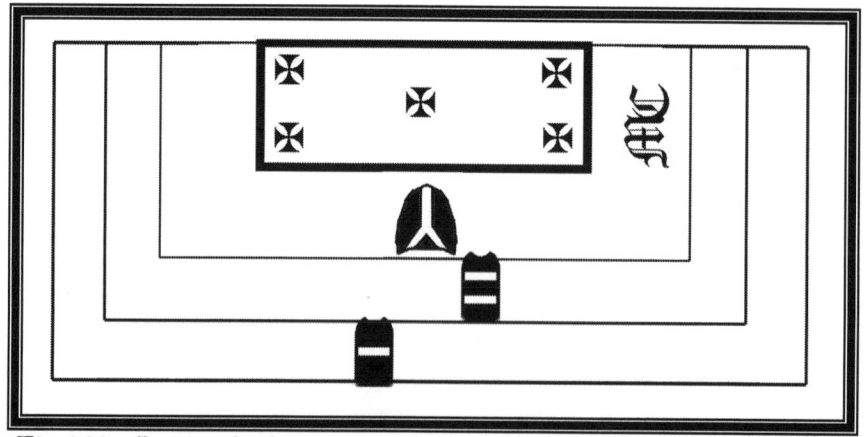

Fig. 6.38 – Positions for the Dominus vobiscum before the Post-Communion, and for the Dismissal and Blessing

HIGH MASS

The Ministers return to their positions as in Fig. 6.36. The servers and all present remain standing. The Celebrant chants *Oremus* at the missal, and then chants the Postcommunions appointed for the mass in the same manner that the Collects were chanted earlier.

DISMISSAL

The Postcommunions having been chanted, the Sacred Ministers return to the center of the altar as in Fig. 6.37. The Celebrant kisses the altar, and turns to the people, the Deacon and Sub-Deacon moving as in Fig. 6.38. The Celebrant chants *Dominus vobiscum*. If the dismissal is to be *Ite Missa Est*, then the Ministers remain as in Fig. 6.38, and the Celebrant or the Deacon, according to local use, chants the dismissal, facing the people with hands extended. If the dismissal is to be *Benedicamus Domino* or *Requiescant in pace*, then the Ministers turn back to the altar as in Fig. 6.37, and the Celebrant or Deacon chants the dismissal with hands joined. The tones are given for *Ite Missa Est* according to the rank of the feast. Tone No. 7 in the Missale Anglicanum 2009 is used for all simple feasts and ferial masses.

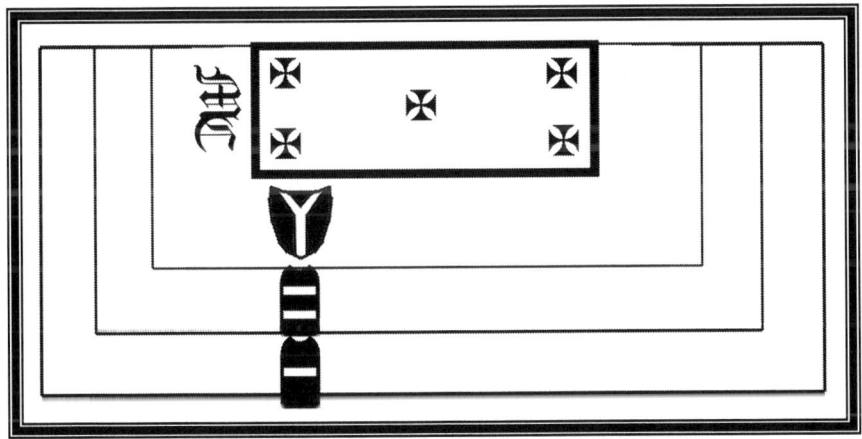

Fig. 6.39 – Positions at the Last Gospel

BENEDICTION

After the dismissal, the Sacred Ministers turn to face the altar (or remain so) as in Fig. 6.37. The Celebrant bows at the altar and recites the *Placeat tibi*. Kissing the altar again, he turns to the people, and the Deacon and Sub-Deacon again move as in Fig. 6.38. All present kneel, except the

Deacon and Sub-Deacon (though they may kneel according to local use). The Benediction is recited, not chanted, and is exactly as at low mass.

LAST GOSPEL

After the Benediction, the Sacred Ministers move to the Gospel corner and stand as in Fig. 6.39. All stand for the Last Gospel. The Celebrant reads the Last Gospel as at low mass.

PROCESSION TO THE SACRISTY

After the Last Gospel, the Ministers move as in Fig. 6.1. If the procession will simply go straight to the sacristy, then the thurifer need not be present. In that case, all present genuflect with the Celebrant, and the servers hand the birettas to the Ministers. Then they walk to the sacristy in the same order they processed in. The crucifer in this case may or may not be used, but if he is, then he stands where the thurifer is indicated in Fig. 6.1, or, if there is a thurifer present, then to his right. There may or may not be music for this type of procession out.

If there will be a long procession, then it is generally the case that there will be music, either sung by the choir or the congregation. If the hymn is too long, then the Celebrant may delay genuflecting until a little later so that the music ends shortly after the procession reaches its final destination. In that case, all simply stand as in Fig. 6.1 until the Celebrant genuflects. Regardless, after the genuflection, the Ministers and servers process out exactly as they processed in, with the thurifer leading the way, and the Celebrant at the end.

The procession ends in the sacristy, even if the Celebrant and others will be present in the narthex to greet the people. The Celebrant leads the sacristy prayer, and then the servers carry out their duties as after low mass.

Sung Mass

ଦେଇଥ

A sung mass contains some or most of the elements of a high mass and is done when there are insufficient clerics to do a high mass. In its most full form, a sung mass is precisely the same as a high mass, except that there is no Sub-Deacon. In its most basic form, there is only the Celebrant, and he chants just one piece of the Canon.

PHYSICAL ARRANGEMENT

The church is set just as for a high mass. Six candles are lit on the altar. Incense may be used (and is best to be used), but need not be. The Sacred Vessels are placed on the altar as at low mass. However, if there is a Deacon, they may be placed on the credence table as at high mass.

ALTAR SERVERS

Altar servers may be those as in high mass, or some part thereof.

CHANT & MUSIC

The Celebrant should still chant everything he is appointed to chant in the high mass. At the very least, just one part of the Canon appointed to be chanted must be chanted. Service music, e.g., Kyrie, Sanctus, etc., may or may not be used. If such a part is to be recited instead of chanted, however, the Celebrant merely begins it by reciting, not chanting. In such a case, the Celebrant also does not go to the sedilia. However, he does still go to the sedilia during the singing just as at high mass if something is being sung instead of recited.

EPISTLE AND GOSPEL

The Epistle and Gospel may be recited or chanted. If the Gospel is chanted, then the Epistle may be recited or chanted. However, if the Gospel is recited, then the Epistle must be recited as well.

WITH OR WITHOUT THE DEACON

If there is a Deacon of the Mass, then he does all as appointed for high mass. He may also chant the Epistle. If there is a Deacon, then he brings the Sacred Vessels from the credence (with or without the humeral veil) if they have been placed on the credence table before mass instead of on the altar.

At a sung mass, the Deacon also has the ability to "float," fulfilling also the role when needed of the Sub-Deacon (though he does not hold the paten with the humeral veil as the Sub-Deacon does at high mass). Also, if there is no MC, then he may also fulfill certain roles of the MC, particularly that of assisting at the missal. In short, the Deacon should stand and move as at high mass, but may move and stand as needed to assist the Celebrant and ensure a good and dignified flow of the mass.

If there is no Deacon, then the Celebrant must do everything, just as at a low mass. He may chant the Gospel and the Epistle. However, if there is only a Celebrant, then the Sacred Vessels must be on the altar before the mass.

FINAL NOTES

A sung mass may contain as many of the elements of a high mass up to but not including a Sub-Deacon. There are many variations possible in a sung mass, and these often develop as a matter of local use, physical arrangement, or other matter of practicality. Care must be taken, however, not to abuse the freedom brought by a sung mass. The sung mass is still a solemn celebration of the Holy Eucharist, and as such must still be treated with utmost respect. It is not a time for liturgical experimentation. Every variation from a high mass done in a sung mass must be done with the thought of maintaining proper tradition and representing doctrinal and Scriptural truths.

Mass with a Bishop Presiding but not Celebrating

ಬಃಡ

Any mass, whether low, high, or sung, may be celebrated by a priest with a Bishop present. Of course, a bishop may simply sit in choir, but especially if the Bishop is the Ordinary, then it is quite typical for him to preside at a mass at which he is not celebrating (though it is even more typical for him to celebrate himself if he is the jurisdictional Bishop).

At a low mass, the Bishop presiding over the mass sits either at his throne or at the faldstool. He wears choir dress, as the mitre is not used at a low mass, and so the cope is not worn, either. The crosier is not carried. He may be attended by servers, but Deacons of Honor (see the sections on Pontifical masses) and the like are not used. The Bishop walks in just after the Celebrant (see the section on Low Mass).

At a high mass or a sung mass, the Bishop presides at the throne or faldstool and also processes in right after the Celebrant. He wears either the rochet or, as at mass, an amice, alb, and cincture. Over this is a stole and a cope in the color of the mass, and a golden mitre (except at masses at which the simplex mitre must be worn). Pontifical gloves are not worn. The crosier, however, is carried. The bishop may be (and should be) attended by the usual four chaplains (see the sections on Pontifical Masses), and may have Deacons of Honor (though an Assistant Priest is not needed).

At any mass, the Bishop participates with the Celebrant at the Prayers at the Foot of the Altar, and then goes to the throne or faldstool. He gives the absolution after the Confession and the Benediction at the end, just as at a pontifical mass. If it is a high mass or sung mass, then the benediction may be the Pontifical Blessing, chanted by the Bishop and the choir and/or congregation.

HOW TO SAY MASS IN THE ANGLICAN RITE

Mass in the Presence of the Exposed Sacrament

ೞଔ

Mass may be celebrated when the Most Blessed Sacrament is exposed on a throne (see the Rituale for a description of this under Forty Hours Devotion). The Sacrament is not exposed on the altar if mass will be celebrated.

First, the Sacrament is exposed, just as at the Sacred Benediction. It is then transferred to its throne, as at the Forty Hours Devotion. At this point, the mass continues as usual.

Points to Remember:

1. The biretta is not worn. Bishops also do not wear the zucchetto.
2. Benediction candles may be lit upon the altar and elsewhere, within reason.
3. All present should kneel through the entire mass unless necessary to perform a function. (For example, the servers participating in the Gospel procession still stand at the Gospel procession, as to kneel would render it impossible to perform their duties.)
4. The Celebrant, Deacon, and Sub-Deacon still stand when appointed to in the mass.
5. The Sacrament may be incensed after the altar is incensed and after the offerings and altar are incensed.
6. All present should remember to genuflect as they pass the exposed Sacrament.
7. After the mass, the Benediction with the Most Blessed Sacrament may be given as at the Sacred Benediction.

Pontifical Low Mass

Low mass celebrated by a Bishop is precisely as a low mass celebrated by a priest with only a few minor changes. The Bishop should arrive as usual in choir dress, and may vest for mass at the throne or faldstool (see the section on Pontifical High Mass), even if a Daily Office is not said or sung, or in the sacristy.

The maniple is not placed on until after the Prayers at the Foot of the Altar, just as at pontifical high mass. The Bishop does not wear the pontifical dalmatic, but rather only a chasuble. Pontifical gloves are also not worn, and archbishops with the pallium do not wear it. In lieu of the mitre is worn the purple biretta, and the crosier is not carried. The pectoral cross and episcopal ring are, of course, still worn. (See the section on Vestments.)

For a low mass celebrated by a Bishop, four candles are lit on the altar instead of the customary two. There should be two altar servers instead of one. Assistant Deacons and the Assistant Priest are not used, and there are no Bishop's Chaplains. The exception to this is that there may be a Candle Bearer, who stands at the book with the candle. The Bishop may have other attendants vested in choir dress as needed.

A Bishop celebrating the mass bows instead of genuflects when crossing in front of the tabernacle from the time he arrives for the mass until either after he removes his vestments or until he leaves, as a matter of local custom. However, if it is the local custom that the Bishop genuflect, then he does so (and he does, of course, genuflect when crossing in front of the reserved sacrament at all other times, except where given in the rubrics or ceremonial). The Bishop certainly still genuflects at all times as called for in the missal, e.g., at the elevations and when covering and uncovering the chalice.

The Bishop says the mass as any priest would, at the altar, with the same actions (see the section on Low Mass). At the salutation before the Collects, if the *Gloria in Excelsis* is sung, the Bishop may optionally say *Pax vobis*, in lieu of *Dominus vobiscum*. The zucchetto is removed after the

Comfortable Words and before the Sursum Corda begins. It is taken again before the General Thanksgiving is begun. At the end, the benediction is given as a priest would at low mass, that is, the sung Pontifical Blessing is not given.

PONTIFICAL HIGH MASS
☙❧

The Pontifical High Mass is the same in general as the solemn high mass sung by a priest, but with considerably more solemnity. This additional grandeur comes from the fact that a Bishop is a successor of the Apostles and represents the fullness of Christ's Holy Priesthood. Indeed, pontifical rites are typically older than those of priests. By carrying out pontifical functions with the utmost of respect, we do honor to God and preserve the most complete form of the sacred rituals that teach us the faith and help us grow on our spiritual journey.

SYMBOLS *(In addition to those given for High Mass)*

Bishop, whether vested in cope or chasuble

Assistant Priest
(vested in cope without stole, unless he is to preach)

First Assistant Deacon (First Deacon of Honor)
(vested in dalmatic without stole or maniple, over cassock and surplice)

Second Assistant Deacon (Second Deacon of Honor)
(vested in dalmatic without stole or maniple, over cassock and surplice)

Mitre Bearer
(vested in cassock and surplice with optional cope)

Crosier Bearer
(vested in cassock and surplice with optional cope)

Book Bearer
(vested in cassock and surplice with optional cope)

Candle Bearer
(vested in cassock and surplice with optional cope)

HOW TO SAY MASS IN THE ANGLICAN RITE

ATTENDANTS

See the section on Altar Servers for the complete list of attendants at a pontifical high mass. As a matter of local use (with basis in tradition), only the Ordinary (or jurisdictional Bishop, or any Bishop with the privilege of celebrating from the throne) uses Assistant Deacons and an Assistant Priest. Other Bishops, celebrating from the faldstool, may or may not have the privilege of Assistant Deacons and an Assistant Priest, depending on local custom and the authority granted by their jurisdictional Bishop. If there are no Assistant Deacons or Assistant Priest, then those functions are fulfilled by the Deacon and Sub-Deacon of the Mass (the duties of the Assistant Deacons) and the MC (the duties of the Assistant Priest).

SOLEMN ARRIVAL OF THE BISHOP

The Bishop arrives at the front of the church in choir dress, rochet and mozzetta or rochet and chimere, both with purple biretta. Given that this is an arrival, not a liturgical function, the Bishop may wear an appropriate Bishop's cape. The cope and mitre are generally not worn, but may as a matter of local custom. This may be outside or in the narthex. He is greeted by the Senior Canon or Dean if it is his (or another) cathedral, or by the Rector if it is a parish. If the asperges will not be done in the mass, then he takes the aspergillum from the person greeting him, sprinkles himself with the holy water, and then sprinkles the Canons or other clergy around him.

Leading the procession, the Bishop goes to the Blessed Sacrament chapel and prays. He then goes either to the throne/faldstool, or to a chapel for vesting. He is followed by the cathedral chapter or other clerics and may be attended as needed. When passing in front of the tabernacle during the arrival, he bows low instead of genuflecting. Canons and other prelates do similarly, while all others genuflect (if the sacrament is reserved, else they bow).

If the chapel is to be used for vesting, then the Bishop should have a faldstool already prepared for him. He will preside over the singing of the appropriate Daily Office while he vests. Upon arrival, the Sacred Ministers, if they participated in the arrival procession and are not vested, retire to the sacristy to vest for mass. Else, they remain in the chapel with the Bishop.

PONTIFICAL HIGH MASS

During the solemn arrival, the choir and/or congregation may sing suitable hymns. The introit of the mass should not be chanted at this point.

VESTING IN THE CHAPEL OR AT THE THRONE

The Bishop vests while the appropriate Daily Office for the time of day is said. Under the Tridentine Rite, for example, this was Terce. Here, for morning masses, this will be Morning Prayer. For afternoon masses, this will be Noonday Prayer or Afternoon Prayer. For evening masses, this will be Evening Prayer or, in rare cases, Compline (though the latter is really only appropriate for vigil masses).

The Bishop, upon arrival at the altar in the chapel (secretarium), bows to the cross. The altar should have six lighted candles upon it. He then goes to his appointed seat and sits with the biretta. The other clergy and ministers reverence the cross, reverence the bishop (with a genuflection, unless they are Canons or are holding something, in which case they bow) go to their seats, and sit. The Assistant Deacons and the Assistant Priest remain near the Bishop. The Bishops Chaplains are not at this time holding their appointed items, all of which are in the chapel.

The cleric appointed to lead the Daily Office should be vested in cope (for Morning or Evening Prayer) or in cassock and surplice for the other minor offices. However, if he is a Sacred Minister of the mass, then he may already be vested for mass.

The Daily Office begins. The Bishop then rises, gives up the biretta, and hands it to the First Assistant Deacon. His cape, if any, and his mozzetta or chimere are taken away by the MC. The pectoral cross is removed by the Assistant Priest and either placed aside or placed back on the Bishop over the rochet. The Bishop then sits again with the biretta. The Assistant Priest removes the pontifical ring and places it aside. His hands are then washed by the Assistant Deacons (who first place a towel in his lap), if he has not already washed them. The Bishop says the proper vesting prayer for the washing of the hands if he has not already done so (this continues throughout the vesting, though the prayers are omitted if he said them earlier). The Assistant Priest places the ring back on the finger of the Bishop.

The Deacon and Sub-Deacon of the Mass should now be present in the secretarium. They approach the Bishop and make the proper reverence. The Assistant Deacons and Assistant Priest retire to the sacristy to vest for mass if they are not already vested. Else, they remain in their position. Altar servers bring the vestments in the order given below, and they are placed on the Bishop by the Deacon and Sub-Deacon of the Mass. The Bishop rises, giving up the biretta to the First Assistant Deacon or the Sub-Deacon, who takes it away or puts it aside. The pectoral cross, if still worn, is removed by the Assistant Priest or the Deacon of the Mass and laid aside. The rochet is not removed. (Note: If the Anglican long rochet is used, some Bishops use this in lieu of the alb. In this case, it is still most proper to put the amice on. Therefore, the rochet should be removed, the amice placed on, and the rochet then taken again. However, the rochet, even the long Anglican one, is most properly worn underneath an alb, not in place of it.)

The servers bring the vestments in order, making a reverence to the Bishop upon arrival. The Bishop is vested by the Deacon and Sub-Deacon in the following order:

    Amice

    Alb

    Cincture

    Pectoral Cross *(handed by the Assistant Priest, if present)*

    Stole

    Cope

    Mitre *(brought by the mitre bearer)*

At this point, the Bishop sits with the mitre, if the Daily Office has not progressed to the prayers. The Book Bearer brings the Book of Daily Offices to the Bishop and holds it for him to chant the appointed prayers. He gives up the mitre to either the Deacon or the First Assistant Deacon before chanting the prayers.

After the collects, the Daily Office continues, led by the cleric appointed to lead it. The Bishop gives up the cope and finishes being vested by the Deacon and Sub-Deacon in the following order:

PONTIFICAL HIGH MASS

Pontifical Dalmatic

Episcopal Gloves *(the ring is first removed, and then replaced after the gloves are taken)*

Chasuble

Pallium *(if so entitled and it is not already pinned to the chasuble)*

Mitre *(again brought by the mitre bearer)*

At the end of the Daily Office, the Crosier Bearer brings the crosier and presents it to the Bishop directly. The procession forms in the chapel to go to the sanctuary for the mass. If the vesting is done instead at the throne, it is done in precisely the same manner as above. For Bishops celebrating without Assistant Deacons and Assistant Priest, all those functions are done by the Deacon and Sub-Deacon.

PROCESSION

The procession is done in the following order:

Thurifer
Acolyte – Crucifer – Acolyte
Torchbearers (without torches)
Other Servers
MC and AMC
Clergy in Choir
Acolyte – Crucifer *(with Chapter cross)* – Acolyte
Cathedral Chapter
Sub-Deacon *(carrying the Book of Gospels with the Bishop's maniple)*
Deacon of the Mass – Assistant Priest
Second Assistant Deacon – Bishop – First Assistant Deacon
Train Bearer *(if needed)*
Crosier Bearer – Mitre Bearer
Candle Bearer – Book Bearer
Other attendants of the Bishop *(vested only in cassock and surplice)*

The Bishop carries the crosier and wears the mitre. The Deacon and Sub-Deacon of the Mass wear their birettas. All other clergy do not wear the biretta except when sitting. The cross is carried in front of an Archbishop, with the figure facing the Archbishop. In that case, the cross in the front of the procession is omitted unless it is a long procession. Also, if there is no Cathedral Chapter, then that cross is omitted. However, if there is a

HOW TO SAY MASS IN THE ANGLICAN RITE

Cathedral Chapter, then the cross at the front of the procession may also be omitted, unless it is a long procession. The Cross is carried most properly by the Sub-Deacon of the Cross, vested in tunicle over cassock and surplice, without stole or maniple. On the way to the altar, if the procession passes the Blessed Sacrament chapel, all remove the biretta (if they are wearing it) and genuflect. The Bishop, retaining the mitre, bows profoundly. Then the procession continues. The Bishop's maniple, which is not placed on until the Prayers at the Foot of the Altar, is placed in the Book of Gospels and carried in the procession by the Sub-Deacon. During the procession, of course, a suitable hymn may be sung. Or, the choir may begin chanting the Introit.

PRAYERS AT THE FOOT OF THE ALTAR

Upon arrival at the sanctuary/choir, the front portion of the procession reverences the altar and goes to their place. The Bishop, when passing the clergy in choir, salutes them with a slight bow (not removing the mitre), and they salute him with a deep bow. Upon arrival at the foot of the altar (see Fig. 11.1) the Bishop hands the crosier to the Crosier Bearer.

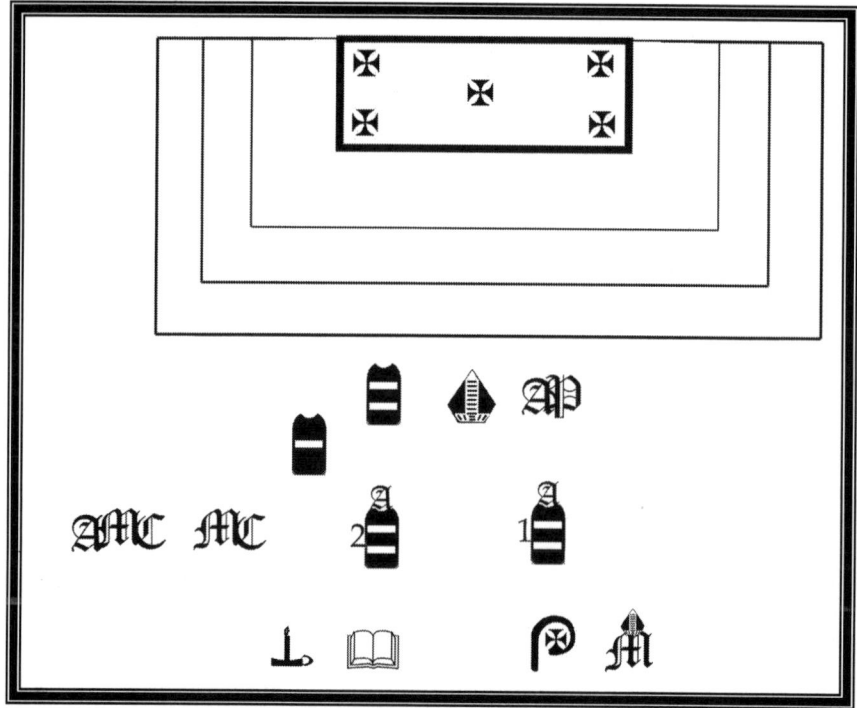

Fig. 11.1 – Positions at the Prayers at the Foot of the Altar

PONTIFICAL HIGH MASS

The Deacon removes the mitre and gives it to the Mitre Bearer. Then the ministers in Fig. 11.1 all reverence the altar with the Bishop. The Bishop bows low, as do all Prelates. Others genuflect if the sacrament is reserved, else they bow. Also, the Bishop's Chaplains, if they are holding something, only bow. Acolytes an the Thurifer go to the Credence table and stand. After the Indulgentiam (or after all the Prayers at the Foot of the Altar), the MC takes the maniple from the Sub-Deacon and places it on the left arm of the Bishop. *(The Asperges may also be done from this location.)*

THE BISHOP ASCENDS THE ALTAR

The Bishop says *Oremus* as usual and ascends the altar. The Deacon crosses to the right behind him, and the Sub-Deacon goes up to the Gospel side on the left of the Bishop. The Sub-Deacon holds open the Book of Gospels on the predella as at the reading of the Gospel for the Bishop to kiss.

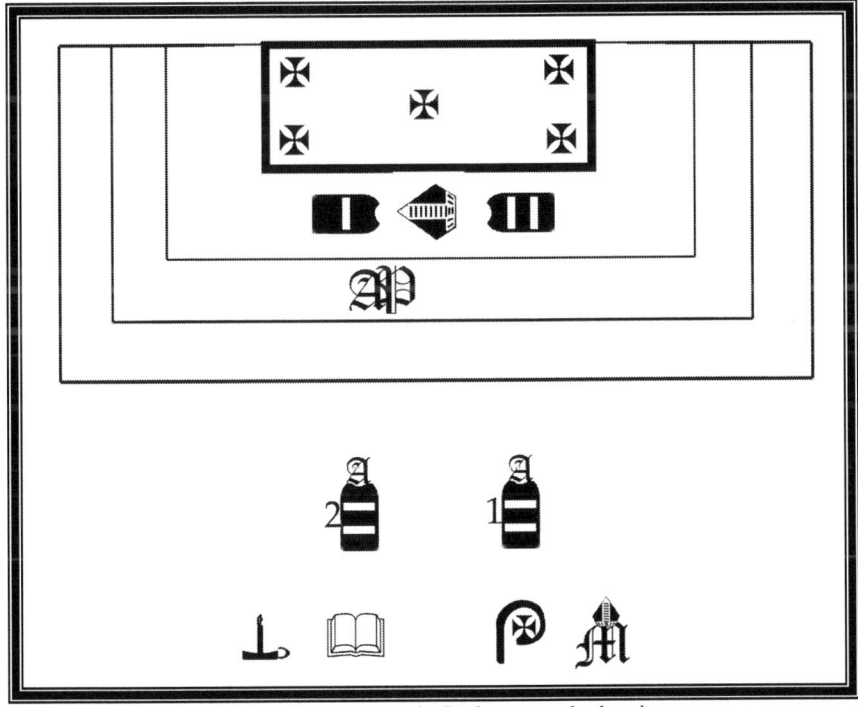

Fig. 11.2 – Positions as the Bishop ascends the altar.

After the Bishop kisses the altar in the usual manner, he then places both hands on the Book of Gospels and kisses the text of the Gospel pointed out by the Assistant Priest (who is standing on the second step). The Assistant Priest (AP) then retires to the pavement and hands the Book of Gospels to the MC, who takes it to the credence table. See Fig. 11.2 for positions of the ministers after the Bishop ascends the throne. See Fig. 11.3 when the AP retires to the pavement.

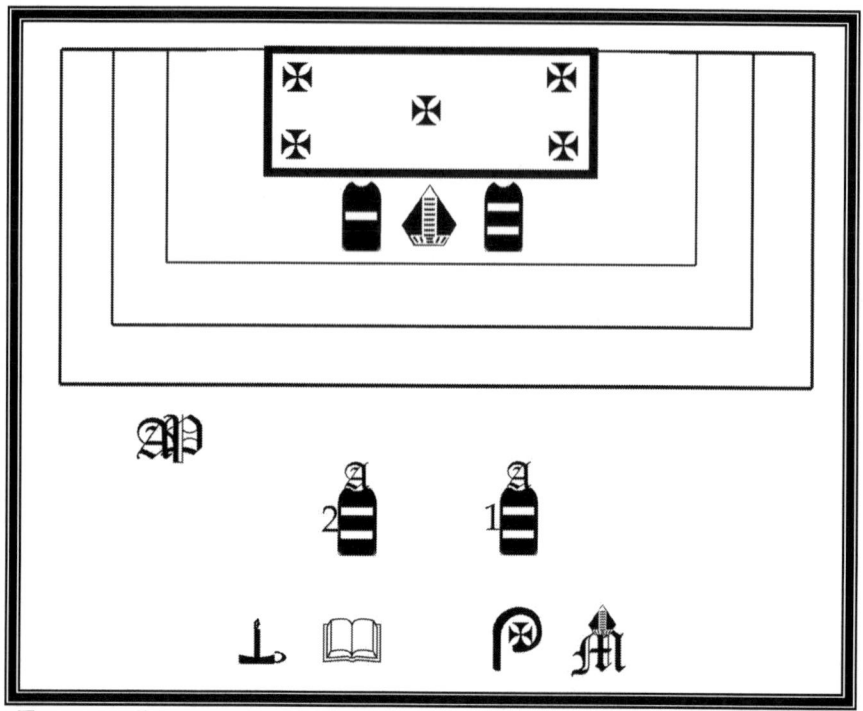

Fig. 11.3 – Positions after the Assistant Priest retires to the pavement. The Acolytes are at the credence table. The MC and AMC, as usual, are at the credence or wherever they are needed.

The thurifer ascends to the predella, and the altar is censed in the usual manner (see the section on High Mass). The AP, First Assistant Deacon (1AD), Second Assistant Deacon (2AD), Mitre Bearer (MB), Crosier Bearer (Crib), Book Bearer (BB), and Candle Bearer (CaB) remain as in Fig. 11.3. When it is time for the Bishop to be censed, the MB brings the precious mitre (except when the precious mitre cannot be worn) to the 1AD, who places it on the Bishop. Then the Bishop is incensed by the Deacon. After he is censed, he blessed the Deacon with the sign of the cross as the Deacon bows to him.

PONTIFICAL HIGH MASS

THE BISHOP GOES TO THE THRONE

After the altar is censed, the CrB brings the crosier to the Bishop. Going to the center of the altar, the Bishop bows to the cross (retaining the mitre and crosier), and then goes to the throne. He is preceded by the AP and followed by the 1AD and 2AD, walking as usual, side-by-side behind him, and the chaplains, walking behind the Assistant Deacons. The Deacon and Sub-Deacon of the Mass follow, but go to the sedilia, with the Deacon on the right of the Sub-Deacon. The positions of the party at the throne are given in Fig. 11.4.

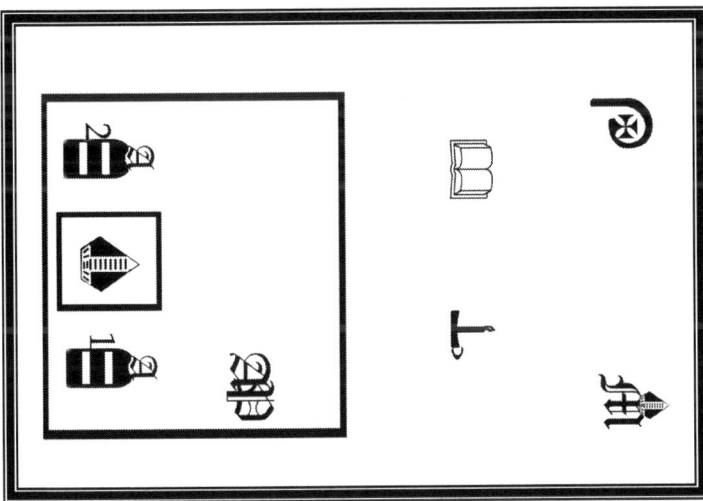

Fig. 11.4 – General Positions at the throne.

The four Bishop's Chaplains stand as in Fig. 11.4 above. If there is a train bearer, he stands to the right of the CaB (at the Prayers at the Foot of the Altar, he stands behind the MB and CrB). If there is a gremial bearer, he stands to the left of the BB (at the Prayers at the Foot of the Altar, he stands behind the BB and CaB).

Immediately upon arrival at the throne, the Bishop hands the crosier directly to the CrB. Then the 2AD removes the precious mitre and hands it to the mitre bearer, who takes it to the Epistle corner of the altar or the credence table, and then returns to his place, now with the golden mitre (unless the precious mitre is to be worn throughout the mass at the discretion of the Bishop). If the precious mitre is not used, as in any mass with the color purple or a mass celebrated by a non-jurisdictional Bishop, then only the golden mitre is used. When the simplex mitre is appointed, then only that mitre is used.

After giving up the mitre and crosier, the Bishop reads the Introit from the missal with hands joined. (At all times when the Bishop stands, all at the throne stand, as do the Deacon and Sub-Deacon of the Mass. The Assistant Deacons and AP may sit when the Bishop sits. The Chaplains stand in their positions in Fig. 11.4. If they are to sit, then they sit as convenient to the left of the throne, but first must put away whatever they are holding.) The book is held by the BB (who holds the book whenever the Bishop reads, but not when he chants). The BB holds the book open with both hands by the bottom, the top of the book resting against his chest. If the music is continuing, then the Bishop sits. The 1AD places the mitre on the Bishop after he sits, and the 2AD places the gremial on his lap. The Assistant Deacons and AP may sit. If the music has finished (or when it finishes), the 1AD removes the gremial, the 2AD removes the mitre, and the Bishop rises. (This is the order in which the mitre and gremial are removed when the Bishop rises, and the above-described manner of taking the mitre is the manner in which it is taken when the Bishop sits).

SUMMARY OF THE LAW AND KYRIE

Standing without the mitre, the Bishop extends his hands and says the Summary of the Law. As the choir sings the *Kyrie*, he recites the *Kyrie* with the party at the throne. The BB holds the book. The Deacon and Sub-Deacon (the Deacon beginning) recite the *Kyrie* at the sedilia. If the music is still continuing, the Bishop sits, taking the golden mitre and gremial.

GLORIA IN EXCELSIS

If the *Gloria* is appointed, the Bishop rises, giving up the mitre (and always the gremial first), and intones the *Gloria* in the usual manner. The AP holds the book. The Bishop continues reading the Gloria, and when he is finished, he sits and takes the mitre. Those sitting with the biretta take it off when appointed to bow (while still sitting) in the rubrics in the missal, but the Bishop bows while sitting and retaining the mitre.

SALUTATION AND COLLECTS

After the *Gloria* has been sung (or after the *Kyrie* if the *Gloria* is not sung), the Bishop rises and gives up the mitre. Turning to the people or continuing to face forward from the throne, he chants *Dominus vobiscum* or, if the *Gloria* is sung, optionally *Pax vobis*. The latter is chanted in the following tone:

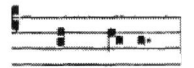

Pax vo-bis.

Then those at the throne and all present respond as usual with *Et cum spiritu tuo*. The Bishop says *Oremus* with joined hands and then, with hands extended and either facing the altar or forward from the throne, chants the collects as usual. Since he is chanting, the book is held in front of him by the AP, who always holds the book when the Bishop chants at the throne. The CaB holds the candle to the right of the book, which he always does when the Bishop reads or sings from the book, both at the throne and at the altar.

EPISTLE

At the conclusion of the last Collect, the Sub-Deacon takes the Book of Epistles from the MC. He goes as described in the section for High Mass to the place from which he will read the lesson, first making the proper reverence to the altar and to the Bishop. After chanting the Epistle, he goes to the throne and lays the Book of Epistles closed on the lap of the Bishop. The Bishop lays his right hand on the book, and the Sub-Deacon kisses it. Then the Bishop blesses the Sub-Deacon with the sign of the cross. Then the Sub-Deacon takes the Book of Epistles to the MC. During the Epistle, the Bishop sits with mitre.

GRADUAL

As the Sub-Deacon goes to the throne, the Deacon rises and takes the Book of Gospels from the MC and goes to place it in the center of the altar as usual (see the section on High Mass). He then descends the steps and says the *Munda cor meum* as usual. During this time, the Assistant Deacons and the AP rise. The BB and CaB go before the Bishop, the BB holding the missal open to the Gradual. (The BB kneels with the book resting against his forehead.) The Bishop, seated with the mitre, reads the Gradual. The choir may begin chanting the Gradual (or the congregation may begin the gradual hymn) at any time after the Epistle is finished. When the Bishop has finished the Gradual, the BB and CaB retire to their places. After saying the *Munda cor meum*, the Deacon ascends the steps, making the proper reverence, takes the book of Gospels, and descends to the pavement as in Fig. 11.5. He holds the book in the same manner the BB holds the missal. The Sub-Deacon, acolytes, and AMC join him.

HOW TO SAY MASS IN THE ANGLICAN RITE

Meanwhile, the thurifer presents himself at the throne, making the proper reverence to the Bishop, and the Bishop blessed and places incense in the thurible with the AP assisting. The thurifer then goes to the pavement as in Fig. 11.5.

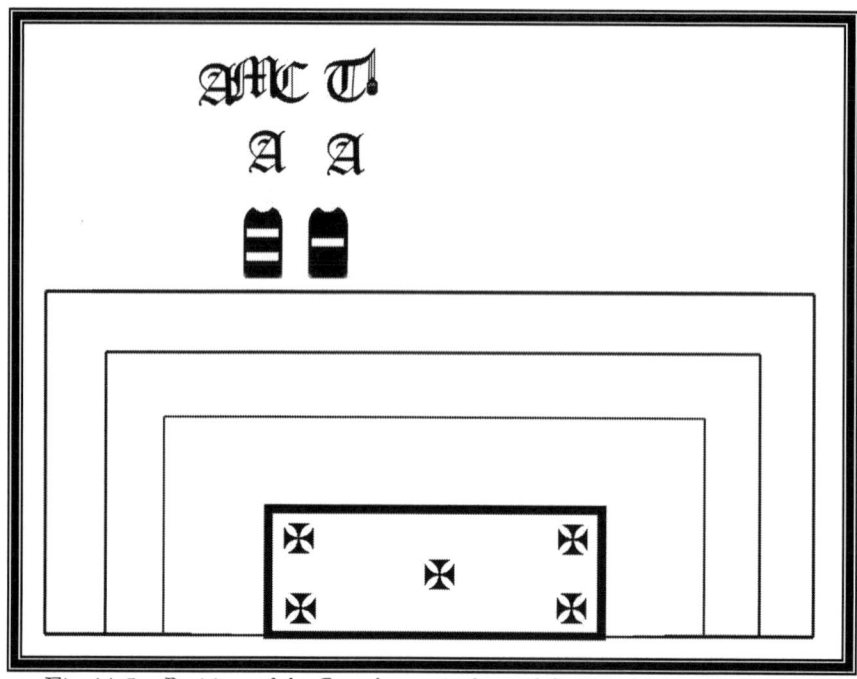

Fig. 11.5 – Positions of the Gospel party in front of the altar before going to the throne. The thurifer joins them as soon as the blessed incense has been placed in the thurible at the throne.

The Gospel party goes to the throne in the order shown in Fig. 11.5. They reverence the altar cross. Upon arrival at the throne, the AMC and thurifer reverence the Bishop and then stand to the left, the thurifer behind the AMC. The two acolytes (who, just as in the section on High Mass, are holding candles) reverence the Bishop and then stand directly in their place as in Fig. 11.6. The Sub-Deacon passes through the center of the two acolytes before the Deacon, reverences the Bishop, and then stands in his place. The Deacon passes through, reverences the Bishop, and then kneels on the pavement before the throne, holding the Book of Gospels. When the Deacon kneels, the Gospel party kneels as well. After the Deacon passes through, the AMC and thurifer take their positions as in Fig. 11.6. The Bishop's chaplains step aside if needed to make room.

PONTIFICAL HIGH MASS

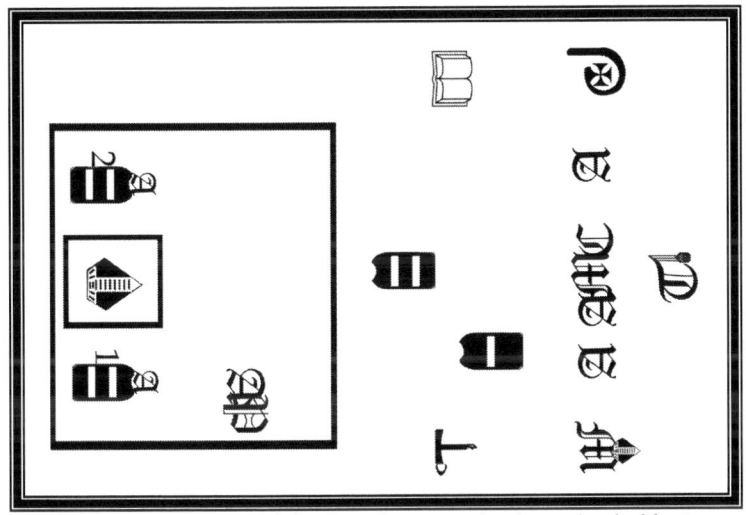

Fig. 11.6 – Positions of the Gospel party at the throne for the blessing before the Gospel

The Deacon says *Jube domne benedicere*, and the Bishop gives the blessing as usual, seated with the mitre. The Deacon does not take the book to the Bishop to kiss, nor does he kiss the episcopal ring. This blessing having been done, the Deacon and the Gospel party rise and go as described in the section on High Mass to the place where the Gospel will be sung.

GOSPEL

The actions of the Gospel party are exactly the same as given in the section on High Mass. The Bishop, before the Deacon gives the salutation, rises, giving up the mitre. The CrB brings him the crosier. He stands, holding the crosier with both hands, and faces the location where the Gospel is being sung. All of the throne party face in the same direction.

When the Gospel is finished, the Sub-Deacon brings the Book of Gospels to the Bishop without making any reverence. The Bishop gives the crosier to the CrB and then kisses the book in the usual manner, saying the *Per evangelica delicta*, etc.. The Sub-Deacon then gives the Book of Gospels to the MC and rejoins the Gospel party, as given in the section on High Mass. The Deacon and Sub-Deacon, the acolytes in the Gospel party, the AMC, and the thurifer take their positions at the throne as in Fig. 11.7. The AP takes the thurible from the thurifer and censes the Bishop with three double swings. The Bishop stands with hands joined, without the mitre and crosier. The Bishop then blesses the AP with the sign of the cross. The thurifer and acolytes retire to the credence table, and the Deacon and Sub-Deacon go to the sedilia.

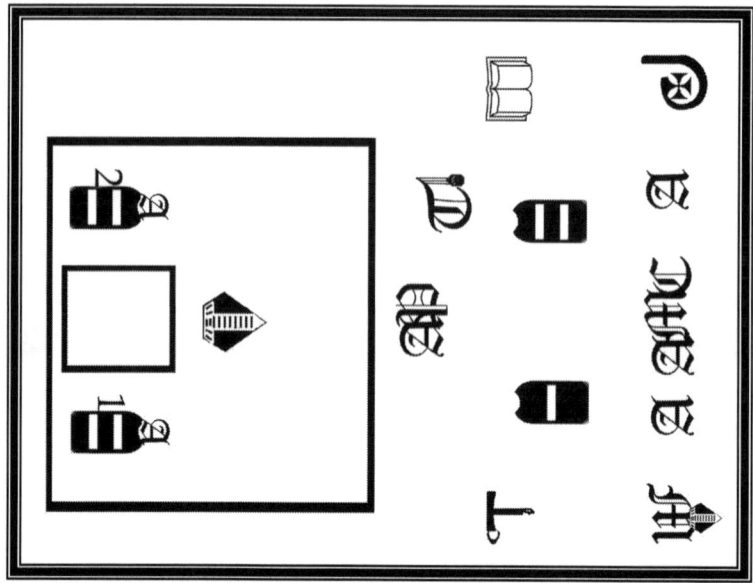

Fig. 11.7 – Positions after the Gospel for the censing of the Bishop

SERMON

If the Bishop preaches the sermon from the throne, then all remain in their places, seated. The Bishop's Chaplains may remain in their places before the throne, standing, or may put away their items and sit. The Bishop preaches the sermon seated, wearing the mitre. If he reads the sermon from notes, then these should be attractively covered and held by the BB.

If the sermon is preached by the Bishop from the pulpit, then he rises, retaining the mitre, but giving up the gremial, takes the crosier from the CrB, and proceeds to the pulpit. He is preceded as usual by the AP, walks between his Assistant Deacons, and is followed by his chaplains. Upon arrival at the pulpit, he gives up the crosier to the CrB. He retains the mitre throughout the sermon, unless he gives an oration at the beginning or the end. However, he retains the mitre if he only makes the sign of the cross at the beginning of the sermon, and he retains it for any blessing he may give at the end. The Assistant Deacons, AP, and chaplains sit nearby as convenient. The chaplains, however, must stand if they are holding something, and may only sit if they can put away their items (including the crosier) conveniently.

If the sermon is to be preached from the faldstool somewhere before the altar, he goes as to the pulpit as above, except that the Deacon and Sub-Deacon of the Mass walk in front of the AP (first the Sub-Deacon, then the Deacon). He sits with the mitre, giving up the crosier to the CrB as above. See Fig. 11.8.

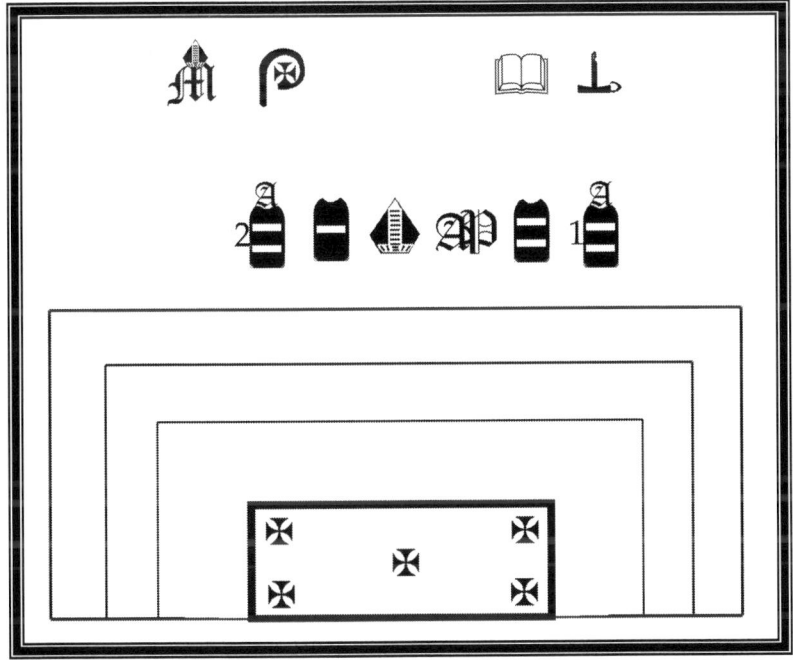

Fig. 11.8 – Positions for the sermon at the faldstool.

If another priest is to preach:

In the case that another priest is to preach, it is often the case that this priest serves as AP for the mass (in which case he also wears a stole, the AP usually not wearing a stole). If another priest other than the AP is to preach, then he should be vested in choir dress, with or without the cope, and a stole in the color of the mass. The Bishop remains at the throne, seated with mitre, during the sermon.

CREED

If the sermon was preached at the pulpit or faldstool, then the Bishop returns to the throne in the same manner that he left it. Upon arrival, he gives up the mitre and crosier and remains standing to begin the Creed. If he preached from the throne, then he simply rises, giving up the mitre.

The AP holds the book with, of course, the CaB standing to the right holding the candle. The Bishop intones the Creed, and then continues reciting it himself while the choir and/or congregation sings the Creed. When he makes the genuflection, all genuflect with him. When he is seated, he bows profoundly while seated when the choir sings the *Et incarnatus*, etc., and all bow profoundly with him. He retains the mitre for this bow, but all those wearing the biretta remove it.

Towards the end of the Creed, the Deacon goes to the altar and spreads the corporal. For a detailed description of this, see the section on High Mass.

OFFERTORY

Shortly before the singing of the Creed is finished, the Bishop's chaplains, on a signal from the MC, present themselves before the Bishop, and the acolytes go before the throne with the ewer and basin and reverence the Bishop. (If there is no Creed, then the Bishop begins the Offertory immediately after the sermon. If there is no sermon, then the Bishop begins the Offertory immediately after the Gospel.)

After the Creed, the Bishop rises, giving up the mitre. He sings *Dominus vobiscum* as usual, and then after the response, sings *Oremus*. Then, from the book being held by the BB (with, as usual, the CaB on the right holding the candle), he reads the Offertory verse appointed for the mass. Also as soon as he sings *Oremus*, the choir and/or congregation either begin to sing the Offertory verse or a suitable offertory hymn. Also during this time, the mitre bearer should take the golden mitre to the credence table and take the precious mitre.

When the Bishop has finished reading the verse, he sits and takes the mitre. In lieu of the usual gremial, a white towel (linen, or at least of attractive form) is spread in his lap by the 2AD. The episcopal ring is removed by the AP and temporarily laid aside. The episcopal gloves are removed by the Assistant Deacons. The 1AD removes the right glove, and the 2AD removes the left glove. See Fig. 11.9.

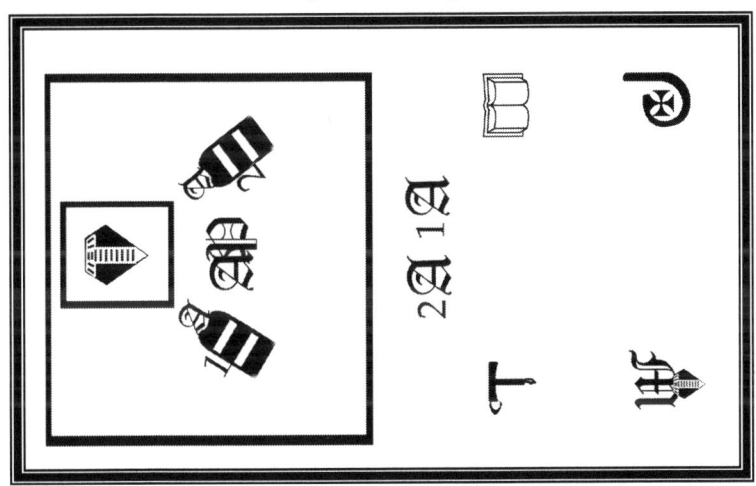

Fig. 11.9 – Positions at the removal of the ring and gloves.

Then the acolytes with the ewer, basin, and towel present themselves, bowing to the Bishop before ascending the platform to the throne. They wash his hands in the usual manner and then retire, after making the proper reverence to the Bishop. See Fig. 11.10.

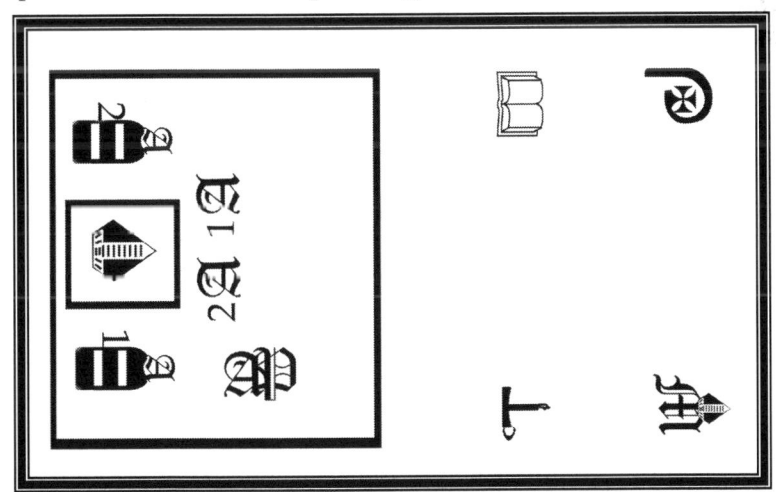

Fig. 11.10 – Positions at the washing of the Bishop's hands at the throne

HOW TO SAY MASS IN THE ANGLICAN RITE

During this time, the AP takes the missal and, if it is not already on the altar, the missal stand, to the altar and places it (them) on the Gospel side in the usual position for the Offertory and Canon of the Mass. He then returns to the throne. Also as the Bishop's hands are being washed, the Sub-Deacon rises and goes to the credence table, where he takes the humeral veil from the MC (see the section on High Mass). He takes the Sacred Vessels in the usual manner and times his movements to arrive at the altar in the prescribed position as in solemn high mass at the same time that the Bishop arrives.

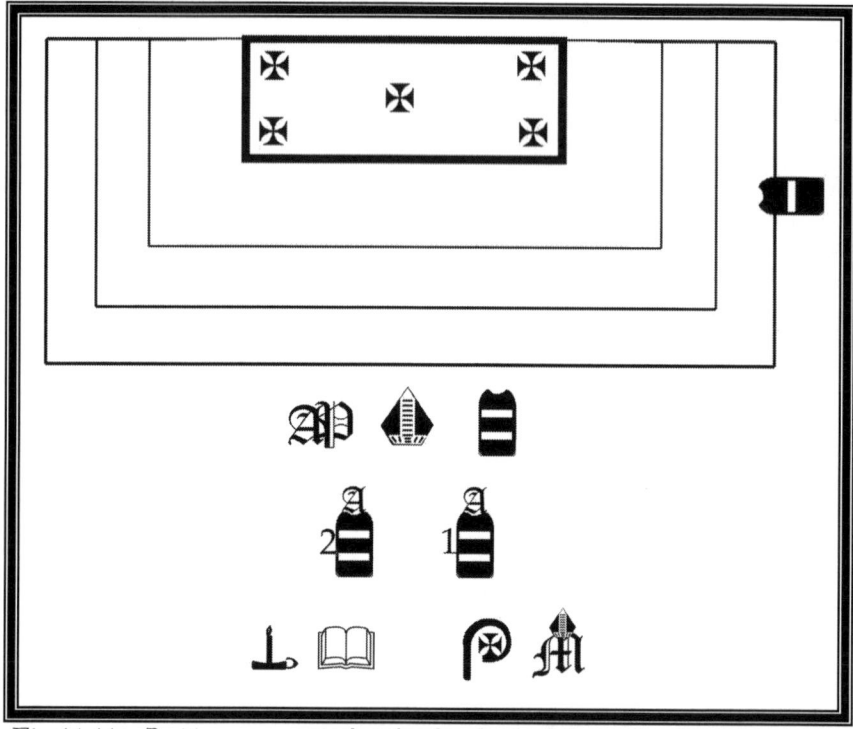

Fig. 11.11 – Positions upon arrival at the altar for the Offertory. In this position, the Bishop and all above reverence the altar. Note the Sub-Deacon, on the pavement on the Epistle side of the altar. He bows with the rest, and then ascends the steps.

After the Bishop's hands are washed, he stands, and the 1AD places the mitre as usual on his head. He takes the crosier from the CrB, and the throne party prepares to go to the altar. Also at this time, the Deacon rises. The timing should be such that the Deacon joins the procession to the altar to walk either in front of or to the side of the AP. The AP and Deacon are followed by the Bishop, between the Assistant Deacons, and the Bishop's chaplains follow in the usual manner. Upon arrival at the altar, the Bishop first gives up the crosier, and then he gives up the mitre. He bows to the cross, and all walking with him reverence the altar as well. He then ascends the altar steps to the predella. The Deacon and Sub-Deacon stand as in high mass for the offertory. The Assistant Deacons stand on the pavement, and the chaplains behind him. The AP stands on the predella to the left of the Bishop and assists at the missal. See Figs. 11.11 (above) and 11.12 (below).

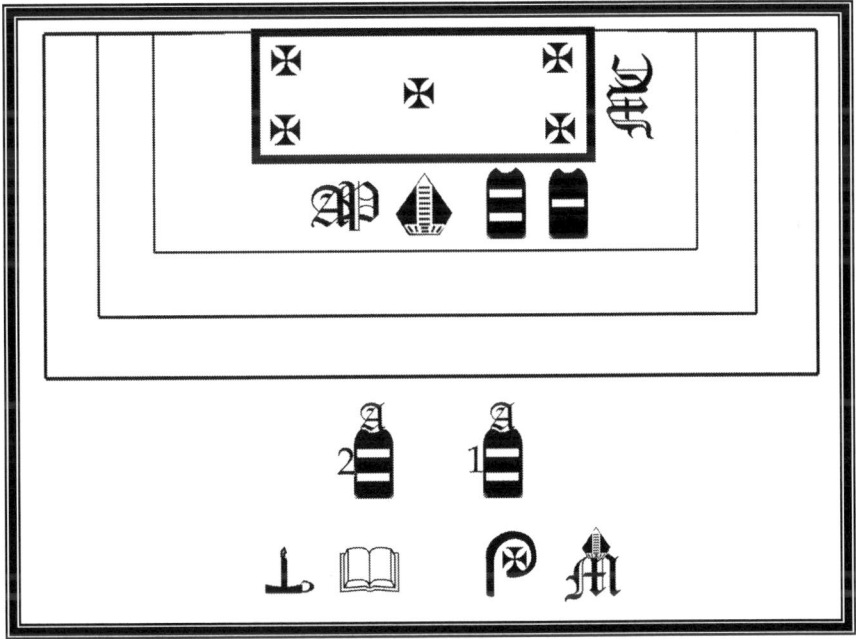

Fig. 11.12 – Positions for the beginning of the Offertory. If the Chaplains do not stand in their positions as above, then they must lay aside their items and retire to the credence table, where their actions are the same as those of the acolytes.

The Offertory proceeds exactly as at high mass, with a few exceptions. When the Bishop censes the altar, he is assisted by the AP on his left and the Deacon of the Mass on his right. The MC moves the missal. The Bishop takes the precious mitre when he is censed at the Offertory. This he takes from the 1AD as usual, except if there are no Assistant Deacons, the Bishop takes the mitre from the MC while he is at the altar. The Bishop makes the sign of the cross over the Deacon after being censed. The Deacon then incenses the AP, the Assistant Deacons, the clergy in choir, and then the Sub-Deacon. Then the Deacon himself is incensed by the thurifer. The incensation continues from there as at high mass.

When the Bishop has been censed, he goes to the Epistle corner and recites the *Lavabo*, still retaining the precious mitre, up to but not including the *Gloria Patri*. Alternatively, the Bishop may recite the *Lavabo* from the missal at the center of the altar. The AP, as soon as he can been censed, goes to the Epistle corner to assist. The acolytes bearing the ewer, basin, and towel approach the Bishop at the Epistle corner and, making the proper reverence, wash the Bishop's hand. The AP first removes the episcopal ring, placing it on after the hands have been washed (the AP presents the towel). Before the Bishop says the *Gloria Patri*, the 2AD removes the mitre and gives it to the MB. During the *Gloria Patri*, the Bishop bows, and the AP bows with him. Otherwise, the Offertory is exactly like that of a solemn high mass celebrated by a priest.

CONFESSION AND ABSOLUTION & PREFACE AND SANCTUS

This is exactly the same as at high mass, except that the Bishop takes the crosier to give the absolution. He gives the crosier back to the CrB before reciting the Comfortable Words. The mitre is not used. After the Absolution and Comfortable words, the Bishop gives up the zucchetto, which is removed by the MC and taken to the credence table. Alternatively, the MC may give the zucchetto to a zucchetto bearer, who takes it away. The zucchetto having been removed, the Bishop returns to the center of the altar to chant the *Sursum corda* and proper preface. The AP remains at the missal, the Deacon and Sub-Deacon in their places as given in the section on High Mass. At the Sanctus, the Deacon moves up to the right of the Bishop as usual, but the Sub-Deacon remains on the lowest step (the AP is still on the left of the Bishop). Torchbearers, if used, should be four, six, or eight in number and arrayed as given in the section on High Mass.

CANON OF THE MASS THROUGH THE AGNUS DEI

The actions of the Canon are essentially the same as those given in the sections of High Mass and Low Mass. There are only slight differences. The Assistant Deacons and Chaplains remain in their positions as given in Fig. 11.12 above. However, the CaB may, if physical arrangements permit it, stand to the left of the AP by the missal with the candle. If this option is used, then he remains there whenever the Bishop is at the altar (though he goes to the pavement for the peace) and holds the candle at the missal. Also, when at the altar, when the Bishop genuflects, the CaB bows.

PONTIFICAL HIGH MASS

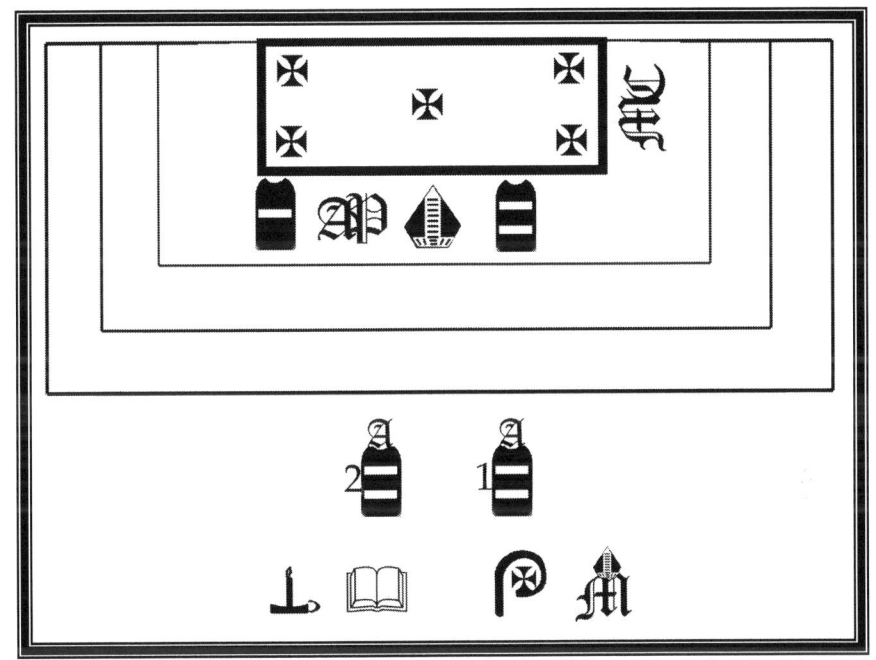

Fig. 11.13 – Positions at the Agnus Dei. If the Candle Bearer is at the altar, he stands between the Sub-Deacon and AP.

The AP assists at the missal and genuflects whenever the Bishop does. At the *Pax Domini*, when the Sub-Deacon is appointed to come to the left of the Celebrant in high mass, he now comes to the left of the AP. See Fig. 11.13. *Nota bene:* If there is no AP, then the actions of the Canon are exactly the same as those given in the section on High Mass, except that the Bishop still follows the procedure for giving the Peace as given in this section as much as is possible.

THE PEACE

After the *Agnus Dei*, the AP and Deacon change places. The Sub-Deacon genuflects and returns to the center of the altar on his own step. See Fig. 11.14. The Bishop turns to the right after saying the proper prayer and gives the peace to the Assistant Priest. The Bishop then turns to the left to give the peace to the Deacon. The Bishop then descends and gives the peace to the Sub-Deacon and the Assistant Deacons. Meanwhile, the AP gives the peace to the MC, who passes it to the Bishop's chaplains in order, then the thurifer, and then the acolytes. The AMC receives the peace from the Sub-Deacon.

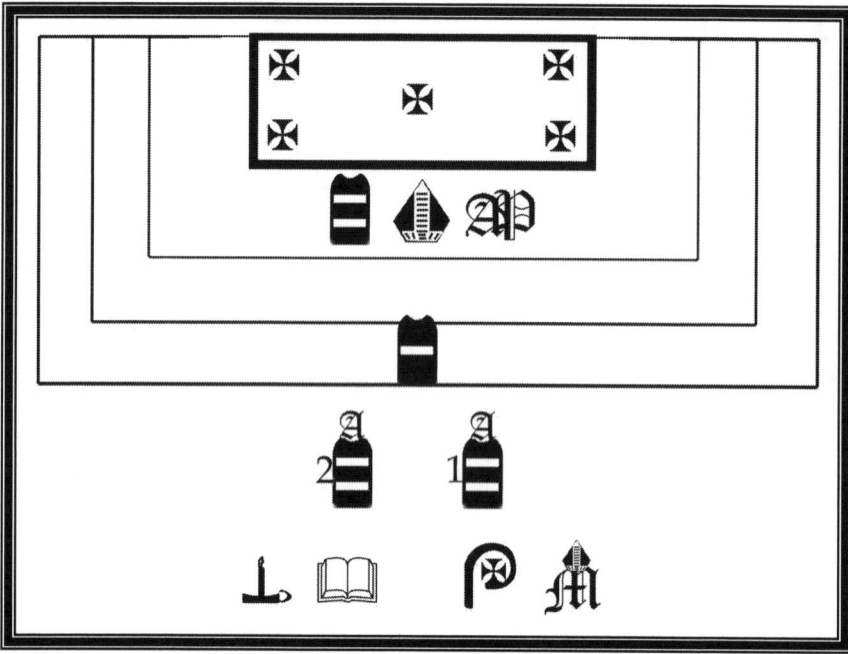

Fig. 11.14 – Positions at the beginning for the Peace

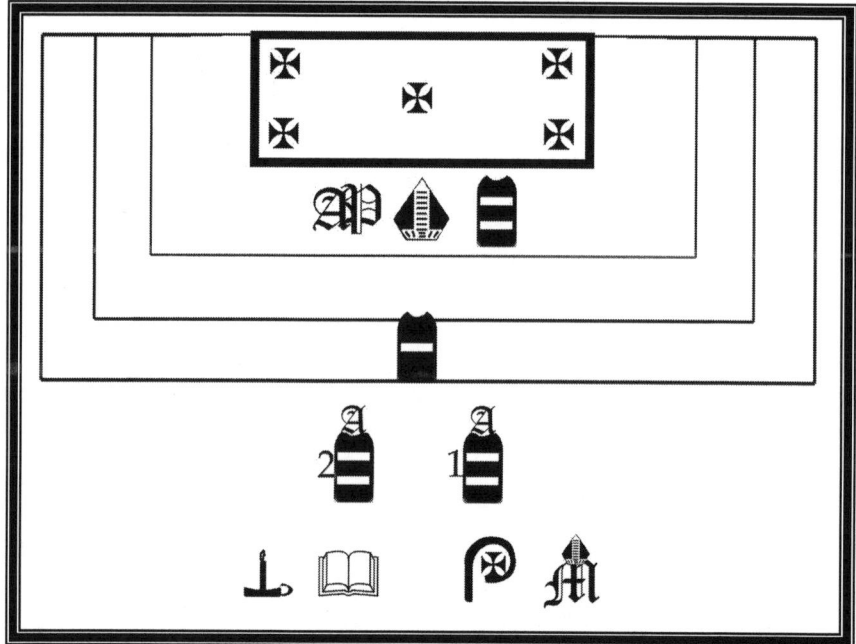

Fig. 11.15 – Positions after the Peace when the AP has returned to the altar

The AP gives the peace to the senior member of the clergy in choir, and then returns to the missal. While the AP is away, the Deacon assists at the missal, and the Bishop continues with the prayer. When the AP returns, the Deacon goes to the Bishop's right. The Sub-Deacon remains on his own step in the center of the altar. See Fig. 11.15.

COMMUNION

For the Communion, the Deacon, standing to the right of the Bishop, removes the pall (instead of the Sub-Deacon as in the section on High Mass). As the Bishop receives the host and Precious Blood, the Deacon, Sub-Deacon, and AP bow, as do the MC and AMC.

After the Bishop receives communion, the AP, Deacon, and Sub-Deacon kneel on the platform, the AP to the left of the Deacon, and the Sub-Deacon to the left of the AP. After the *Ecce Agnus Dei*, the Bishop then communicates them, as in the section on High Mass. Communion follows as at High Mass, beginning with the Assistant Deacons, then the clergy, then the servers, and then the faithful.

ABLUTIONS

Ablutions are done as at High Mass. The AP stands to the left of the Deacon before he transfers the missal, and then on the pavement on the Gospel side once he transfers the missal back to the throne. The missal is transferred once the Bishop has read the second ablution prayer. The MC replaces the zucchetto either before or after the ablutions are done.

The Bishop takes the precious mitre from the 1AD or the Deacon of the Mass, the crosier from the CrB. The AP leads the way back to the throne. Then the Bishop, between the two Assistant Deacons, and followed by the Bishop's Chaplains. They return to their positions at the throne as in 11.4.

If the Pontifical Blessing is to be sung, then the Bishop again takes the pontifical gloves. See the positions in Fig. 11.9. The AP removes the ring, the 1AD replaces the right glove, the 2AD the left glove, and the AP replaces the ring. The gloves are brought by servers, the MC, or AMC as convenient. If the Blessing is simply to be recited, then the gloves may or may not be taken, according to local custom.

GENERAL THANKSGIVING, COMMUNION VERSE, POST-COMMUNIONS, & DISMISSAL

The Bishop, having arrived at the throne, gives up the mitre and crosier. He chants the General Thanksgiving from the throne (see the section on High Mass), with the AP holding the book. After the Thanksgiving, the choir may chant the Communion Verse or the choir and/or congregation may sing a suitable hymn. The Bishop reads the Communion Verse from the missal (held still by the AP as a matter of convenience), and then sits with the precious mitre (and, of course, the gremial, if it is used).

When the music has ended, the Bishop rises, giving up the mitre, and chants *Dominus vobiscum* as for the collects. He then chants the Postcommunion prayers in the same manner as the collects, the AP holding the book. After the orations, the AP returns the missal to the BB, who will hold it for the Last Gospel.

The Bishop again chants *Dominus vobiscum*. Either he or the Deacon (it is usually the Deacon) chants *Ite missa est*, with hands extended, facing the people (if the Bishop chants it, then he may face the people or face forward from the throne). If *Benedicamus Domino* or *Requiescant in pace* is appointed, then the Deacon (or Bishop) faces the altar to chant the dismissal with hands joined.

PONTIFICAL BENEDICTION

The Bishop takes the mitre and crosier. Turning to the people or facing forward from the throne, he begins the chant *Sit nomen*, etc. with his right hand on his breast (see Fig. 11.16). At *Adjutorium nostrum*, etc., he makes the sign of the cross (see Fig. 11.17). Alternatively, he may hold his right arm extended pastorally for the entire introduction (see Fig. 11.18). Then he gives the blessing by first extending his right hand (if it isn't already extended), and then raising it, bringing it in and then down before his breast in one fluid motion. As he chants ✠*Pater, et* ✠*Filius, et* ✠*Spiritus Sanctus*, he makes the sign of the cross three times with the index and middle fingers of the right hand. These crosses are on the small side relative to the cross made by a priest at the benediction. The first cross is made to the Bishop's left. The second in the center, and the third to the right. See Figs. 11.19-11.24. All kneel, except prelates, who bow low.

PONTIFICAL HIGH MASS

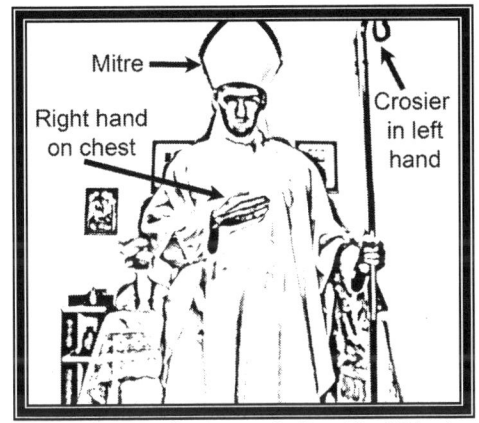

Fig. 11.16 – Position at the introduction to the Pontifical Blessing for Sit nomen, etc.

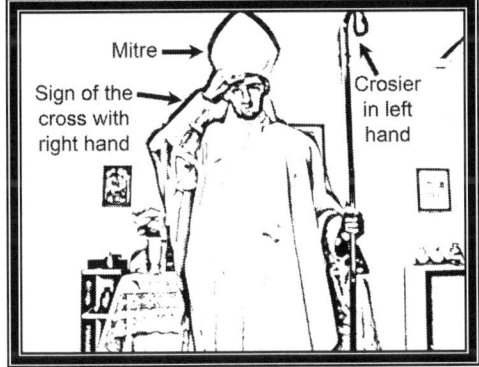

Fig. 11.17 – Position at the introduction to the Pontifical Blessing when the Adjutorium nostrum is said.

Fig. 11.18 – Alternative option for the Introduction to the Pontifical Blessing

HOW TO SAY MASS IN THE ANGLICAN RITE

Fig. 11.19 – After being extended, the right arm is raised as Benedicat vos, etc. is begun.

Fig. 11.20 – The arm continues to be raised…

Fig. 11.21 - …and then brought down in front of the breast as omnipotens Deus is sung.

PONTIFICAL HIGH MASS

Fig. 11.22 – The sign of the cross is made to the left with two fingers at "Pater"

Fig. 11.23 – Then to the center for "et Filius"

Fig. 11.24 – Then to the right for "et Spiritus Sanctus."

If the Benediction is to be given from the throne as described above, then the *Placeat tibi* is recited standing, without mitre, in an inclined position at the throne, the BB holding the book. If he takes this option, then he will kiss the altar as described below after the Last Gospel and before processing out.

If the Benediction is to be given from in front of the altar, then the Bishop returns to the altar as described at the Offertory during the music for the Communion verse. He recites the *Placeat tibi* from the center of the altar as usual and kisses the altar in the center. The Deacon and Sub-Deacon stand as given for this in High Mass. The Assistant Deacons and Chaplains are on the pavement. The AP stands on the second step on the Gospel side. Then the Bishop takes the mitre and crosier. He stands on the predella as in Fig. 11.25. If this option is used, then the Last Gospel should be read from the altar.

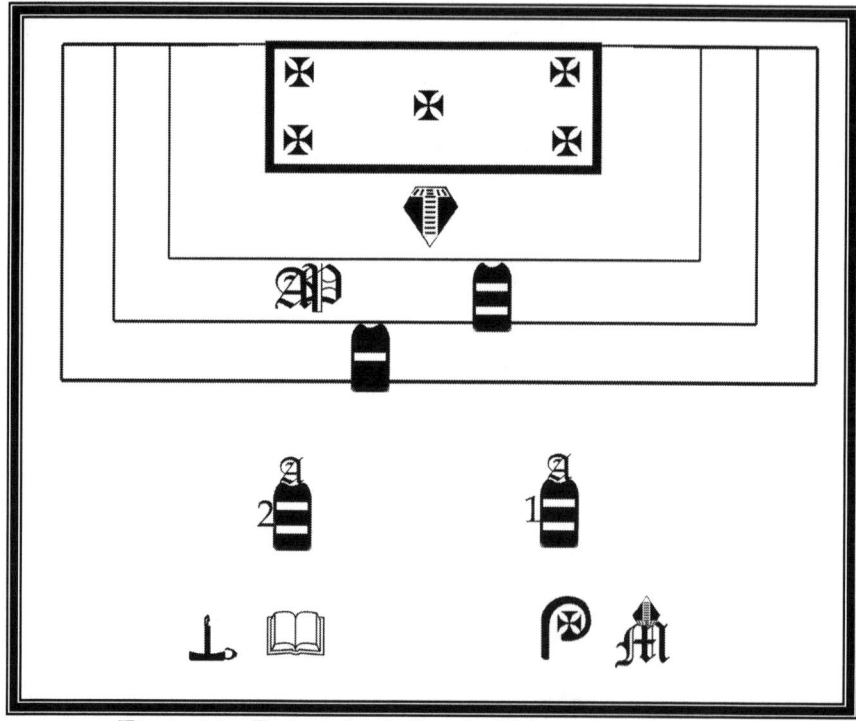

Fig. 11.25 – Positions for the Pontifical Blessing from the altar

If the Pontifical Blessing is not to be sung, then the Bishop gives the spoken Benediction, using the motions as in Figs. 11.19-11.24 above,

PONTIFICAL HIGH MASS

either from the throne or in front of the altar. He wears the mitre and holds the crosier.

If the Bishop wishes to say the entire Conclusion of the Mass from the altar, then the AP transfers the missal to the Epistle side after the Ablutions, and the Conclusion is exactly as given in the section on High Mass. The AP, however, assists at the missal on the Epistle side instead of the MC. The Assistant Deacons and Chaplains remain in their positions on the pavement. If this option is used, the pontifical gloves are not used again after the Offertory. See Fig. 11.26 for positions at the Thanksgiving, Communion Verse, and Post-Communions. The positions for the Salutations and Dismissal are exactly as in High Mass. It is also best, should this option be used, that the Bishop reads the Communion verse and then immediately begins the Post-communions, with no music. Otherwise it becomes awkward, as the Bishop must return to the throne and sit during the music and then return to the altar for the Post-communions. However, a split option exists, in which the Thanksgiving and Communion are read from the altar, music is sung during which the Bishop returns to the throne, and the Post-communions, etc. are done from there. These are matters of local custom and episcopal decision.

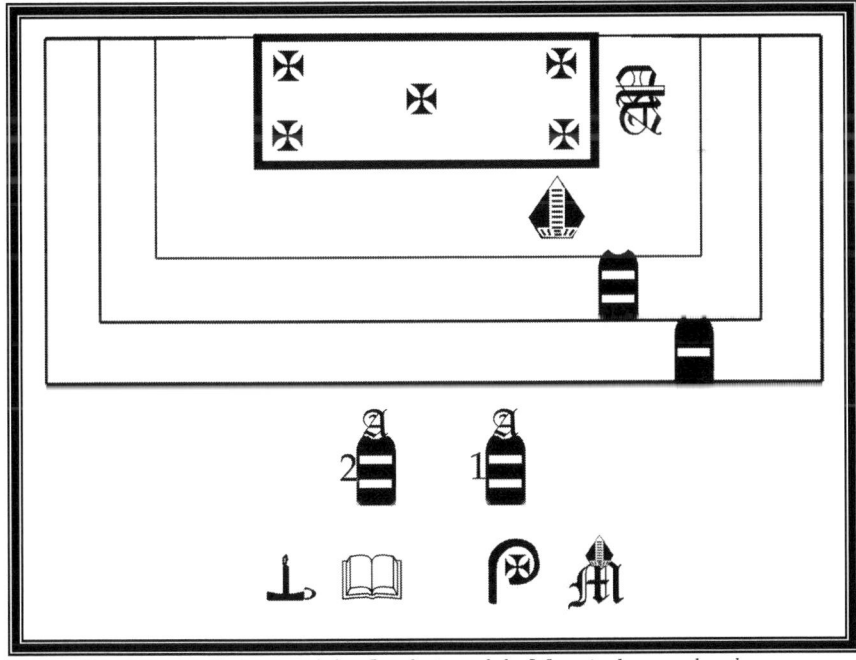

Fig. 11.26 – Positions if the Conclusion of the Mass is done at the altar

LAST GOSPEL

If the Last Gospel is to be read from the altar, then the Bishop goes to the altar in the usual manner (see the part on the Offertory) if he is not already there. He reads the Last Gospel in the same manner as in the section for High Mass. The Deacon and Sub-Deacon stand behind him as at High Mass, and the AP stands on the Gospel side to the left of the Bishop. If the Last Gospel is read from the throne, the BB holds the book. Positions for all are the usual ones while at the throne. The Bishop genuflects in either case at the appropriate time, and all genuflect with him.

PROCESSION TO THE SACRISTY

The ministers move to positions as at the Prayers at the Foot of the Altar, Fig. 11.1. The Bishop reverences the altar, and then the procession forms in the same order as for the procession to the sanctuary given above, and they process to the sacristy. The sacristy prayer is done as at high mass.

If, however, the Bishop recited the *Placeat tibi* at the throne, then before the above, he processes again to the altar with mitre and crosier, giving them up at the foot of the steps. He ascends the steps alone and kisses the altar in the center. He then takes the mitre and crosier again, and all take their places as in Fig. 11.1. From there, all is as above. The Bishop is devested of mass vestments by the Deacon and Sub-Deacon of the Mass, the Assistant Deacons, and the AP. He returns to choir dress to greet the people and exit the church.

IF THE VESTING IS NOT DONE DURING THE DAILY OFFICE

If the Daily Office is not sung while the Bishop vests, then he still vests in the chapel or at the throne. Hymns may be sung by the choir and/or congregation. He also may vest in the sacristy. The manner of vesting is exactly the same as that described for the vesting during the Daily Office. The solemn arrival may also be done as well. In any case, most properly the Bishop arrives in choir dress for liturgy.

PONTIFICAL HIGH MASS

NOTES ON VESTURE OF SERVERS & EXTRA MINISTERS

Vesture on servers is also detailed in the section on Altar Servers. Lay servers at a pontifical mass may wear black or red cassocks, though only black should be used in penitential seasons. Blue-purple (not Roman purple) cassocks may be worn at cathedral churches regardless of the season. Servers in Holy Orders wear black cassocks or the habit of their order. Over the cassock goes a surplice, either plain or with lace. In some areas, the altar boys wear small shoulder capes. Other local variations exist. Albs should not generally be worn by servers, but if they are, they must be plain and not adorned or made of lace. The use of lace in an alb is best reserved to the dignity of those in Holy Orders.

The MC and AMC may wear a cope, though the AMC may only do so if the MC does. The MC may wear white gloves and, if the MC does and it is permitted by local custom, the AMC may do so as well. These gloves are simple, white kid gloves with no ornamentation other than the typical three white seams found on such gloves.

The Bishop's Chaplains may wear copes. It is best for aesthetic reasons that they either all wear copes or they all do not wear copes. The chaplains of the mitre and crosier should wear a vimpa.

The Assistant Deacons wear the dalmatic over choir dress, i.e., cassock and surplice, unless they are bishops, in which case it is cassock and rochet. They do not wear the biretta except while sitting. They may carry it in procession. They do not, however, wear a stole or maniple. Similarly, the Assistant Priest does not wear a stole or maniple.

The preacher at a pontifical mass, if it is not the Bishop, may wear a stole over his cassock and surplice. Typically if the Bishop does not preach, the preacher is the Assistant Priest. Usually an Assistant Deacon will not be the preacher.

NOTES ON THE MITRE

The precious mitre is worn only by jurisdictional bishops. It is also not worn at masses when the color is purple, rose, or black. More precisely, it is not worn at all during penitential seasons, even on feast days. Whether it is used on feasts that impede September Ember Days is a matter of local use and episcopal authority. However, it would not be used at the Ember Day mass in such a case anyway.

When the precious mitre is used, it is worn from the time the Bishop vests until he sits and takes the mitre for the singing of the *Kyrie* exclusive. At that point, he takes the golden mitre. This usage is grounded in tradition, coming no doubt from the heavy nature of many precious mitres. However, the Bishop may wear the precious mitre throughout if he wishes. The golden mitre, if taken as above at the *Kyrie*, is retained until the Bishop goes to the altar at the Offertory. From then on, the precious mitre is again used. If the precious mitre is not used at all, as in the case of penitential seasons or masses celebrated by non-jurisdictional Bishops, then the golden mitre is used throughout.

The simplex mitre is appointed on three occasions. It is mandatory to be used on Ash Wednesday and Good Friday. It is also the proper mitre for all Masses of the Dead, i.e., when the color of the mass is black. This includes seasonal Masses of the Dead, such as All Souls' Day, and all Requiem masses.

If the Deacon of the Mass is a Bishop (and this applies also if the Sub-Deacon of the Mass is also a Bishop, though he may rightly only be a Bishop if the Deacon of the Mass is a Bishop), then he wears the mitre as well. Its usage follows precisely that of the Bishop. His mitre should be removed before the Bishop Celebrant and put on after. He uses the gremial only if permitted by local use. He should have an attendant to assist him with the mitre, and that attendant should be vested in choir dress with a vimpa. The mitre use should be a golden mitre or a simplex mitre, never a precious mitre. The simplex mitre must be used when the Bishop Celebrant uses the simplex mitre.

If other ministers, such as the AP and Assistant Deacons, are Bishops, then they also wear the mitre. Which mitre to use is a matter of local custom. However, the same general rule applies. The precious mitre is never used. The simplex mitre is really the most appropriate. Each such minister may also have an attendant to manage their mitre, vested in choir dress with a vimpa.

Regarding the precious mitre and golden mitre, the distinction is the level of ornamentation. A plain gold mitre is clearly a golden mitre, and a mitre with jewels or icons is clearly a precious mitre. From there the distinction can be difficult. A mitre of gold or white with an orphrey of any suitable color is classed as a golden mitre. A mitre of white or gold with a simple religious symbol, such as an AΩ or a cross, would likely count as a golden mitre, provided it is of simple design. The simplex mitre is plain white, usually of linen or a linen blend, and without any ornamentation whatsoever. The only permissible addition to the simplex mitre is red fringe on the lapits.

AT THE FALDSTOOL

If the mass is celebrated at the faldstool, as would be the case for a Suffragan Bishop or a Bishop celebrating outside his jurisdiction (unless he was invited to use the throne), all is essentially as was given for mass at the throne. The positions at the faldstool are rotated 180 degrees from those at the throne, as the faldstool is placed on the Epistle side as a general rule. There are usually no Assistant Deacons and may be no AP, as non-jurisdictional Bishops typically do not have Assistant Deacons. In the case of no Assistant Deacons, the Deacon and Sub-Deacon of the Mass sit on either side of the Bishop, the Deacon to his right, and the Sub-Deacon to his left. If there are Assistant Deacons, then they sit on either side of the Bishop as usual, and the Deacon and Sub-Deacon sit at the sedilia. The AP, if there is one, sits in his usual position to the right and front of the Bishop (though now this is on the side closest to the altar). The Chaplains stand in front of the Bishop exactly as at the throne, only rotated 180 degrees. See Figs. 11.27 and 11.28.

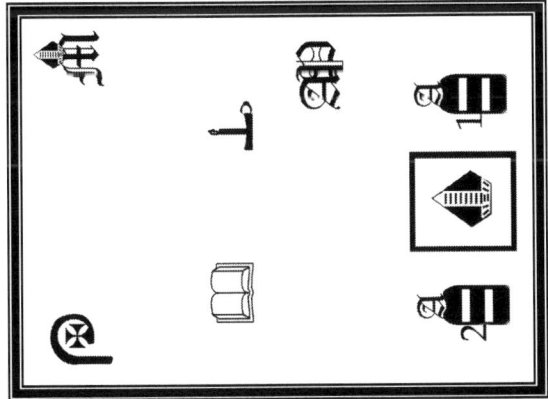

Fig. 11.27 – Positions at the faldstool if there are Assistant Deacons

HOW TO SAY MASS IN THE ANGLICAN RITE

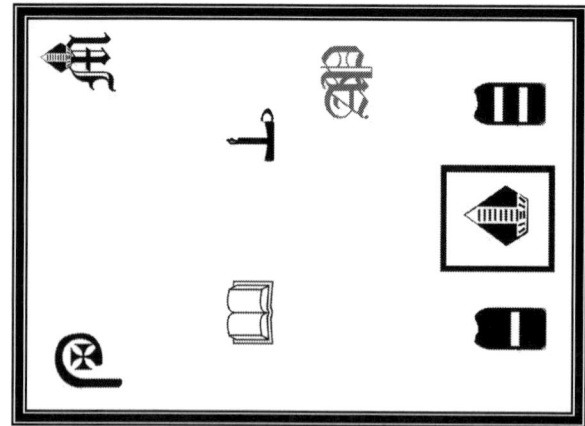

Fig. 11.28 – Positions at the faldstool if there are no Assistant Deacons. The Assistant Priest is shown in grey, as he may or may not be present.

All aspects of the pontifical mass celebrated from the faldstool are the same as those from the throne, except they are done at the faldstool. The portions of the mass at the altar are precisely the same. If there is no AP, then the MC fulfills the role of the AP. If there are no Assistant Deacons, then the positions and movements of the Deacon and Sub-Deacon at the altar are exactly the same as those given in the section on High Mass.

IF THERE ARE NO ASSISTANT DEACONS

If there are no Assistant Deacons, then the Deacon and Sub-Deacon of the Mass may either remain at the sedilia or sit on either side of the Bishop at the throne. The Deacon sits to the right of the Bishop, and the Sub-Deacon sits to the left. This is generally the best option, as the Deacon and Sub-Deacon of the Mass are expected to fulfill the roles of the 1AD and 2AD when there are no Assistant Deacons. The Deacon fulfills the duties of the 1AD, and the Sub-Deacon fulfills the duties of the 2AD. In a procession with no Assistant Deacons, it may go with the Sub-Deacon, followed by the Deacon, followed by the Bishop walking alone, or the Bishop walking in between the Deacon (on his right) and the Sub-Deacon (on his left), the AP in front (if there is an AP). In the latter case, though, the Book of Gospels, containing the Bishop's maniple, must already be in place at the foot of the altar in a suitable location (or it may be at the credence table, to be brought by the MC. Another option is for the Bishop to walk with the AP on his right, the Deacon of the Mass on his left, and the Sub-Deacon of the Mass in front carrying the Book of Gospels.

Pontifical Sung Mass

ಸಿರ

The details of a sung mass are given in general in the section on Sung Mass. For a Bishop, the seventh candle, if it would be used at a pontifical high mass, may or may not be used. The episcopal gloves are optional. There may or may not be Assistant Deacons or an AP. Elements of the mass may be altered, as at any sung mass, as needed. The variations are far too numerous to mention. However, if the Bishop chooses to celebrate a sung mass from the altar, then the actions before the Offertory are exactly the same as those given for a priest in high mass. The Assistant Deacons, if any, and Chaplains stand as they do when the Bishop goes to the altar after the Offertory. The AP, if there is one, stands where the MC is to stand in a high mass celebrated by a priest.

The pontifical sung blessing may certainly still be given. The mitre should be worn, and the crosier carried. Bishop's Chaplains are needed. If there are fewer than four, they must do double or triple duty. The first to omit is the candle bearer, and then the book bearer. The CaB's duties are simply not fulfilled. Those of the BB are done by the MC. It is possible for the mitre bearer and crosier bearer to be one person, but this is most difficult, and he must generally put the crosier away nearby to make this feasible.

When there are three chaplains, they stand in the place they should stand as in the section on Pontifical High Mass. If there are two, the senior one stands on the right side of the Bishop, the junior to the left. If there is only one, then he stands on either side as convenient. As a reminder, the rank of chaplains is, from highest to lowest, mitre bearer, crosier bearer, book bearer, and candle bearer (and then train bearer, gremial bearer, and zucchetto bearer).

The formal vesting before the mass may or may not be done, according to the wishes of the Bishop. It still may, of course, be done.

All the ceremonies may be included or not as possible. The fullest form of a pontifical sung mass is, of course, the same ritual, only without a Sub-Deacon. However, it seems better if one has sufficient priests to have

Assistant Deacons and an AP to have a Sub-Deacon, do a pontifical high mass, and do without an AP or one Assistant Deacon. In general, a pontifical sung mass will be without Assistant Deacons or an Assistant Priest.

Pontifical Mass with a Greater Prelate Presiding but not Celebrating

೧೦೦೩

If a Bishop celebrates a mass, but a Bishop senior in rank presides, then the Bishop celebrates from the faldstool. The Bishop presiding vests in amice, alb, cincture, stole and cope in the color of the mass, and mitre, precious, golden, or simplex according to the mass. The Presiding Bishop sits at the throne or another faldstool. This Bishop is the one who gives the Absolution (taking the crosier) and the Pontifical Blessing (sung or recited, taking the mitre and crosier) at the end of the mass. The Blessing is given from the throne, faldstool, or predella, and the Absolution is given from the throne, faldstool, or in front of the altar. Servers should also reverence the Bishop presiding at the mass whenever they pass him. He is communicated immediately after the Deacon and Sub-Deacon of the Mass.

The Bishop presiding at a mass but not celebrating walks after the chaplains of the Bishop celebrating, and his attendant (mitre and crosier bearer, and others if needed) walk behind him. Alternatively, he may walk immediately behind the Bishop Celebrant, the chaplains of both Bishops walking behind him.

If there is to be a formal vesting, then he also vests with the Bishop Celebrant in the chapel, at the throne, or in the sacristy in the same manner. His attendants vest him.

If the Bishop presiding at the mass has Assistant Deacons (and the Bishop Celebrating cannot have Assistant Deacons unless the Bishop presiding has them), then they walk in procession and sit on either side of him as usual. At the vesting, they assist him in vesting.

HOW TO SAY MASS IN THE ANGLICAN RITE

Requiem Masses

A requiem mass (or any mass of the dead) is as any other mass, low, high, or sung, with a few differences. The color of the vestments should most properly be black, but purple may be used. Masses of the Dead are marked by austerity. The following are the key changes for Masses of the Dead.

Prayers at the Foot of the Altar

1. The *Judica Me* is not said. After the Antiphon, the priest proceeds immediately to the *Adjutorium nostrum*.

Introit

2. The altar is not incensed during the Introit.
3. The Celebrant makes the sign of the cross over the missal instead of on himself.
4. The *Gloria Patri* is not said, but the *Requiem aeternam* is repeated.

Gloria

5. The *Gloria* is not said.

Epistle

6. At a High Mass, the Sub-Deacon does not kiss the hand of the Celebrant, and the Sub-Deacon is not blessed.

Gospel

7. The *Munda Cor* is said.
8. The *Jube Domine, benedicere* and *Domine sit in cordo meo* are not said.
9. The Deacon does not ask for a blessing, nor does he kiss the hand of the Celebrant.
10. Candles and incense are not carried for the reading of the Gospel.
11. The *Per Evangelica dicta* is not said.

12. In High Mass, the Book of Gospels is not incensed, it is not brought to the Celebrant to be kissed.
13. The Gospel is also not kissed by the Priest in Low Mass or the Deacon in High Mass.

Creed

14. The Creed is not said.

Offertory

15. The oblations alone are incensed, not the altar.
16. The Celebrant is incensed, not the servers, clergy in choir, or congregation.

Lavabo

17. The *Gloria Patri* is not said.

Consecration

18. At High Mass, the Sub-Deacon does not hold the paten, but kneel and incenses the elements during the elevations.

Agnus Dei

19. The proper form for the *Agnus Dei* given in the missal is used.
20. The breast is not struck

Communion Prayers and the Peace

21. The prayer *Domine Jesu Christe qui dixisti Apostolis tuis* is not said.
22. The Pax is not given.

Dismissal & Blessing

23. In lieu of the *Ite Missa Est* or the *Benedicamus Domino* is said *Requiescant in Pace*.
24. The *Placeat tibi* is said as usual. The priest proceeds to the Last Gospel.
25. The Blessing is not given.

REQUIEM MASSES

General

26. Acolytes do not kiss the Celebrant's hand not objects.
27. The Sermon, if one is given, is given after the Last Gospel and before the Absolution.
28. The Absolution of the Dead (if the body is present) is the final act of the mass.

ABSOLUTION

After the Last Gospel in the Requiem Mass, the Celebrant lays aside his chasuble and maniple and takes the cope. He then goes to the bier, preceded by the Sub-Deacon and Deacon. The Sub-Deacon carries the cross between two acolytes with lighted candles. He is followed by an acolyte carrying the pot of holy water. The thurifer walks in front of the Sub-Deacon. Other acolytes go before the Deacon if needed. Then the Deacon goes before the Celebrant. Upon arrival, the Deacon stands to his left, and he is accompanied by the thurifer, the Sub-Deacon carrying the cross between two acolytes with lighted candles, and other servers. The Celebrant stands at the head of the bier, while the Sub-Deacon stands with the cross and acolytes at the foot, facing the bier.

The bier is placed differently for laymen and priests. If the deceased is a layman, then it is positioned with the head furthest from the altar, as the layman faced the altar in life and does so in death. If the deceased is a deacon or priest, then the head is placed closest to the altar, as they also faced the people in life. Six candles on stands should be placed around the bier as shown in the figures below. These should remain throughout the mass. See Fig. 14.1 for the positions for absolution of a layman and Fig. 14.2 for the positions for absolution of a deacon or priest.

The details on the absolution rite are given both in the Missale Anglicanum 2009 and the Rituale Anglicanum. The sprinkling rite begins in the positions in Fig. 14.1 or Fig. 14.2 and continues as described therein. The Sub-Deacon should leave ample space between the cross and the bier to allow the Celebrant to pass. If he must move to make room, then he turns by the right, walks forward a few steps, and then turns back by the left. The acolytes accompanying him do similarly. They do not walk backwards. The MC may be present if needed in a convenient location.

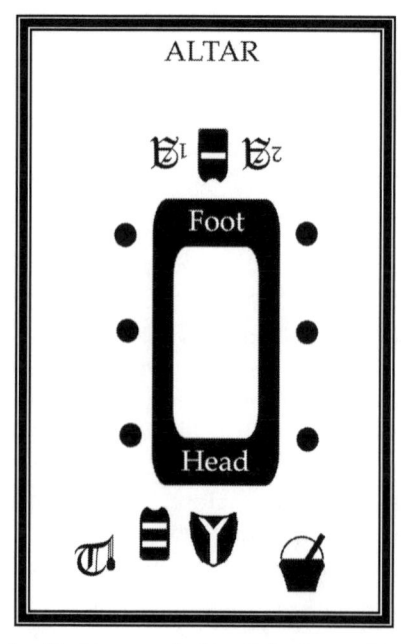

Fig. 14.1 – *Positions at the bier if the deceased is a layman*

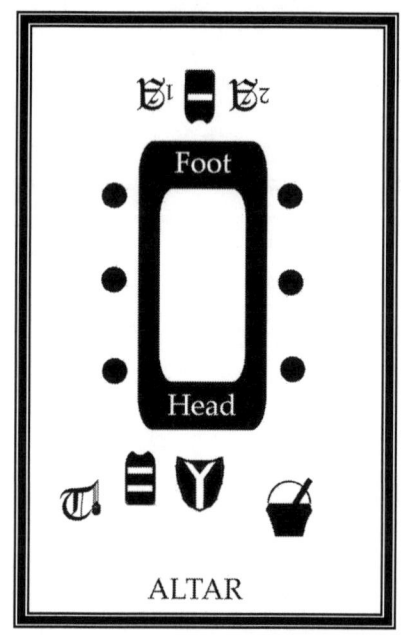

Fig.14.2 – *Positions at the bier if the deceased is a deacon or priest*

REQUIEM MASSES

REQUIEM MASS CELEBRATED BY A BISHOP.

Bishops wear the simplex mitre, and pontifical gloves are not worn. The special changes to the requiem mass are the same as given above. The ministers and chaplains stand with the Bishop as given in Fig. 14.3 (for a deceased layman) and Fig. 14.4 (for a deceased cleric).

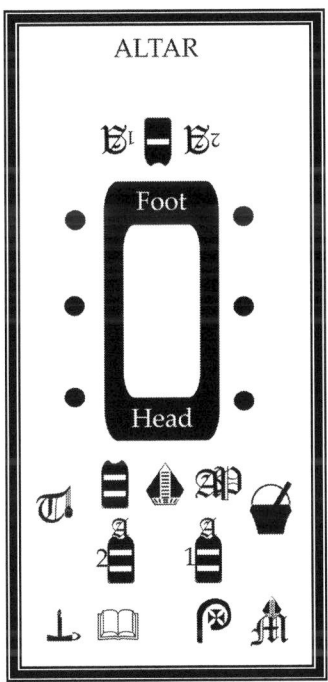

Fig. 14.3 – Positions for the Absolution of a Layman by a Bishop

When the sprinkling and incensation are done, the Bishop walks around the bier as given in the Pontificale Anglicanum, with the Deacon of the Mass to his right and the Assistant Deacons and Assistant Priest walking behind him. The chaplains and other attendants and servers remain in their positions. See Fig. 14.5. Details for this rite are in the Pontificale Anglicanum.

Use of the mitre is in accordance with liturgical customs. Details for this are also in the Pontificale Anglicanum.

HOW TO SAY MASS IN THE ANGLICAN RITE

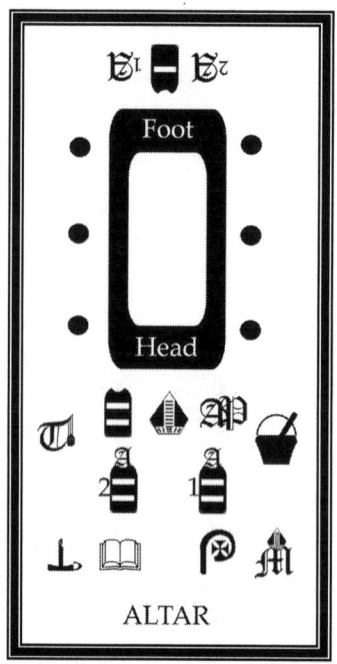

Fig. 14.4 – Absolution of a deacon or priest by a Bishop

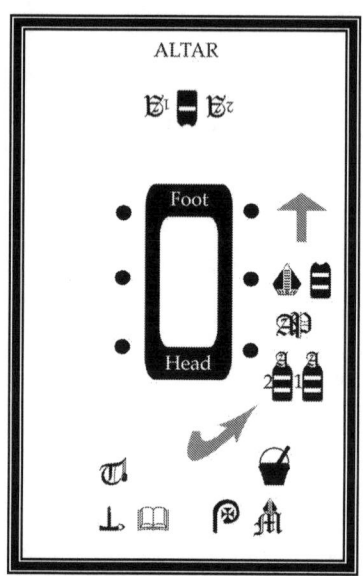

Fig. 14.5 – Movement of the Bishop, Deacon, AP, and Assistant Deacons around the bier for the sprinkling and incensation. Above is the layout for a layman, but the movement is the same for a cleric.

REQUIEM MASSES

ABSOLUTION BY FIVE BISHOPS

This absolution is used only when the mass is said for a deceased Metropolitan or other jurisdictional Archbishop, or a Bishop Ordinary. It is used only at the mass on the day of burial, or at the primary mass without the body if there is no requiem mass with the body present. It is also only used in the Cathedral church, or at another suitable location if that is designated as the official primary requiem mass for the deceased.

The four other Bishops designated to participate in the absolution are vested in the amice and alb, or surplice, a black stole, black cope, and simplex mitre. They are attended by one attendant in choir dress. The four Bishops go before the altar and stand, awaiting the Bishop Celebrant. See Fig. 14.6.

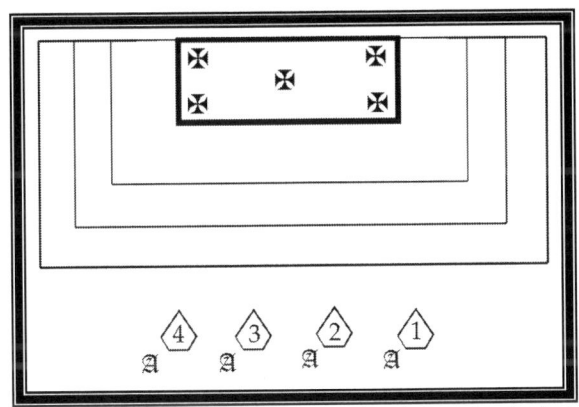

Fig. 14.6 – The four bishops at the altar before the absolution

The Bishop joins the four other bishops. All reverence the altar and then process to the bier. First is the thurifer with the acolyte with the holy water pot to his left, then the processional cross, carried by the Sub-Deacon between two acolytes (unless the celebrant is an Archbishop, in which case it is carried immediately before the Archbishop), then any clergy carrying lighted candles in the outer hand, Bishops No. 3 and 4 (3 to the right), with their attendants behind them, Bishops No. 1 and 2 (1 to the right), with their attendants behind them, The Deacon of the Mass with the Assistant Priest to his right, the Bishop between the two Assistant Deacons, and then the Bishop's Chaplains. Upon arrival at the bier, they take positions as in Fig. 14.7.

HOW TO SAY MASS IN THE ANGLICAN RITE

Fig. 14.7 – Positions of the Bishops at the bier for the Absolution by five Bishops

The First Bishop begins with *Pater Noster*, as described in the absolution above, and sprinkles and censes the bier in the usual manner. The Deacon of the Mass walks on his right, and his attendant remains in place. The MC walks behind them. This is repeated by the 2nd, 3rd, and 4th Bishops in turn in exactly the same manner.

The fifth and final absolution is given by the Bishop Celebrant, accompanied by the Deacon on his right, and followed by the AP and Assistant Deacons (see Fig. 14.5). After the absolution rite is completed, the four bishops then take their mitres and go, accompanied by their attendants, back to the sacristy.

SERMON BY A BISHOP

If there is to be a sermon at the requiem mass, it is preached at the usual time as given in the rubrics. The Bishop preaches from the throne, seated with mitre, or from the faldstool, seated with mitre, or in the pulpit (also with mitre). The sermon comes after the chasuble and maniple have been removed and replaced with the cope. The method for processing to the place for the sermon is done as usual in a pontifical mass.

ABSOLUTION IN THE ABSENCE OF THE BODY

The absolution rites may be done at any requiem mass for a specific individual without the body present. All is as described as above, except that there is a catafalque in lieu of a bier. The catafalque may be decorated similarly to the bier. In some usage, the catafalque is always placed with the head facing the altar, even for a priest. If this is not local use, however, then it is placed in the same manner as it would be if the body were present.

DRESS OF PRIESTS FOR BURIAL

The deceased clergy is traditionally vested by priests when possible. The casket should be covered with a black or purple pall (not white).

VESTURE OF DECEASED DEACONS

The Deacon should be vested in penitential mass vestments, which is black cassock, black rope or band cincture (optional), amice, alb, white rope cincture, purple maniple on the left arm, purple Deacon's stole over the left shoulder, and purple Dalmatic. Upon the feet should be black sock and black shoes. Upon the head is placed the black biretta if space permits. In the hands should be placed a crucifix or rosary.

VESTURE OF DECEASED PRIESTS

The vesture of deceased priests is the same as that of Deacons, except that the purple stole is worn in the manner of a priest, that is around the neck and crossed in the form of an X over the chest. Also, instead of a Dalmatic, the purple Chasuble is used.

If the priest is a prelate, the cassock and fascia should be purple. Where customary, the socks for prelates so-entitled should be purple. The biretta may have a purple or red tuft and, optionally, matching purple or red piping.

VESTURE OF DECEASED BISHOPS

The deceased bishop should be vested in purple cassock, purple band cincture (fascia), amice, alb, rope cincture, purple maniple on the left arm, pectoral cross over the alb, purple stole worn in the manner of a bishop (around the neck and not crossed in the front as a priest), purple Dalmatic, and purple Chasuble. If the Bishop is a Metropolitan or otherwise so entitled, the pallium is placed over the chasuble. The plain white simplex mitre is placed on the head if there is room. Else it is placed in the hands, laying against the torso.

The purple episcopal gloves are placed on the hands, and the episcopal ring is placed over the glove on the right ring finger (4th finger). In the hands is placed a crucifix or rosary.

On the feet shall be the footwear the bishop for mass, i.e., either purple episcopal sandals and purple buskins, or purple prelatial socks and red or black slippers or shoes, according to the use of the individual bishop, in accordance with tradition and canons.

The crosier, as a symbol of jurisdiction, is not placed in the casket (or on the bier), or anywhere near it. Neither is it carried in front of or by the bier (or casket).

VESTURE OF CLERGY IN RELIGIOUS ORDERS

Clergy in religious orders shall be vested as above, according to their rank, except that the biretta is only worn if permitted by the rule of their order, and in lieu of the cassock shall be their habit. In the case of orders with a rule prescribing certain footwear, that footwear is used in lieu of that prescribed above.

HOLY WEEK RITES

PALM SUNDAY

The mass of Palm Sunday is as any other mass, following the rubrics in the missal. However, before the principal mass of the day, the Palm Sunday procession is typically done. If the procession is done, then the church should be arrayed as follows:

1. Crosses, icons, and images veiled in purple (throughout Passiontide)
2. Sacred Vessels covered by a purple chalice veil, with a purple burse, and a red chalice veil covering that
3. If the humeral veil is used to cover the credence table, then it is purple and is further covered by a red humeral veil.
4. The paraments of the church are purple, covered with red paraments
5. The palms are laid on the Epistle side of the altar, and the missal is in its usual place on the Epistle corner. (If a Bishop celebrates, then the palms are placed in front of the altar.) There are also branches for the people places near the chancel gate.
6. There should be three lecterns or desks on the Gospel side for the chanting or reading of the Passion.

The Celebrant is vested in amice, alb, cincture, red stole, and red cope. He wears the biretta. The Deacon and Sub-Deacon wear the red dalmatic and tunicle respectively.

> If the Celebrant is a Bishop: He wears the golden mitre, preferably of very simple design. Deacons of Honor (Assistant Deacons) for a Bishop wear red dalmatics, and the Assistant Priest for a Bishop wears a red cope.

The asperges is not done on Palm Sunday when the procession is to take place. The Celebrant, with the Deacon to his right and the Sub-Deacon to his left, stand facing the people behind the table containing the palms. The MC may stand to the right of the Deacon. See Fig. 15.1. The antiphon *Hosanna filio David* is sung as the ministers come in.

HOW TO SAY MASS IN THE ANGLICAN RITE

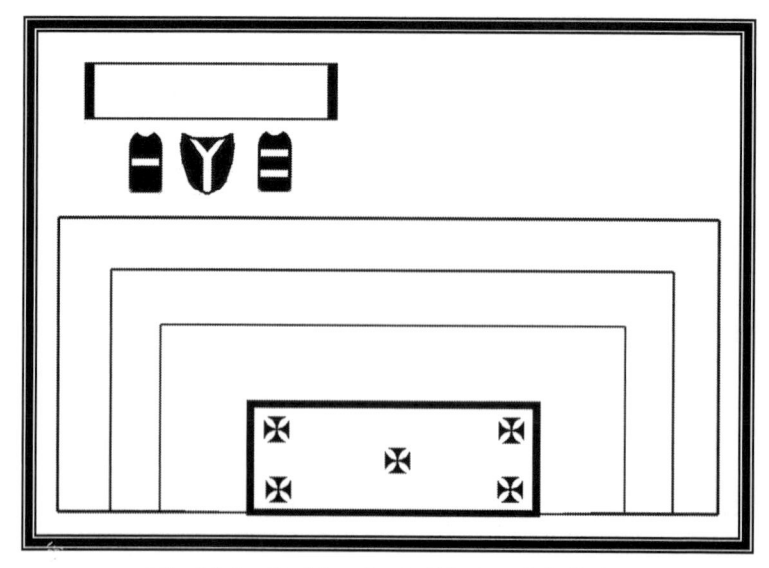

Fig. 15.1 – Positions for the Blessing of the Palms

<u>If the Celebrant is a Bishop:</u> He stands with the AP to his right, the Deacon to his left, and the Sub-Deacon to the left and slightly behind the Deacon. The Deacons of Honor are behind him side-by-side. The MC and AMC may be to the left of the Sub-Deacon. The Chaplains may stand in their usual order behind the Assistant Deacons. See Fig. 15.2. However, if there is no AP, then the Deacon and Sub-Deacon stand in the same position as in Fig. 15.1. The Bishop wears the mitre and carries the crosier as usual until he reaches the table with the palms, which may be in front of the throne or faldstool, but also may be in any convenient location within the chancel rail. The Bishop may vest for the rite in the chapel as described in the section on Pontifical High Mass. He then vests for mass at the throne or faldstool after the procession is finished.

After the Antiphon mentioned above, the Celebrant chants *Dominus vobiscum*, facing the palm branches (in the direction of the people), but with hands joined. Still facing the palm branches, the Celebrant chants the prayer, blessing the palms, in the ferial tone. The Celebrant then takes the aspergillum from a server and sprinkles the branches three times without saying anything; in the center, on the left, and on the right. He sprinkles

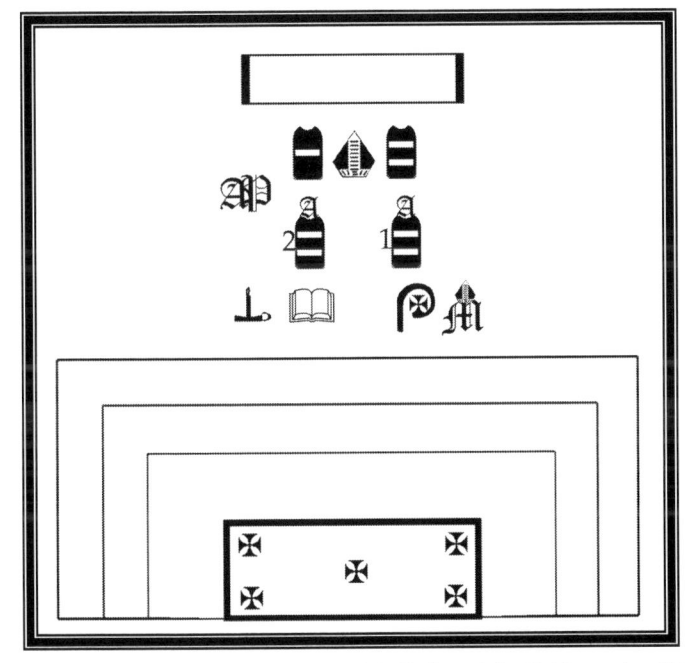

Fig. 15.2 – Positions for the Blessing of the Palms if the Celebrant is a Bishop

first the branches for the clergy on the table, then the branches at the chancel gate for the faithful. Next, taking the thurible, he blesses the incense in the usual manner and censes the palms with three single swings. He first censes the palms on the table, then the palms at the entrance to the sanctuary.

> If the Celebrant is a Bishop: When he moves from the palms on the table to the palms at the chancel gate to sprinkle and cense them, he does not take the mitre or crosier, but processes in zucchetto only.

> Alternatively: The branches for the faithful may be held by them instead of being laid at the chancel gate. In this case, the Celebrant walks through the church sprinkling the branches, as at the Asperges. The branches are censed from the chancel gate with three single swings.

Distribution of the Palms

The palms are distributed by local custom. During this time, the proper antiphons and psalms given in the missal are sung by the choir and/or congregation.

Gospel

When the distribution is complete, the table is removed and the Celebrant washes his hands. The Gospel is chanted by the Deacon. He takes the Book of Gospels, places it on the altar, etc., all exactly as at mass. The Celebrant goes to his place at the altar, kissing it in the center, for the Gospel. All is as given for the Gospel at high mass. The exception is that the Celebrant is not censed by the Deacon.

> <u>If the Celebrant is a Bishop:</u> The Bishop instead goes to the throne or faldstool and takes the crosier, after giving the blessing of the Deacon.
>
> <u>If there is no Deacon:</u> If there is no Deacon, then the Gospel is chanted by the Celebrant. He may chant the Gospel from the Gospel side, chanting from the missal, or use one of the options given in the section on Low Mass.

The Procession

After the Gospel, the procession forms. The Deacon chants *Procedemus in pace (Let us go forth in peace)*, and the choir and people respond *In nomine Christi, Amen. (In the name of Christ, Amen.)*. The clergy wears the biretta. Bishops wear the mitre if they are in Sacred Vestments or the cope, or the biretta if in choir dress.

The order of the procession is as follows, from front to rear:

Thurifer *with smoking thurible*
Acolyte – Sub-Deacon of the Cross *with unveiled cross* – Acolyte
Clergy *in order of rank, lowest to highest*
Sub-Deacon – Celebrant – Deacon
Lay Choir
Faithful

If the Celebrant is a Bishop, then the procession is as follows:

Thurifer *with smoking thurible*
Acolyte – Sub-Deacon of the Cross *with unveiled cross* – Acolyte
Clergy *in order of rank, lowest to highest*
Sub-Deacon
Deacon – Assistant Priest
Second Assistant Deacon – Bishop – First Assistant Deacon
Bishop's Chaplains
Lay Choir
Faithful

During the procession, the proper antiphons are sung. Consult the Liber Processionalis or the Rituale Anglicanum. When the procession again reaches the door of the church, the Sub-Deacon knocks on the door with the base of the staff of the processional cross three times. A cleric or attendant inside the church opens the door (which, of course, was previously shut). The procession continues. As soon as the procession enters the church, the choir begins the *Ingrediente Domino*.

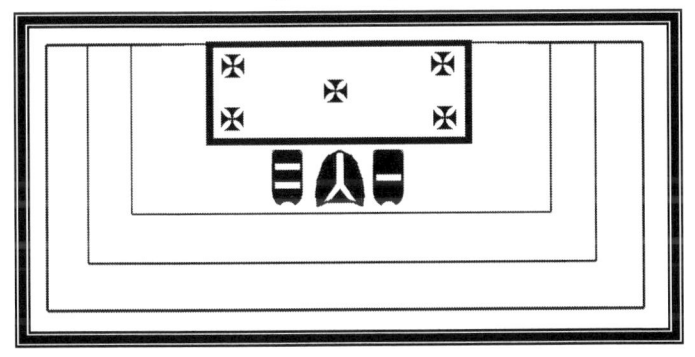

Fig. 15.3 – Positions at the final Collect

When the Sacred Ministers reach the altar steps, the Sub-Deacon gives up the cross to the MC or a server and ascends the steps with the Celebrant and Deacon, after making the proper reverence. The Celebrant stands in the center of the predella facing the people. The Deacon stands on his right, and the Sub-Deacon on his left. See Fig. 15.3.

> If the Celebrant is a Bishop: All is as above, except that he stands as shown in Fig. 15.4. The AP is on his right, the Deacon of the Mass to the right of the AP, and the 1AD to his right. To the Bishop's left is the Sub-Deacon of the Mass and then the 2AD. If, however, there are no Assistant Deacons or AP, then the

Bishop stands on the predella just as a priest. If space does not permit the above, then the Assistant Deacons may stand in their usual positions on the pavement, second step, or lowest step. The Bishop's Chaplains stand in their usual position on the pavement. All face the people except the Bishop's Chaplains.

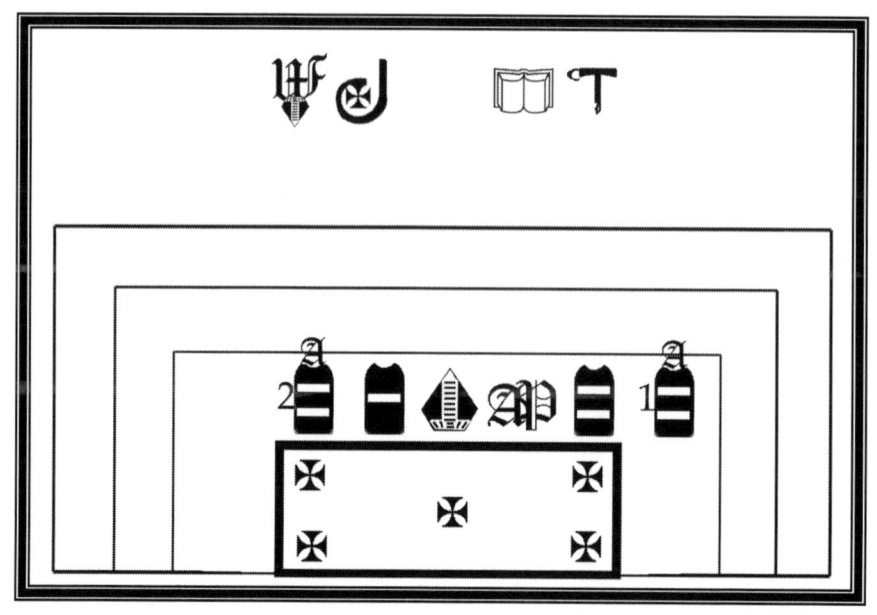

Fig. 15.4 – Positions at the final Collect if the Celebrant is a Bishop

The Mass

After the procession, the Celebrant and ministers retire to the sedilia or sacristy. They exchange their red vestments for purple ones. Meanwhile, the servers remove the red paraments and coverings, exposing the purple ones. There are no Prayers at the Foot of the Altar. The ministers simply continue, without further procession (unless necessary from the sacristy) with the Introit. Standing in front of the altar, the priest says *Oremus*, and the Sacred Ministers ascend the altar. The mass is as usual, except for the Gospel, which is the Passion. (However, at non-principal masses on this day, there is another Gospel appointed in the missal that may optionally be read instead. If it is used, then all is as usual for the Gospel.)

> <u>If the Celebrant is a Bishop</u>: The Bishop may remove the red vestments and vest in purple vestments for mass at the throne, faldstool, or in the sacristy. He is assisted by the Assistant

Deacons and AP while the Deacon and Sub-Deacon vest for the mass in the sacristy. When they return, the Assistant Deacons and AP retire to the sacristy to vest in purple vestments. If there is no AP or Assistant Deacons, then the Bishop is assisted by the MC and AMC while the Deacon and Sub-Deacon are vesting.

The Passion

Three bare desks are placed on the Gospel side. See Fig. 15.5. The part of Jesus is reserved to priests. The Chronicler is also restricted to a deacon or priest. Only the part of the people may be sung or read by a layman. Some local usage involves the congregation as a whole reading the people's part in the Passion. Or, the choir may chant this part.

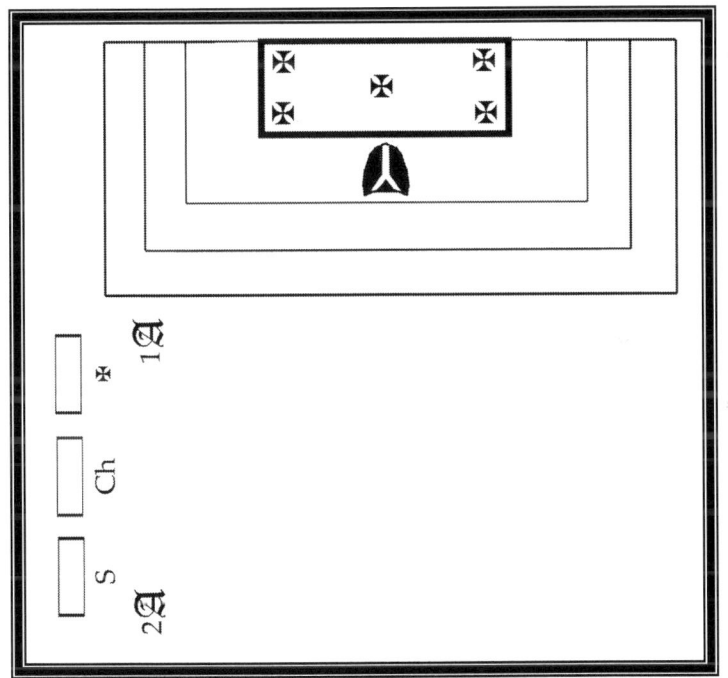

Fig. 15.5 – Positions of the Readers for the Passion. Ch = the Chronicler. S = the people, and the cross is the part of Jesus.

Those to read the Passion present themselves before the altar and kneel on the lowest step. The Chronicler is in the center, the priest reading the part of Christ is to his right, and the reader for the people is to the left. The *Munda cor* is not said, and the blessing is not given. The Celebrant says over them *Dominus sit in cordibus vestris, et in labiis vestris: ut digne et competenter annuntietis evangelium suum: in nomine Patris, et Filii,* ✠ *et Spiritus Sancti.* If the Celebrant is reading the part of Jesus, then the above is still done, but turning to the altar, the Celebrant says the *Dominus sit* for himself as well. If the Celebrant is reading the entire Passion himself, then he only says the *Dominus sit* for himself. If the congregation is reading the part of the people, then they are including in the *Dominus sit in cordibus vestris* above.

> <u>If the Celebrant is a Bishop:</u> The above is done from the throne.

After the above, the readers rise and go to their desks. The Celebrant, if he is not reading, remains in his position in front of the altar as usual for the Gospel. (However, if the Celebrant is reading the entire Passion himself, then he does so from the missal from the Gospel side of the altar, facing the altar, or from some other suitable location as suggested in the section on Low Mass.) The Passion is announced as given in the missal. The sign of the cross is not made over the book or on themselves, and the people also do not make the sign of the cross on themselves. Incense is not used, and the acolytes accompanying the readers (as in Fig. 15.5 above) do not carry candles. All genuflect when called for in the Passion (this is indicated in the missal and in the Evangeliarium). This method of reading the Passion is observed every time the Passion is read during Holy Week.

> <u>If the Celebrant is a Bishop:</u> He remains at the throne as given in the section on Pontifical High Mass, and stands without mitre, holding the crosier.

At the end of the mass, the Last Gospel is not said. The blessing is given in the usual way, and the Sacred Ministers retire to the sacristy, with or without a long procession.

MONDAY, TUESDAY, & WEDNESDAY OF HOLY WEEK

The mass on Monday of Holy Week is as usual for a mass during Passiontide. On Tuesday and Wednesday, the Passion is read at the mass. The rubrics concerning this are given in the missal. The procedure is exactly the same as that on Palm Sunday.

CHRISM MASS

The details for the ritual of the Chrism Mass are given in the Pontificale Anglicanum. This rite takes place only in the cathedral church or another church in lieu of the cathedral designated by the Bishop. It is celebrated only by the jurisdictional Bishop. Most properly, it is celebrated during the day on Maundy Thursday, but may be celebrated on Monday, Tuesday, or Wednesday of Holy Week if so ordered by the Bishop. During this mass, the Holy Oils are blessed for the year (though the Pontificale also gives a rite for blessing the oils outside the Chrism Mass). The Chrism Mass is a mass primarily for the clergy. It is in part a celebration of Holy Orders.

Preparation

There should be a table in the sanctuary, in the center, in front of the altar on the pavement. This may be brought out at the appropriate time or placed there in advance if physical arrangements permit. It should be covered with a white cloth. There should be a faldstool or suitable chair placed in the center of the table facing the altar, with the table in between said chair and the altar.

In the sacristy should be the vessels containing the oil for the Oil of the Sick, Oil of the Catechumens, and Holy Chrism, as well as a container for the fragrance for the Chrism. If the fragrance has already been added, then this latter container is omitted from the ritual. There also should be bread, towels, and perhaps lemon available at the table for cleaning the fingers.

Participants

In addition to the usual participants at a pontifical mass, there should be 12 priests, vested in choir dress with stole, 7 deacons vested in choir dress with diaconal stone, and 7 sub-deacons vested in choir dress without stole. Two deacons and two sub-deacons have special roles. One deacon will carry the oil for the Chrism, who may optionally wear a gold dalmatic. One deacon will carry the oil for the Oil of the Catechumens, who may optionally wear a purple dalmatic. On sub-deacon will carry the oil for the Oil of the Sick, and he may optionally wear a green tunicle. One sub-deacon will carry the fragrance for the Chrism, and he may optionally wear a gold tunicle.

The Bishop should be attended by all of his Suffragan Bishops, as well as his entire Chapter, sitting in choir if they are not otherwise participating. The entire clergy as much as is possible should be present in choir dress. This is, after all, a mass for the clergy.

The Bishop vests in full pontifical mass vestments in white, silver, or gold, viz., amice, alb, cincture, pectoral cross, stole, dalmatic, gloves, ring, chasuble, pallium (if a jurisdictional archbishop), and gold mitre (the jeweled/precious mitre is not used). If the Bishop is an Archbishop, then the archiepiscopal cross should not be omitted in procession.

Procession

The procession for the Chrism Mass is as at any other pontifical high or sung mass, with the exception that there are the special participants detailed above. They process, the seven sub-deacons first, then the seven deacons, then the twelve priests, immediately before the Sacred Ministers (specifically immediately before the Sub-Deacon of the Mass, who carries the Book of Gospels). The twelve priests walk two-by-two, the deacons walk singly, with the two Deacons of the Holy Chrism and the Oil of the Catechumens walking singly behind the other Deacons, the Deacon of the Oil of the Catechumens walking first. The Sub-Deacon of the Oil of the Sick walks behind the other sub-deacons, with the Sub-Deacon carrying the Balsam walking in front of him. The other Sub-Deacons walk singly. These participants, after reverencing the altar (they do not wait for the Bishop and his assistants) go immediately to the choir or other appointed seats for them.

The Mass

The mass itself is as any other mass. However, despite being in Passiontide, the *Gloria in excelsis* is appointed to be sung, as given in the rubrics of the missal. The blessing of the oils is carried out as appointed during the mass, according to the rubrics in the missal and the Pontificale. The ceremonial details are also expounded upon below. The Preface of the Chrism Mass is used, and the Last Gospel is not said. Also, the Creed is not said, according to the rubrics.

Blessing of the Oil of the Sick

The mass proceeds in the usual fashion until the Canon. The Bishop continues until just before the words *Per quem haec omnia, Domine, semper bona creas*. First the Bishop cleans his hands in a bowl of water on the altar so that he may disjoin his thumbs and fingers. This water is then put into the sacrarium later. The Bishop, genuflecting to the Blessed Sacrament now laying upon the corporal, turns, and descends to the lowest step of the altar. The Deacon and Sub-Deacon of the mass stand on either side of him, the Deacon on the Epistle side, the Sub-Deacon on the Gospel side, with the AP on the Gospel side in between the Bishop and the Sub-Deacon. There he accepts the mitre (but he does not take the zucchetto), which is placed on his head by the First Assistant Deacon or another attendant. Proceeding to the pavement, first the AP goes, then the Sub-Deacon, then the Deacon, then the Bishop. Then follow his Assistant Deacons and chaplains.

The Bishop sits at the faldstool before a table facing the Blessed Sacrament. The twelve priests, seven deacons, and seven sub-deacons stand in order behind him; first the priests, then the seven deacons, then the sub-deacons. The Deacon of the Oil of the Catechumens is to the left of the rest of the Deacons, and the Deacon of the Chrism is to the right of them. The Sub-Deacon of the Oil of the Sick is to the right of the rest of the Sub-Deacons, with the Sub-Deacon of the Balsam to the left of them. In front of these clergy are the Deacon and Sub-Deacon of the Mass. The Assistant Deacons stand immediately behind the Deacon and Sub-Deacon of the Mass. The Assistant Priest stands to the left of the Bishop. The Archdeacon stands in front of the table, taking care not to turn his back to the Blessed Sacrament. The four Bishop's Chaplains stand in their usual order behind the seven Sub-Deacons. See Fig. 15.6.

It should be noted, though, that the BB and/or CaB are needed at the table. When they are, they stand generally on the same side of the table as the Bishop. The BB holds the book so that the Bishop may read, and the CaB holds the candle. As a matter of practicality, the CaB will stand to the left of the BB. If the book, however, is on a stand on the table, then only the CaB stands to the right of the Bishop. However, they remain behind the clergy as shown in Fig. 15.6 until the Bishop needs to read from the book.

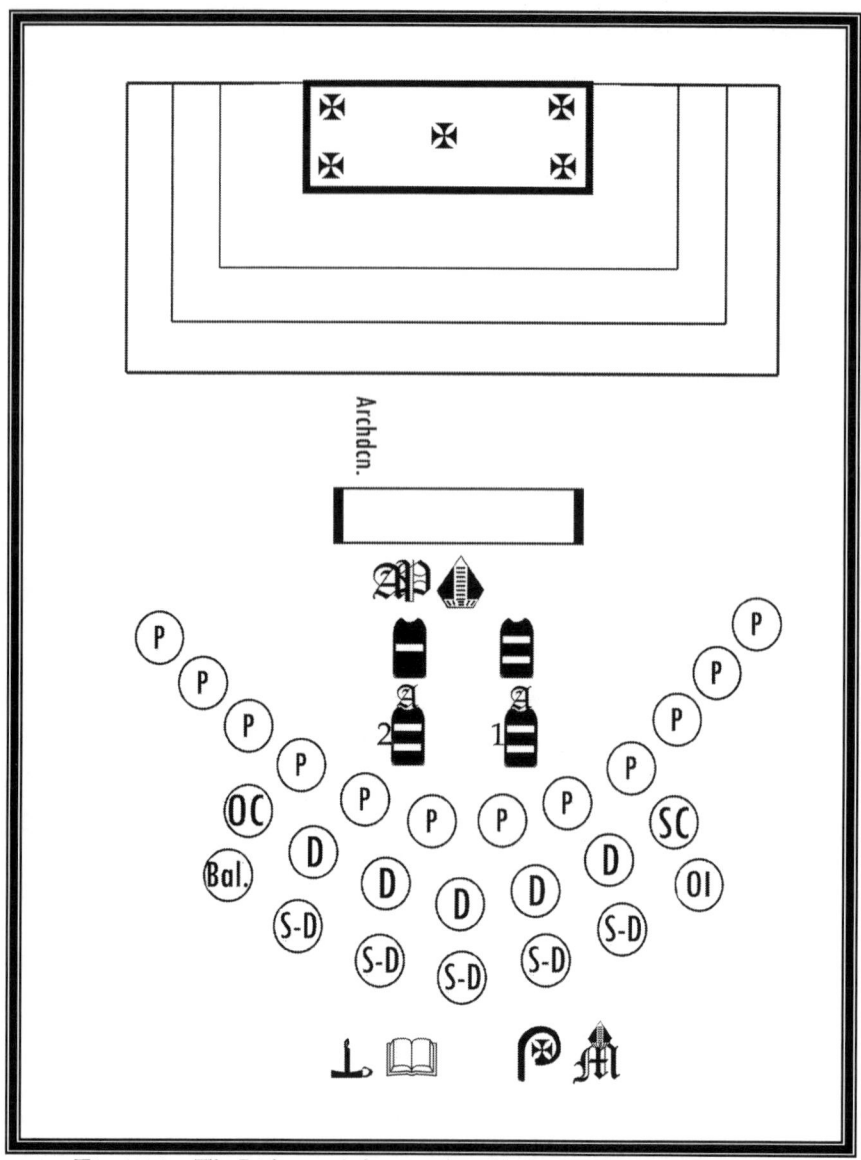

Fig. 15.6 – The Bishop and clergy at the table for the blessing of the oils.

In Fig. 15.6, and elsewhere for the Chrism Mass, the circle with "P" are priests, with "D" are Deacons, and with "S-D" are Sub-Deacons. The Deacon appointed for the Chrism is "SC," and that appointed for the Oil of the Catechumens is "OC." The Sub-Deacon for the Oil of the Sick is "OI," and the Sub-Deacon for the balsam is "Bal."

When the Archdeacon calls for the Oil of the Sick, as given in the Pontificale Anglicanum, the Sub-Deacon appointed for the Oil of the Sick goes to the sacristy, flanked by two acolytes with lighted candles. He returns carrying the contained with the pure olive oil to be blessed as the Oil of the Sick. Depending on the nature of the container, it may be simply the container itself, or the container may be carried upon a silver tray. The Sub-Deacon of the Oil of the Sick goes before the table, taking care not to turn his back to the Blessed Sacrament, and says (but does not sing) *Oleum infirmorum*. He then hands the oil to the Archdeacon, who places it in the center of the table for the Bishop to bless. See Fig. 15.7. During this time, an appropriate hymn may be sung by the choir and/or congregation.

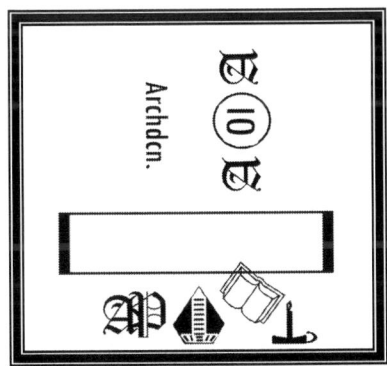

Fig. 15.7 – Positions at the presentation of the Oil of the Sick. Note the Book Bearer and Candle Bearer are present on the right side of the Bishop. They should time their arrival, coming around the back of the clergy and up the Epistle side, to arrival shortly before the Bishop will begin the prayers.

The Bishop stands with the mitre for the exorcism. He should speak loudly enough so that those around him, i.e., the clergy assisting him, may hear him, but no louder. When this is finished, he gives up the mitre. The Second Assistant Deacon removes it. As a matter of practicality, the MB need not approach and take the mitre. However, the MB may reposition himself to the right of the Bishop (but also to the right of the BB and CaB) in time to take the mitre from the 2AD. The Bishop continues with the blessing. Then, taking the mitre from the 1AD, the Bishop sits and cleans his hands. In the case that the Bishop did not purify his hands at the altar, then his hands have now been purified. This water in either case should be thrown in the sacrarium.

Resumption of the Canon of the Mass

Having cleaned his hands, the Bishop takes the mitre, but not the crosier, and goes with the ministers back to the altar. The AP goes first, then the Sub-Deacon, then the Deacon, and then the Bishop. The Assistant Deacons and chaplains take their places as usual. The clergy assisting at the blessings go back to the choir or their appointed seats. The Sub-Deacon of the Oil of the Sick goes between two acolytes holding lighted candles back to the sacristy to return the Oil of the Sick. He holds the oil with both hands at the level of his breast. This manner of carrying the oil is observed whenever an oil is carried, either before or after it is blessed.

The Bishop gives up the mitre at the top step of the altar to the Deacon, who gives it to the MB. Then the Bishop, the Sacred Ministers, and attendants nearby genuflect together to the Blessed Sacrament. The mass resumes where it left off. From the moment the priest again takes the host, he must keep his thumb and forefinger joined on each hand as usual until the ablutions.

Mass proceeds through the communion. After his own communion, the Bishop communicates the Sacred Ministers, clergy, and servers as usual. Excepting those laymen who are servers or attendants, the faithful do not receive communion at this mass. After communion, the Bishop receives the ablutions as usual.

Presentation of the Oil for the Oil of the Catechumens and the Holy Chrism

After the ablutions, the Bishop proceeds as described above, taking the mitre (with the zucchetto this time), back to the table before the altar. All array themselves as before in Fig. 15.6. The thurifer should also present himself before the Bishop, making the proper reverence, on the right side of the Bishop (the BB and CaB are typically in their place behind the clergy at this time, but if they are to the right of the Bishop, then they must step back). The Bishop sits at the table as before, wearing the mitre. The Archdeacon calls out as before (in the tone of the Epistles) *Oleum ad sanctum Chrisma* and *Oleum Catechumenorum*. As the procession described below begins to form, the Bishop rises, giving up the mitre to the 2AD, and blesses the incense, which is held by the thurifer. He then sits again with the mitre. During the procession below, the *O Redemptor* is sung by the choir.

After the oils have been called for by the Archdeacon, the seven Sub-Deacons and the Deacons process to the sacristy in the following order:

Thurifer
Acolyte – Sub-Deacon of the Cross – Acolyte
Torchbearers *walking two-by-two, up to eight in total number*
5 Sub-Deacons *walking singly*
Sub-Deacon of the Oil of the Sick
5 Deacons *walking singly*
12 Priests *walking side-by-side*
Acolyte – Sub-Deacon of the Balsam – Acolyte
Acolyte – Deacon of the Holy Chrism – Acolyte
Acolyte – Deacon of the Oil of the Catechumens – Acolyte

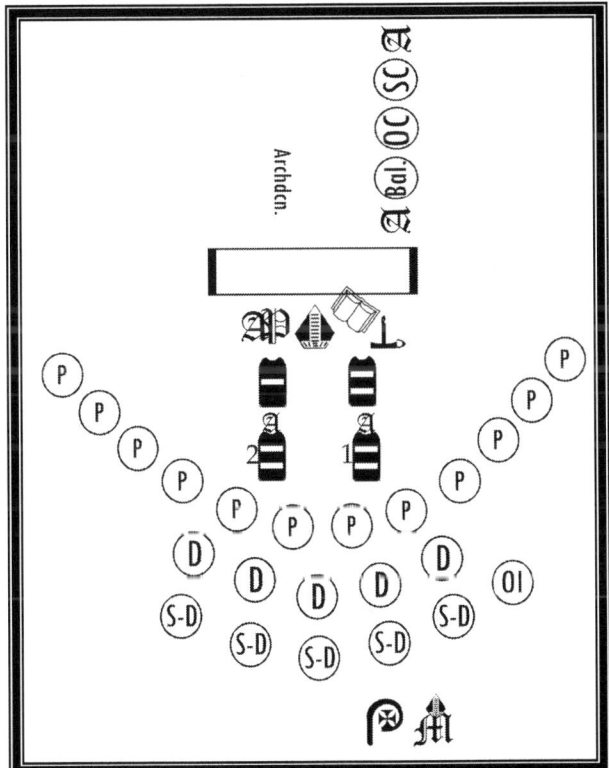

Fig. 15.8 – Positions as the ministers of the oil return

Upon arrival in the sacristy, the ministers appointed to carry the oils receive them. The procession forms back in the same order and returns to the table before the altar. The ministers of the oils carry the oil with both hands before their breast. Upon return to the table, all stand in their usual positions except for the ministers of the oils. See Fig. 15.8 above.

Blessing of the Oils

The ritual continues as given in the Pontificale. When each minister of the oil has presented it to the Archdeacon, they genuflect to the cross and return to their place as in Fig. 15.8. When the balsam is mixed with a small amount of Chrism, the container of oil for the Holy Chrism is presented to the Archdeacon, the oil is poured, and the container is returned to the Deacon of the Chrism. For both the Holy Chrism and the Oil of the Catechumens, the Bishop breathes on the oil as described in the Pontificale. The twelve priests come forward and do similarly, following the motion as described below for reverencing the oils. Upon arrival before the table, they genuflect to the cross and then turn to the table and breathe on the oil.

Reverence of the Holy Chrism

Once the Chrism has been consecrated, the Deacon of the Chrism, standing in the center in front of the altar, holds up the container of the Chrism for all to see. The Bishop sings in the tone of the Epistles (see the Epistolarium for this tone) *Ave sanctum Chrisma*, as appointed in the Pontificale. This is sung three times, each time on a higher note. Then he kisses the lip of the ampulla held by the Archdeacon. See Fig. 15.9.

Fig. 15.9 – The Deacon of the Chrism holds the ampulla before the Bishop

Next, each of the twelve priests comes around to the front of the table by the Epistle side, genuflects to the cross, and then to the Holy Chrism. They sing *Ave sanctum Chrisma* just as the Bishop did, kiss the ampulla containing the oil, genuflect again to the cross, and return to their place via the Gospel side. The movement of the twelve priests is a simple one, in a single-file line, progressing in a circular path from their place, around the table via the Epistle side, to the oil, and then completing the circular path via the Gospel side back to their place. The Bishop sits with the mitre during this time.

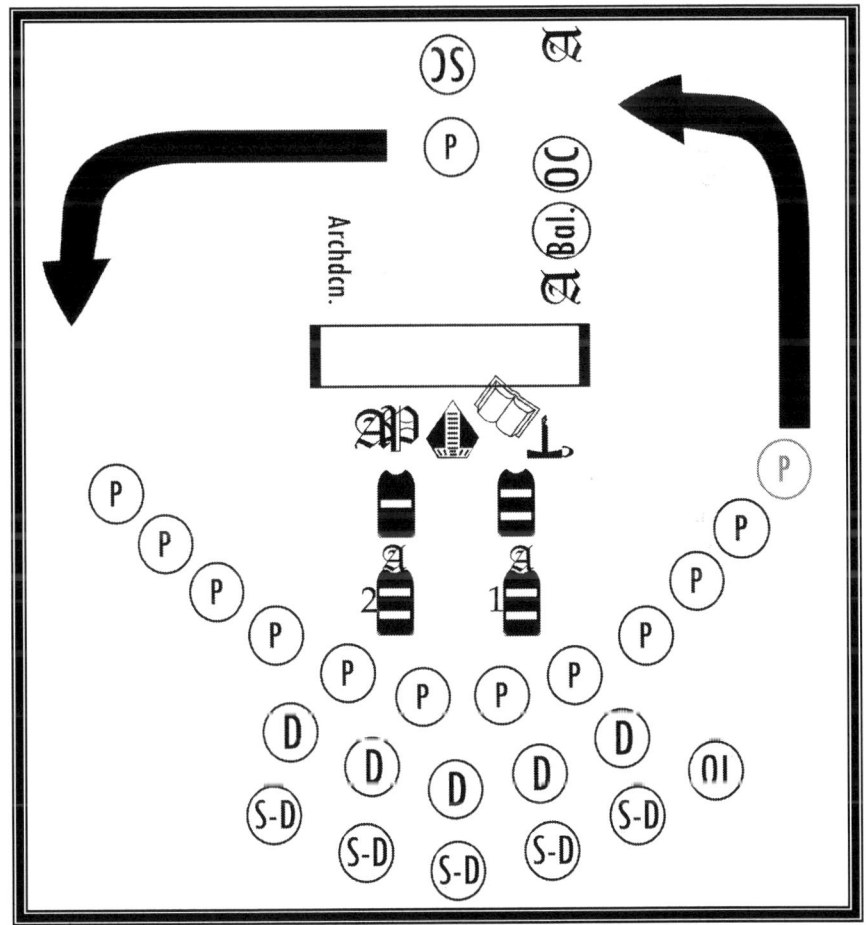

Fig. 15.10 – Movement of the priests to reverence the Holy Chrism

Reverence of the Oil of the Catechumens

This is done exactly as for the Holy Chrism, except the Deacon of the Oil of the Catechumens holds the ampulla. All is as described above, except

Ave sanctum oleum is sung instead. The twelve priests come around just as for the Holy Chrism.

Return of the Oils to the Sacristy

After the above, the holy oils are returned to the sacristy. During this, the choir sings O *Redemptor, sume carmen*, etc. The Deacon of the Oil of the Catechumens, flanked by two acolytes, takes the Oil of the Catechumens, holding it as usual before his breast. He is followed by the Deacon of the Chrism, holding the Holy Chrism, flanked by two acolytes. The procession forms to the sacristy as given below.

Thurifer
Acolyte – Sub-Deacon of the Cross – Acolyte
Torchbearers *walking two-by-two, up to eight in total number*
5 Sub-Deacons *walking singly*
Sub-Deacon of the Balsam
Sub-Deacon of the Oil of the Sick
5 Deacons *walking singly*
12 Priests *walking side-by-side*
Acolyte – Deacon of the Holy Chrism – Acolyte
Acolyte – Deacon of the Oil of the Catechumens – Acolyte

Resumption of the Mass

As the Holy Oils are being returned, the Bishop cleans his hands at the table. Then he returns to the throne or faldstool with mitre and crosier. He is proceeded as usual by the AP and followed by his Assistant Deacons and chaplains. The Deacon and Sub-Deacon go to the sedilia. When the assistants at the blessing of the oils have taken the oils to the sacristy, they return to the choir or their appointed places. When the choir has finished singing, the mass resumes with the General Thanksgiving. All else is as usual at the end of the mass, except that the Last Gospel is not said.

HOLY WEEK RITES

MAUNDY THURSDAY

The mass begins as usual. The finest white, silver, or gold mass vestments should be used. Clergy in choir wear white, silver, or gold stoles. Bishops in choir do not wear the stole over the mozzetta or chimere.

> <u>If the Celebrant is a Bishop:</u> He wears full pontifical mass vestments as described for the Chrism Mass above.

The crosses, icons, and images, remain veiled in purple. The tabernacle, if it is on the altar, should be entirely empty (that is, all consecrated hosts should be either consumed at an earlier mass or removed to another place of reposition). As a matter of local use, it may be the custom that all consecrated hosts (except perhaps a small umber for use in Visitation of the Sick) be consumed. This has certain symbolic merit, as the Mass of the Lord's Supper celebrated this evening is a special rite pertaining to our Lord's institution of the Sacrament of Holy Communion. In preparation for the mass, a second priest's host should be placed on the paten. All hosts used in the distribution of communion at this mass should be consecrated at this mass.

At the *Gloria in excelsis*, the bells are set ringing. After this, no musical instruments or bells (including the altar/Sanctus bells) are used until the *Gloria* at the Easter Vigil mass. The Creed is also not said during this mass, according to the rubrics. This mass, however, has a special Canon, as given in the Propers of the Season in the missal. This includes special words of consecration. The Peace is not given, and the prayer *Domine qui dixisti* is not said.

After the priest's communion of both the host and the Precious Blood, the Sub Deacon brings a second chalice from the credence table, using the humeral veil in the usual manner. The second host the priest consecrated upon the paten is placed inside this chalice. It is placed on the corporal towards the back (behind the chalice) until after the ablutions.

After the ablutions, the chalice (the one used in the mass, not the one containing the consecrated host) and paten are taken to the credence table by the Sub-Deacon (using the humeral veil). The corporal is left at this point upon the altar, as the chalice containing the host is still upon it. All other consecrated hosts in the ciborium should be consumed, the ciborium purified, and then taken back to the credence table. All should take care to genuflect when passing in front of the altar, as the sacrament is exposed. The Celebrant also genuflects upon arrival in the center of the altar.

> **If the Celebrant is a Bishop:** The zucchetto is not taken after the ablutions, as the sacrament is still exposed upon the altar in the chalice.

Ending of the Mass

The end of the mass is said as usual. The only difference is that, at the Last Gospel, the priest signs only himself, and not the missal or altar. The people remain kneeling throughout, as the Blessed Sacrament is exposed. The servers remain kneeling as well unless their duties require them to be standing.

Translation of the Sacrament to the Altar of Repose

After the mass, is completed, the Celebrant shall exchange his chasuble for a cope. He shall kneel in front of the altar with the Sacred Ministers. The Deacon is on his right, and the Sub-Deacon on his left. The acolytes kneel on either side or behind. The thurifer brings incense and the thurible. The Celebrant puts incense into the thurible without blessing it (because only the Blessed Sacrament is to be censed). He then censes the Blessed Sacrament with three triple swings, returning the thurible to the thurifer afterwards. All present should be kneeling throughout

> **If the Celebrant is a Bishop:** The arrangement of persons is as for the Prayers at the Foot of the Altar in a pontifical high mass.

After the censing above, the party rises and forms the procession to transfer the sacrament. The Celebrant takes the humeral veil, and then ascends the altar to take the ciborium. The acolytes take 2, 4, or 6 candles off of the altar, and these should be the only lights carried. The Blessed Sacrament is most properly carried under a canopy. The order of the procession is as follows:

Acolyte – Sub-Deacon of the Cross – Acolyte
Lay Choir
Clergy
Thurifer
Sub-Deacon – Celebrant *(with the sacrament)* – Deacon
Acolytes with candles *(2, 4, or 6, walking here or on either side of the canopy)*

A second thurifer may be employed, as this is a procession of the Blessed Sacrament (see the Corpus Christi procession in the Liber Processionalis). If this is done, then the thurifers walk side-by-side.

> <u>If the Celebrant is a Bishop:</u> His Assistant Deacons walk side-by-side immediately behind him, and his Assistant Priest either behind them or to the right and in front, depending on physical restrictions.

During the procession, the choir and/or congregation should sing *Pange lingua*. When the procession comes to the altar of repose, the acolytes place their candles upon it. If the total number of candles they brought is less than six, then additional candles should be ready upon the altar to bring the total number to six. These additional candles are lit from the candles the acolytes bring. When the candles are arrayed on the altar, the Celebrant places the chalice containing the consecrated host in the tabernacle, leaving the door open. (These candles must be left lit on the altar as long as the sacrament is present there, i.e., until the Mass of the Pre-Sanctified on Good Friday.) He genuflects and retires to the pavement before the altar. The Celebrant and all present kneel. He takes the thurible from the thurifer and censes the Blessed Sacrament with three triple swings as usual. If there are two thurifers, different customs deal with what they should do. Here, it is suggested that the second thurifer, if there is one, cense the sacrament simultaneously with the Celebrant. See Fig. 15.11. Or, the Celebrant censes it first, and then the two thurifers cense it with three triple swings, kneeling on one on each side of the altar, acting in unison. See Fig. 15.12. The positions for a Bishop are in Fig.15.13.

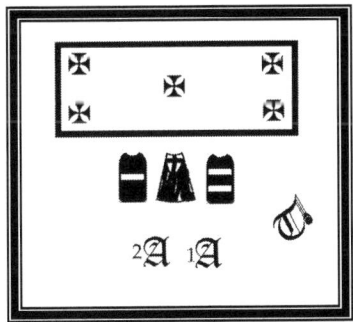

Fig. 15.11 – One option with two thurifers: Here the Celebrant censes the altar, and the thurifer on the right censes it simultaneously with him. The thurifer on the left is not shown, but his position is as shown in Fig. 15.12.

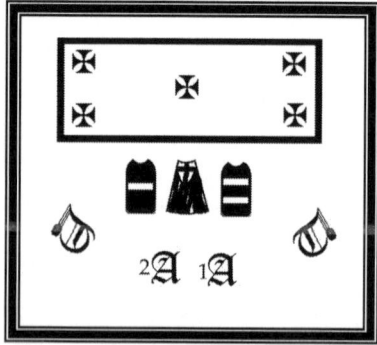

Fig. 15.12 – Another option with two thurifers: First the Celebrant takes the thurible from one thurifer and censes the sacrament. Then the two thurifers, in the positions shown in this figure, cense the sacrament again simultaneously.

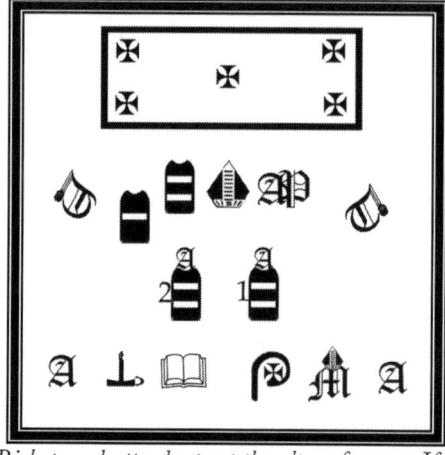

Fig. 15.13 – The Bishop and attendants at the altar of repose. If there is no AP, then the Deacon and Sub-Deacon are as in Figs. 15.11 and 15.12.

After the sacrament has been censed, the Celebrant rises, with all others still kneeling. He goes to the tabernacle and genuflects. Then he closes the door of the tabernacle and veils it as usual. Here all rise and form the procession in the same order as they came to the altar of repose. No lights are carried. The canopy should be left near the altar of repose, and the altar most properly should not be left unattended until the Mass of the Pre-Sanctified on Good Friday. The procession returns to the sanctuary. The ministers remove their vestments and take the violet stole. The Celebrant should be wearing the alb and priest's stole, the Deacon wears the alb with diaconal stole, and the Sub-Deacon wears the alb with no stole. The maniple is not worn. All others who were wearing a stole should either change it for a purple one or lay it aside all-together.

> If the Celebrant is a Bishop: The Bishop removes his vestments as do the other Sacred Ministers. He takes the purple stole over the alb. The chasuble, dalmatic, pallium, and gloves are not used. The mitre is not worn, but the zucchetto is retained. The Bishop may take the zucchetto again once the procession returns from the altar of repose. His Assistant Priest removes the cope and, if he was wearing a stole, either lays it aside or exchanges it for a purple one. The Assistant Deacons remove their white dalmatics, but do not take the purple dalmatic. The chaplains remove the cope if they were wearing one.

Once the choir has finished the *Pange lingua*, no further music should be chanted. The procession returns to the sanctuary in silence.

Stripping the Altar

When the ministers have changed into purple stole, the altars are laid bare. If there are multiple altars to strip, then the different clergy may be assigned to different altars, including the clergy in choir. Everything is removed from the altar, unless it is permanently attached. The candlesticks, frontals, altar cloths, relics, and cross (if not permanently attached) are all removed. Nothing should be left on the altar. In some congregations, it is the custom to scour the top surface of the altar once it has been laid bare. This is a matter of local use. The stripping of the altars is done in silence.

Evensong

Evening Prayer is appointed to be said without chant after the stripping of the altars. The Celebrant takes the purple cope and leads Evening Prayer in solemn format, but again, without chant or any singing whatsoever. Other clergy not attending the celebrant sit in choir or in other appointed seats.

> If the Celebrant is a Bishop: He takes the cope and golden mitre and then leads Evening Prayer from the throne or faldstool. He may use the crosier at his discretion.

The Maundy

After Evening Prayer, a signal on a wooden instrument may be given to signal that the Maundy is about to begin and that the participants for the Maundy should assemble as instructed prior to the ritual. Evening Prayer having been finished, the Celebrant lays aside the purple cope. He takes the white linen gremial and, following the example of Christ, ties it around his waist.

> <u>If the Celebrant is a Bishop</u>: The Bishop lays aside the purple cope and gives up the mitre. He takes the purple dalmatic and then ties the linen gremial over that. The mitre is not worn, but the zucchetto is retained.

Meanwhile, the Deacon and Sub-Deacon, or two servers, or the MC and AMC, lead the twelve men who have been chosen to the benches. See Fig. 15.14. For the Maundy, it should be performed on men only. The twelve men have clear symbolism of the twelve disciples whose feet Christ washed at the Last Supper. If twelve men are not available, then fewer may be used. The men may be priests or laymen.

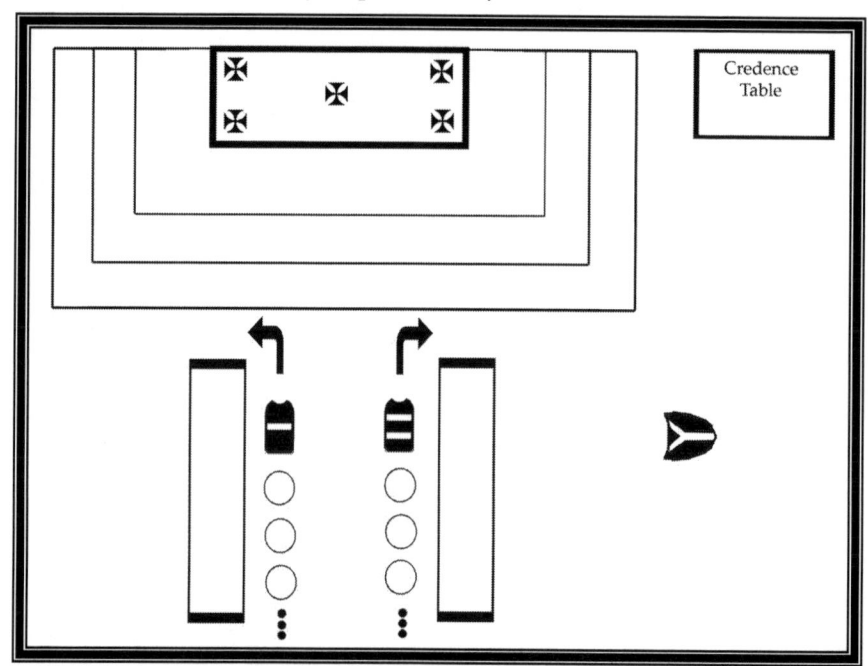

Fig. 15.14 – Entrance of the twelve men for the Maundy. The Celebrant remains seated at the sedilia.

Two benches or suitable chairs should be set up as shown in Fig. 15.14 above. A small table may be set up nearby with necessary supplies. The basin and pitcher should be on this table, along with sufficient towels. The Deacon and Sub-Deacon (or the two servers) take the men down the center in between the benches. At the top, each reverences the altar and then bows to the Celebrant, who is seated at the sedilia or another suitable location. The men then turn and walk away from the altar to take their seats, i.e., the man immediately behind the Deacon goes to the seat furthest from the altar. This is not a matter of symbolism, of course, but of simple logistics. If physical arrangements at any particular church require different movement, then there is no reason it cannot be done as needed. When the men are seated, the Deacon and Sub-Deacon go to the sedilia and bow to the Celebrant. The Celebrant rises (he is not wearing the biretta) and goes to perform the Maundy with the Deacon on his right and the Sub-Deacon on his left. At the top of the benches, they reverence the altar together. They also do this when crossing from one bench to the other.

> If the Celebrant is a Bishop: He sits at the throne or faldstool without mitre. His attendants are around him as usual. When he goes to perform the Maundy, the Deacon and Sub-Deacon are on either side of him. The AP walks in front of him, the Assistant Deacons walk behind him. They will maintain this arrangement throughout performing the Maundy. When they reach the altar, they reverence the altar together, standing as at the Prayers at the Foot of the Altar.

The Celebrant, walking with the Deacon on his right and the Sub-Deacon on the left, approaches each man in turn, kneels before him, and washes his feet. Each man should remove his right shoe and sock. One acolyte holds or positions the basin to catch the water, and another ministers the pitcher of water that is handed to the Celebrant. The Sub-Deacon holds the right foot of each man, and the Celebrant pours some water over it. The Deacon presents a towel, which the Celebrant then uses to dry the foot. Additional servers may keep a steady supply of towels and fresh pitchers of water coming as needed. See Fig. 15.15 for the order of washing. During this time, beginning when the twelve chosen are presented, the choir sings the antiphons appointed in the missal. After the washing is completed, the Celebrant lays aside the linen gremial and recites the appointed prayers in the missal. The Celebrant leads the prayers from the center of the altar on the predella, the Deacon and Sub-Deacon standing behind him on their own step. The MC stands to the left of the Celebrant, assisting at the missal. They step to the side (see the section on High Mass) when the Celebrant turns to the people to say *Dominus vobiscum*. After these prayers, the twelve men are led away. Nothing further is said in this ritual. The tenebrae office appointed for the day, if it is to be said, may be said from anytime after this service and Compline until the end of the following morning.

> <u>If the Celebrant is a Bishop:</u> He leads the prayers from the center of the altar on the predella, facing the altar. The Deacon and Sub-Deacon stand behind him as described above. The AP stands to his left at the missal.

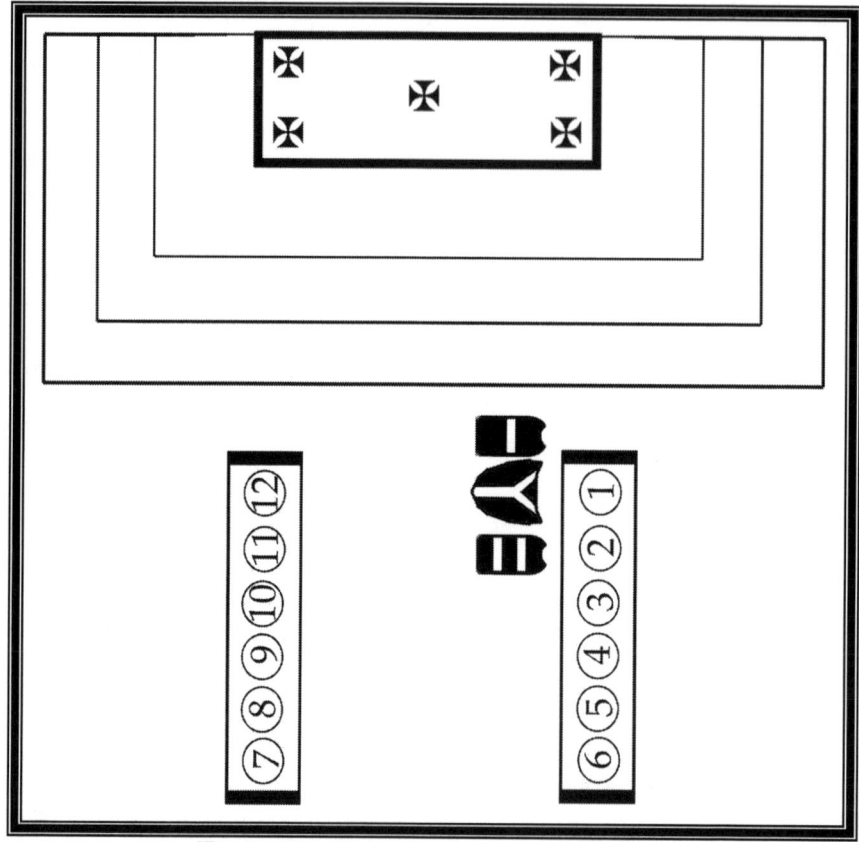

Fig. 15.15 – Order of performing the Maundy

Compline and Adoration

Compline follows the Maundy as above. It should be said in choir without chant. Public adoration of the Blessed Sacrament should continue at the altar of repose at least until midnight. The Sacrament is not exposed, however, and should remain in the tabernacle. If it is not possible that the altar of repose be attended the entire night, then when the adoration is finished, the candles may be extinguished if necessary for safety. However, at least one white votive-style candle (the kind that usually can be left burning unattended) should be left. Better is to place six such candles on the altar, replacing the usual tapers that were on the altar from the earlier ritual. These should be again exchanged for the tapers before the Good Friday office.

Variations and Notes

In some uses, the Maundy is performed during the mass. In this case, it is typically performed after the sermon. The only differences are: the Celebrant removes the chasuble, the Deacon removes the dalmatic, and the Sub-Deacon removes the tunicle. All remove the maniple. They retain their white stoles. After the Maundy, they take the maniple and their vestments again, and then the Celebrant leads the prayers.

> If the Celebrant is a Bishop: The Bishop removes the chasuble, leaving the white dalmatic, with the gremial over it. The other ministers retain their vestments.

The Maundy is a ritual of great symbolic importance. Excessive inclusiveness, e.g., attempting to invite anyone in the congregation who wishes to participate to do so is to destroy the great significance of what the Maundy is designed to impart. The Celebrant in all humility acts in the part of Christ, washing the feet of the twelve chosen men, representing the twelve disciples at the Last Supper. To do otherwise removes this symbolism and denigrates the ritual and relegates it to mere theatrics.

GOOD FRIDAY

Good Friday Office and Mass of the Pre-Sanctified

The altar should be completely bare, with no cross (excepting any crosses that cannot physically be removed, in which case they should be veiled completely), altar cloth, candles, or any other decoration. The Celebrant vests in amice, alb, cincture, black stole, and black chasuble, with biretta. The Deacon vests similarly, only with the black diaconal stole and black dalmatic. The Sub-Deacon wears the black tunicle. They do not wear the maniple. Purple high mass vestments should be laid out near the sedilia for the mass. Other clergy wear choir dress. If black vestments are not available, then purple may be used (but without the maniple, which is taken for the mass only).

<u>If the Celebrant is a Bishop</u>: He vests as above, but with the black dalmatic under the black chasuble. The simplex mitre is worn. This is the only mitre that may be worn on this day. Archbishops should omit the pallium. The crosier typically is not carried. Typically the episcopal ring is omitted, but this is a matter of local custom and personal choice. The pectoral cross is not omitted. The AP vests in black cope. The Assistant Deacons vest in black dalmatic over choir dress as usual. The Bishops chaplains may wear the black cope or simple choir dress.

<u>Local Variation</u>: In some localities, it is the custom that the ministers do not vest as above, but instead wear the black cope. If this is done, then after they reverence the altar, they retire to the sedilia to remove the cope and prostrate (see below) wearing only the alb and stole. They then take the cope again for the remainder of the office and change into purple mass vestments before the mass.

Entry and Prostration

The Good Friday office takes the place of Afternoon Prayer and follows anytime after Noonday Prayer but before Evening Prayer. Most traditionally, this office begins at the ninth canonical hour, i.e., 3pm. When the office begins, the procession goes in the usual manner. If there is a processional cross, remember that it is veiled (as it should be for the entirety of Passiontide anyway). The Sacred Ministers and servers reverence the altar as usual (see the section on High Mass). Then the Sacred Ministers, but not the servers or anyone else, prostrate themselves before the altar. They do this in the positions they are in for the reverence, i.e., the Deacon to the right and the Sub-Deacon to the left. For this, there should be three purple cushions laid out in advance on the pavement. These are taken away later by a server. While they prostrate, all others should kneel and profoundly bow. This is a time of prayer and reflection that should not be omitted. When they have finished, they rise, go to the sedilia, and sit with the biretta. The proper length of the prostration is up to the individual priest, but should be at least a few minutes.

<u>If the Celebrant is a Bishop:</u> All is as above with minor exception. The reverence of the altar is done from the positions as at the Prayers at the Foot of the Altar. The AP is to the right, and the Deacon and Sub-Deacon both are to the left. After the reverence, the Deacon comes to the Bishop's right, and the Sub-Deacon moves closer to the Bishop's left, just as for a priest Celebrant as

above. The AP goes to the left and behind the Sub-Deacon, but in front of the Assistant Deacons, and kneels.

Lesson

As the Celebrant and ministers go to the sedilia, the reader goes to the desk for the Lesson. The desk should be bare an uncovered. It is placed conveniently in the center of the sanctuary, facing the people or facing the altar according to local custom. If necessary, a server moves the desk into position after the ministers go to the sedilia. Alternatively, the lesson may be read from the usual lectern. If there is no reader, one of the ministers may read the lesson. The lesson is read without any announcement whatsoever. *Deo gratias (Thanks be to God)* is not said or sung after the lesson. All should sit for the lesson.

<u>If the Celebrant is a Bishop:</u> He goes to the throne or faldstool.

Response and Collects

The response given in the missal is chanted by the choir (recall that no instruments are to be used). Towards the end, the Sacred Ministers rise in the usual manner and go to the Epistle corner of the altar, standing as for the Introit and Collects in a high mass. The Celebrant sings *Oremus*, and the Deacon then sings *Flectamus genua (let us bow the knee)*. The Celebrant and all present shall genuflect and remain so until the Sub-Deacon sings *Levate (Arise)*. This is chanted as below:

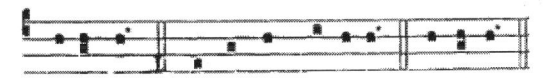

O-re-mus. Flec-ta-mus ge-nu-a. Le-va-te.

The Celebrant chants the first Collect in recto tono. Then after *Amen*, the Celebrant, Deacon, and Sub-Deacon chant *Oremus*, *Flectamus genua*, and *Levate* as before. The Celebrant chants the second Collect in recto tono. Again after *Amen*, the Celebrant, Deacon, and Sub-Deacon chant *Oremus*, *Flectamus genua*, and *Levate* as before.

<u>If the Celebrant is a Bishop:</u> He chants the Collects from the throne or faldstool. The Deacon and Sub-Deacon stand with hands joined as usual at the sedilia and chant *Flectamus genua*, and *Levate* as given above.

Epistle and Response

The Celebrant and Deacon go to the sedilia and sit (with the biretta), and the Sub-Deacon goes as usual to read the Epistle. This is begun without any introduction. When he is finished, he returns to the sedilia and sits with the other Sacred Ministers for the response. Towards the end of the response, the Celebrant rises and goes to the center of the altar. The readers of the Passion go before him. All is as described for the Passion in the section on Palm Sunday above.

Passion

All is as described for Palm Sunday. Lights are not carried, incense is not used, and the Celebrant does not kiss the book. The people should stand. At the words *Et inclinato capite tradidit spiritum*, all genuflect and pause for awhile. When the Celebrant rises, the Passion continues.

> <u>If the Celebrant is a Bishop:</u> He stands without mitre at the throne or faldstool for the Passion. As he generally is not using the crosier on Good Friday, he stands with hands joined. If the Bishop reads part of the Passion, then he may do so from the throne or faldstool (as may be done anytime a Bishop reads part of the Passion).

Solemn Collects

After the Passion, the Sacred Ministers go to their positions at the Epistle corner as for the collects in a high mass. The Celebrant then chants the Solemn Collects as appointed in the missal. These each come with a special introduction that is chanted after *Oremus*. The chants for these are given in the missal. After the introduction is *Oremus, Flectamus genua*, and *Levate*, chanted as before by the Celebrant, Deacon, and Sub-Deacon. The introduction is chanted with the hands joined. Then, when the Celebrant chants the Collect, he extends his hands as usual. Joining his hands at the conclusion. Keeping his hands joined, he immediately begins the next introduction with *Oremus*, as given in the missal.

Veneration of the Cross

After the Solemn Collects, the Celebrant lays aside his chasuble at the sedilia, and the Deacon and Sub-Deacon remove their dalmatic and tunicle. The Deacon then goes to the sacristy and takes a cross veiled with a purple cloth. The cross should be sufficiently large that the figure of

HOLY WEEK RITES

Christ upon it is clearly visible by the faithful. The Celebrant and Sub-Deacon remain standing, uncovered, at the sedilia.

The Deacon is preceded to the sacristy by two acolytes, and two other acolytes walk on either side of him. When they return from the sacristy, the procession is in the same order. The Deacon carries the cross. Now the two acolytes on either side of him carry lighted candles. See Fig. 15.16. If there is no Deacon, then the Celebrant goes in the same manner to the sacristy to get the cross.

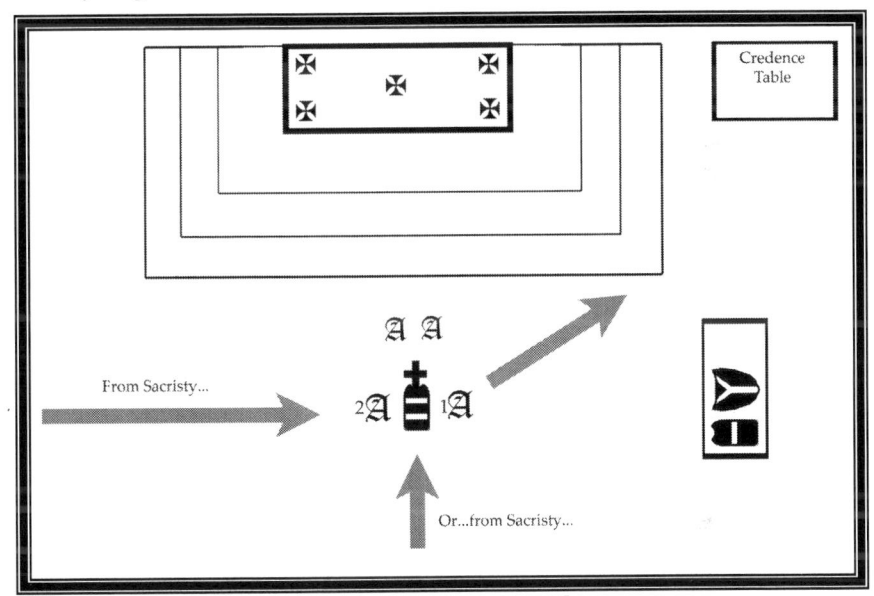

Fig. 15.16 – Procession of the Cross

If the Celebrant is a Bishop: He rises from the throne and goes with his attendants to the Epistle corner, just as a priest Celebrant does. He stands with the AP on his right, the 1AD to the right of the AP (leaving enough space for the Deacon in between), the Sub-Deacon to his left, and the 2AD to the left of the Sub-Deacon. When the Deacon hands to cross to the Bishop, the Deacon goes to stand to the right of the AP and the left of the 1AD.

HOW TO SAY MASS IN THE ANGLICAN RITE

Ecce Lignum Crucis

The Celebrant uncovers the top of the cross. The head of Christ is not uncovered at the first unveiling. The Celebrant sings *Ecce lignum crucis* as given in the missal. The other Sacred Ministers then join in for *in quo salus*, etc. Then the choir sings *Venite adoremus*. The congregation stands at these words (or at the *Ecce lignum crucis*, according to local custom or regulations). All kneel in silent adoration and meditation.

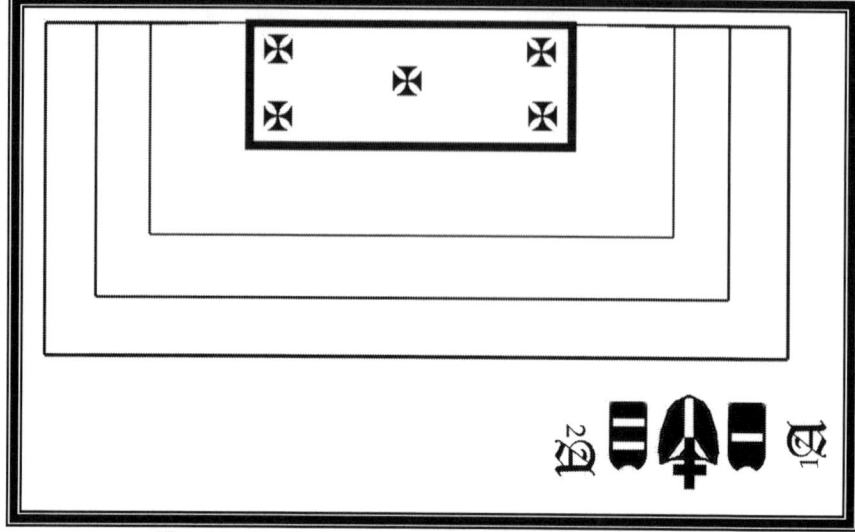

Fig. 15.17 – Position for the first Ecce Lignum Crucis

Then the Celebrant goes with the Deacon, Sub-Deacon, and acolytes to the Epistle side on the predella, standing as in the left frame of Fig. 15.18 below. He uncovers the right arm of the cross and the figure of Christ and lifts the cross a little higher. The ministers assist if necessary. The *Ecce lignum crucis* is sung again in the same manner as described above, but preferably is begun on a higher note than before (and all stand on the final part of the chant as before).

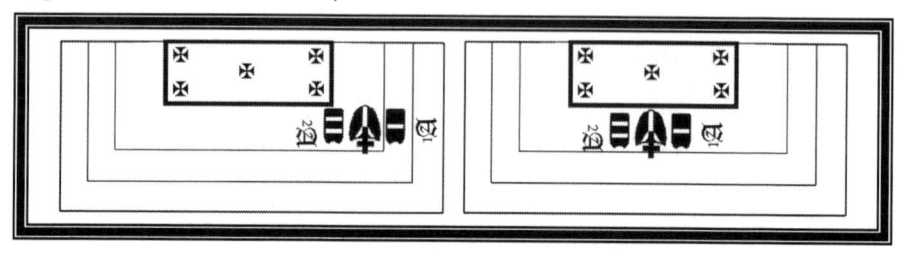

Fig. 15.18 – Left: Position at the second Ecce lignum
Right: Positions at the third Ecce lignum.

After another period of silent adoration and meditation (all kneeling), the Celebrant and ministers go to the center of the altar on the predella, again maintaining the configuration as in the right frame of Fig. 15.18 above. Here the Celebrant uncovers the entire cross completely, lifting it still higher. The *Ecce lignum crucis* is sung again in the same manner, preferably begun on a still higher note than before. Then all kneel in silent adoration and meditation. (If there is not a Deacon or Sub-Deacon, then the acolytes assist with all that is described above.)

> If the Celebrant is a Bishop: All is as in Figs. 15.17 and 15.18 above, except that the AP, Deacon, Sub-Deacon, and Assistant Deacons stand as described earlier.

During the above exposition of the cross, the Celebrant does not kneel. The Deacon and Sub-Deacon do not kneel if they are assisting the Celebrant. Else, they kneel, facing the cross. The acolytes holding the candles on either side kneel with the rest.

Veneration of the Cross

After the *Ecce lignum crucis*, the Celebrant hands the cross to two acolytes or servers. They stand on either side of the cross and hold it by the arms. They stand on the predella, facing the people. The acolyte on the Epistle side holds the cross with the right hand, and the acolyte on the Gospel side holds the cross with the left hand. If the cross is sufficiently large, then the foot of the cross may rest on the predella. The acolytes who were holding the candles during the *Ecce lignum crucis* place them on the predella on either side of the cross. They remain kneeling, facing the cross, on the predella. Meanwhile, the Celebrant descends the altar steps and lays aside his shoes. He approaches the cross from the chancel gate (or outside the chancel gate, depending on physical arrangement and local use). He makes three single genuflections on the way. Ascending the altar steps, he kneels before the cross and kisses the figure of Christ. The traditional place to kiss the figure is on the feet. (Note: In some places, the tradition is that the genuflection should be a double genuflection, i.e., kneeling on both knees.) The Celebrant walks alone to venerate the cross. The Deacon and Sub-Deacon go to the sedilia, remove their shoes, and go to the chancel rail and wait. See Fig. 15.19.

> If the Celebrant is a Bishop: He walks to the cross alone or in between the Assistant Deacons, preceded by the AP. If he uses the Assistant Deacons, they and the AP do not venerate the cross at this time. They wait on the pavement as the Bishop ascends the

altar. The AP waits on the pavement on the Gospel side or on the first step on the Gospel side. They then accompany him back to the throne or faldstool.

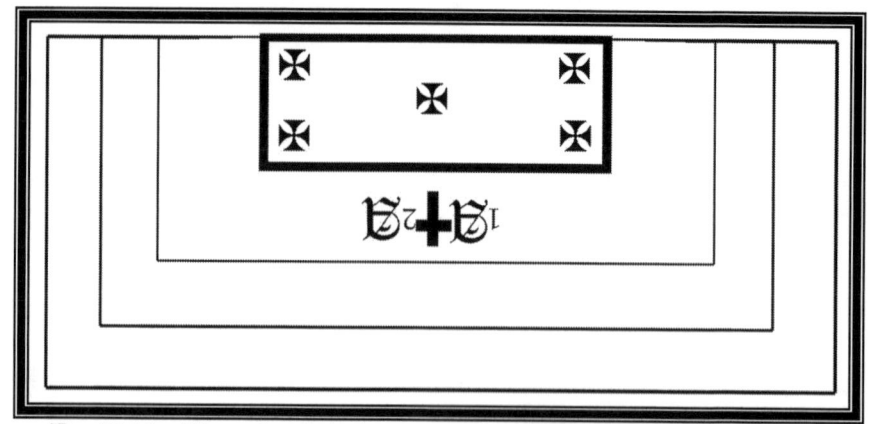

Fig. 15.19 – The acolytes hold the cross on the predella for the veneration by the Sacred Ministers, clergy, and servers

While the veneration takes place, the choir sings the Reproaches. This may be commenced as soon as the Celebrant hands the cross to the acolytes. Once the Celebrant has venerated the cross, he goes to the sedilia and takes his shoes and the black chasuble. The Sacred Ministers, clergy, and servers come in order to venerate the cross (in the same manner as the Celebrant, i.e., kissing the feet of the Christ figure). The order is: Deacon of the Mass, Sub-Deacon of the Mass, clergy serving in order of rank, clergy in choir in order of rank, MC, AMC, thurifer, Sub-Deacon of the Cross, servers in order of rank. The removal of the shoes may be optional, depending on local custom. Similarly, a single genuflection is all that is required by the Missale Anglicanum 2009, though a triple genuflection may be required by local custom. Both the removal of shoes and the triple genuflection (or double genuflections at each instance) may be done by each individual as a matter of personal devotion.

> <u>If the Celebrant is a Bishop</u>: The order of veneration is the Assistant Priest, the Deacon of the Mass, the Sub-Deacon of the Mass, the First Assistant Deacon, the Second Assistant Deacon, the other clergy serving in order of rank, the clergy in choir in order of rank, the MC, the AMC, the thurifer, then the Sub-Deacon of the Cross, and finally the servers in order of rank.

HOLY WEEK RITES

After the clergy and servers have venerated the cross, the acolytes holding it move to the chancel gate. See Fig. 15.20. The acolytes carry the candles and kneel on either side as on the predella. They either place the candles on the pavement as they did on the predella, or they hold them, depending on which is more convenient. The faithful approach the cross one by one. As above, the removal of shoes is optional.

Fig. 15.20 – The acolytes hold the cross at the chancel gate, facing the people.

They must make a single genuflection before kneeling before the cross to kiss the figure. They may optionally make a triple genuflection. During this time, the Celebrant, Deacon, and Sub-Deacon sit at the sedilia with the biretta. They wear the black chasuble, black dalmatic, and black tunicle.

> <u>If the Celebrant is a Bishop:</u> He sits at the throne or faldstool in black dalmatic and chasuble, with the simplex mitre. His attendants come to the throne after they have venerated the cross.

Preparation for the Mass of the Pre-Sanctified

Towards the end of the veneration, the servers make ready the altar. A single linen altar cloth is placed upon the altar. The acolytes carry the cross to the altar, accompanied by the acolytes carrying the candles. They place the cross, unveiled, in the center of the altar so that it may be seen by the faithful. The candles on placed on either side. Only two candles are on the altar. When this has been done, the Sacred Ministers change their vestments for purple for the mass.

When this is completed, the Deacon of the Mass goes to the credence table (which does not have a cloth or candles on it) and takes the purple burse to the altar. He spreads the corporal in the center of the altar in the usual manner. The Sub-Deacon places an empty paten in the center of the corporal in front of where the chalice will go. A server places a bowl of water with a purificator next to it on the Epistle side of the altar for purifying the priest's fingers after communion. Another server places the missal stand and missal on the Gospel side of the altar in the usual place

HOW TO SAY MASS IN THE ANGLICAN RITE

for the Canon of the mass. After this has been done, the procession forms to the altar of repose. The Celebrant and Sub-Deacon, as well as the clergy in choir remain in their places. The procession forms in this manner.

Thurifer*
Acolyte or Cleric to carry the small canopy**
Acolyte – Deacon – Acolyte

* There may be one or two thurifers, as for the procession to the altar of repose on Holy Thursday.

** The number of clerics or acolytes here depends on the type and size of canopy to be used; though the smaller canopy requiring only one acolyte to carry it is more appropriate for the austerity of this service).

The procession goes to the altar of repose while the choir chants the *Vexilla Regis* (the music may be repeated as needed). On the altar of repose should be six lighted candles (two of these will be carried back to the high altar; in some customs there are only two lighted candles on the altar of repose on this day; in either case, when the procession forms to go back to the high altar, any candles that are not carried should be extinguished). Also on the altar or a nearby table should be the white humeral veil for the deacon. Upon arrival at the altar, all genuflect together and then kneel (except the Deacon). See Fig. 15.21.

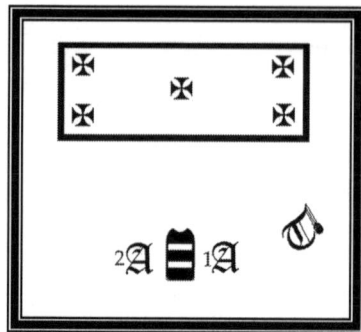

Fig. 15.21 – Positions of the party at the altar of repose on Good Friday. The acolytes shown are those to carry the candles. The other server or servers kneel to either side or behind them. If there is a second thurifer, then he does just as is given above for Maundy Thursday at the altar of repose.

The Deacon goes straight to the tabernacle. He unveils it, opens it, and then genuflects. The chalice is left in the tabernacle. He goes back to his position and kneels, takes the thurible, and censes the sacrament with

HOLY WEEK RITES

three triple swings (if there are two thurifers, then the options for censing are the same as one Holy Thursday). Additionally, the thurifer may optionally cense the sacrament with three triple swings as soon as the Deacon opens the tabernacle. This is in addition to the censing done by the Deacon.

After the sacrament has been censed, a server rises and goes to the altar or table to get the humeral veil. Then he brings it to the Deacon and puts it on him over the dalmatic. The Deacon rises and goes back to the tabernacle. The servers rise. Those appointed to carry the candles go up to the altar with the Deacon and take the candles from the altar. The server(s) appointed to carry the canopy go to get the canopy. Upon arrival at the tabernacle, the Deacon genuflects, and the servers by him genuflect with him. The Deacon takes the chalice containing the consecrated host using the humeral veil. The procession forms again to the sanctuary. The Deacon walks carrying the chalice at the level of his breast with the acolytes carrying the candles on either side. The server(s) carrying the canopy hold it over the sacrament.

If there is no Deacon, then the Celebrant must do all of the above himself, accompanied by the servers. The humeral veil is not used over the chasuble. So, he removes the chasuble before the procession and wears either just the alb and stole or takes the purple dalmatic, exchanging it again later for the chasuble. Alternatively, he may wear the purple cope.

Mass of the Pre-Sanctified

When the Deacon and his attendants have returned to the sanctuary, they go up the altar steps without any reverence. The acolytes place the candles on the altar on either side of the cross. The acolytes retire to the credence table, and the Deacon goes to the Epistle corner, facing the altar and holding the chalice with the host, and waits for the Celebrant and Sub-Deacon. The Celebrant and Sub-Deacon rise and go to the pavement in front of the altar. They genuflect on both knees and then ascend the altar steps to the predella, the Sub-Deacon to the left of the Celebrant. The Celebrant takes the chalice from the Deacon and places it on the corporal. The Celebrant, Deacon, and Sub-Deacon then genuflect together. They retire to the pavement and kneel, Deacon on the right and Sub-Deacon on the left as usual. The Celebrant takes the thurible and censes the sacrament with three triple swings. The Celebrant then again ascends to the predella, standing in the center of the altar for the Offertory. The

Deacon stands to the right of the Celebrant, and the Sub-Deacon to the right of the Deacon. The Offertory is performed in the usual manner, except that no blessings are given and the offertory prayers are not said. The Celebrant holds the chalice with his left hand and takes the host out with his right hand, placing it on the paten. From this moment until the ablutions, his tombs and forefingers should remain joined.

> <u>If the Celebrant is a Bishop:</u> The AP stands on the predella to the left of the Bishop. He remains there through the ablutions.

Then Acolytes bring the cruets. They hand the wine cruet to the Sub-Deacon, who hands it to the Deacon, who then pours it in the chalice, which is held in the usual manner by the Celebrant (who has turned, as usual, to the right). The Sub-Deacon takes the water cruet. The Deacon takes the chalice in his left hand, still holding the wine cruet in his right hand as usual. The Sub-Deacon pours a little water into it. (Remember, there are no blessings at this mass.) The Sub-Deacon retires to his own step (but without the paten) after the offering of the chalice, and the Deacon retires behind the Celebrant on his own step. When the Celebrant turns to the people to say *Orate fratres*, the Deacon and Sub-Deacon step out of the way as usual. They are on their own step for the *Pater Noster* as usual. Then they come up to the predella towards the end. However, unlike as at high mass, the Deacon is on the right, the Sub-Deacon is on the left. The *libera nos* is done as usual, except that when the Celebrant signs himself with the paten, he must keep it parallel to the altar, not in the usual manner. This is to prevent any particles of the consecrated host from falling. He then wipes his mouth with a purificator (or the Deacon does this). Also, the Deacon and Sub-Deacon do not sign themselves at the *libera nos*. Alternatively, the signing with the paten may be omitted, as it is in some usage.

> <u>If the Celebrant is a Bishop:</u> The Sub-Deacon stands to the left of the AP.

After the *libera nos*, the priest slides the host under the paten as usual. He then elevates the host with his right hand only so that the faithful may see it. The bells, of course, are not rung. The fracture is done as usual, except that the usual prayers are not said. The small piece is broken off and placed in the chalice as usual, but the *Pax Domini* and other prayers are not said. The Peace is not given, and the *Agnus Dei* is not said. The communion devotion given in the missal is said. Then the Celebrant genuflects and receives communion as given in the missal. The Celebrant takes the host in the usual manner, and then the wine. Nothing other than that which is given to be said in the missal for communion on Good Friday is said. The priest does not make the sign of the cross with the host or chalice. The Deacon remains on his right, and the Sub-Deacon on the left.

>   <u>If the Celebrant is a Bishop:</u> The Sub-Deacon stands to the left of the AP.

No one other than the Celebrant receives communion. When the Celebrant receives communion, the ablutions are performed as usual, except that the prayers are not said. The chalice is not veiled. The corporal is folded and placed back in the burse. Nothing further is said.

The Sacred Ministers go to the sedilia and remove their vestments. In silence, the Sacred Ministers wearing alb with stole, but without maniple, the altar is laid bare. Both the burse and the Sacred Vessels are taken to the credence table. The Deacon takes the burse, the Celebrant takes the chalice, and the Sub-Deacon takes the paten. The servers or the Sacred Ministers remove the altar cloth, cross, and candles, which are first extinguished.

Evensong and Compline

Evensong is said without chant, as is Compline later in the evening at the usual time. The Celebrant may take the purple cope over the alb or change into choir dress with purple stole.

Commentary on Good Friday Liturgy

The above ritual is that taken from the Missale Anglicanum 2009. It is a traditional rite for this day. However, there have been many variations in the ritual for this day. As usual, there is usually a core of common ritual and symbolism, and there is plenty of room for variation under episcopal authority. The key elements, though, are the prostration, readings and Passion, Solemn Collects, Exposition and Veneration of the Cross, and the Mass of the Pre-Sanctified. In the mass, some congregations reserve instead of the chalice with host a ciborium containing hosts for communion. In this case, the clergy and people receive communion. All is as described above, except that there is no offering (and hence no need for a chalice or paten) and the Celebrant does not receive the Precious Blood. Ablutions are in the form of a small dish with water and a purificator (as in the Sacred Benediction). The *Ecce Agnus Dei* is said, and then communion distributed without making the sign of the cross over the communicants. All communion wafers not distributed must be consumed by the priest at the altar before the ablutions. The ciborium is purified as well.

MASSES OF SAINTS ON HOLY SATURDAY

Feasts are not celebrated from Palm Sunday through Good Friday inclusive. However, a mass of a Saint appointed for the calendar day that happens to be Holy Saturday may be said during the day before the Holy Saturday/Easter Vigil liturgy. The altar is arrayed as usual in the color of the Saint, with the cross veiled in purple. A wooden instrument may be used in lieu of altar bells. Musical instruments are not permitted. The *Gloria* is not said. All is like a mass during Passiontide. Minimal celebration should take place.

HOLY SATURDAY AND EASTER VIGIL

Similar to Good Friday, this liturgy varies in precise form from congregation to congregation, or diocese to diocese, or from time period to time period. The ritual described here is that given in the Missale Anglicanum 2009 and is highly recommended for its symbolic nature.

Preparations Inside and Outside the Church

The altar should be arrayed as usual with altar cloths, six candles, and an altar cross. The cross and all icons and images should still be veiled in purple. The Sacred Vessels are covered in a white (or silver or gold) veil. Paraments are white. All white coverings and paraments are covered in purple ones that will be removed later. The candles are not lit. On the pavement in the sanctuary, in the center in front of the altar should be placed the paschal candle on a stand. The church should be completely dark, without any lights (excepting any needed for safety purposes).

Outside the front of the church should be built a fire in a safe manner, which will be lit at an appropriate time before the liturgy. A holy water pot and aspergillum, thurible without coals, five grains of incense (for the Paschal candle) in a dish or upon a salver, coals for the thurible (in the fire), and white stole and dalmatic for the Deacon should be prepared and carried to the new fire by the servers.

HOLY WEEK RITES

Blessing of the New Fire

The Celebrant vests in amice, alb, cincture, purple stole, and purple cope. If he does not wear the cope, then he wears only the alb, not the chasuble. The Deacon and Sub-Deacon vest similarly, in purple dalmatic and purple tunicle respectively. If the Celebrant does not wear the cope, then the other ministers wear only the alb and, for the Deacon, the stole. Other clergy are in choir dress. The Celebrant goes from the sacristy to the new fire. If the people can better follow the rite, then he may instead stand in the front of the church or inside the church near the door. The descriptions here, though, assume that all is done outside. The Celebrant faces the fire and the church. See Fig. 15.22 for a priest, Fig. 15.23 for a Bishop. The order of procession is:

Thurifer
Sub-Deacon of the Mass *(with the cross)*
Servers
Clergy
Deacon
Celebrant

Or for a Bishop:
Thurifer
Sub-Deacon of the Mass *(with the cross)*
Servers
Clergy
Deacon – Assistant Priest
Second Assistant Deacon – Bishop – First Assistant Deacon

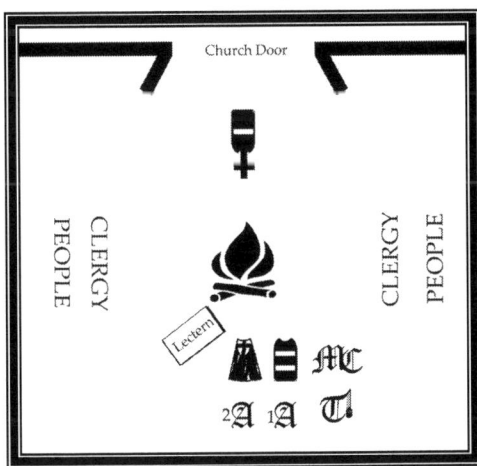

Fig. 15.22 – Positions at the New Fire

HOW TO SAY MASS IN THE ANGLICAN RITE

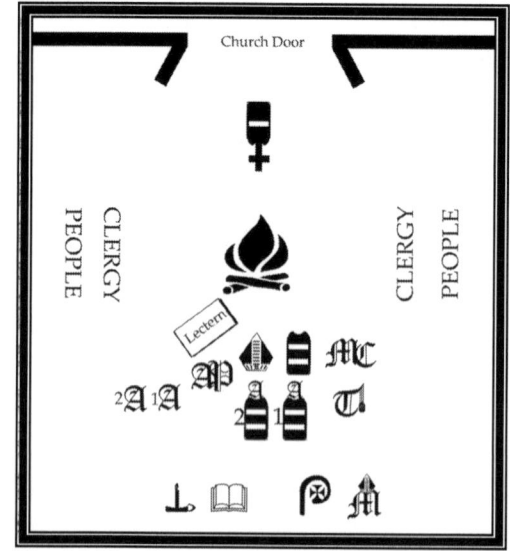

Fig. 15.23 – Positions at the New Fire for a Bishop

At the fire, the Sub-Deacon stands on the opposite side from the Celebrant, holding the cross facing the fire. The Celebrant begins the prayers as given in the missal. These are either spoken or chanted in recto tono. Next, the Deacon (or a server, if there is no Deacon) takes the dish or salver with the five grains of incense for the Paschal candle and holds them up for the Celebrant to bless.

<u>If the Celebrant is a Bishop:</u> The five grains are held by the AP.

The thurifer goes to the fire during this time and takes out the three live coals placed there previously. They needed be far in the fire, given problems of accessibility. It is best if they are placed near the edge of the fire, and they must at least be in a place accessible safely by the thurifer. The thurifer places these coals in the thurifer. Then he approaches the Celebrant and holds up the incense for him to bless in the usual manner. The Celebrant places incense in the thurible. He then sprinkles first the five grains of incense and then the new fire in the usual manner with holy water (three times each). He says the *Asperges me* (not including the Psalm or *Gloria Patri*, and the antiphon is not repeated) while he does this. Taking the thurible from the thurifer, he censes first the five grains of incense and then the new fire with three single swings. The Deacon hands the grains of incense back to the server appointed to carry them as soon as they have been incensed.

The Deacon, having given up the grains of incense, removes his purple dalmatic and stole with the help of a server or the MC. He then puts on the white diaconal stole and dalmatic. He takes the reed, containing three tapers, for carrying the Light of Christ into the church. See Fig. 15.24. Meanwhile, an acolyte lights a candle or other taper from the new fire. (The reed has clear Trinitarian symbolism. The new fire lights the three candles, representing the three heads of the Trinity, and this is used to light the Paschal candle, representing the risen Christ on this earth.)

Fig. 15.24 – The Reed. It should have three candles. The center one is best elevated as shown. Any base or candelabra providing this arrangement is suitable.

The procession forms to carry the light into the church. The order of the procession is as follows:

Thurifer
Acolyte *(with the dish with the five grains of incense)*
Sub-Deacon *(with the cross)*
Deacon *(holding the reed)*
Master of Ceremonies – Celebrant
Clergy *(in order of rank)*
Laity

Or for a Bishop...

Thurifer
Acolyte *(with the dish with the five grains of incense)*
Sub-Deacon *(with the cross)*
Deacon *(holding the reed)*
Assistant Priest
Second Assistant Deacon – Bishop – First Assistant Deacon
Bishop's Chaplains
Clergy *(in order of rank)*
Laity

HOW TO SAY MASS IN THE ANGLICAN RITE

When the Deacon has come into the church, he lowers the reed, and one of the candles is lit by a taper brought by the acolyte who lit it from the new fire. (This should be one of the two lower candles on the reed.) The Deacon holds up the reed, turning to the people (that is, turning around facing the opposite way from that in which the procession is progressing) and all genuflect except the Sub-Deacon, who is holding the cross. The Deacon sings *Lumen Christi (The Light of Christ),* and all respond *Deo gratias (Thanks be to God).* Then all rise, and the procession continues. The Deacon carries the reed at breast level. When the Deacon has reached the center of the church (when the Deacon has, not the entire procession), he lowers the reed, and the acolyte with the taper lights the other of the two lower candles on the reed. The Deacon turns again to the people, elevates the reed, and sings *Lumen Christi* as before. All present genuflect before and respond *Deo gratias.* When he reaches the pavement in the sanctuary, the Deacon again stops, and the third candle (the highest one) is lit by the acolyte with the taper lit by the new fire. He again turns to the people, elevates the reed, and sings *Lumen Christi* as before. All present genuflect before and respond *Deo gratias.* Each time he sings this, he begins on a progressively higher note.

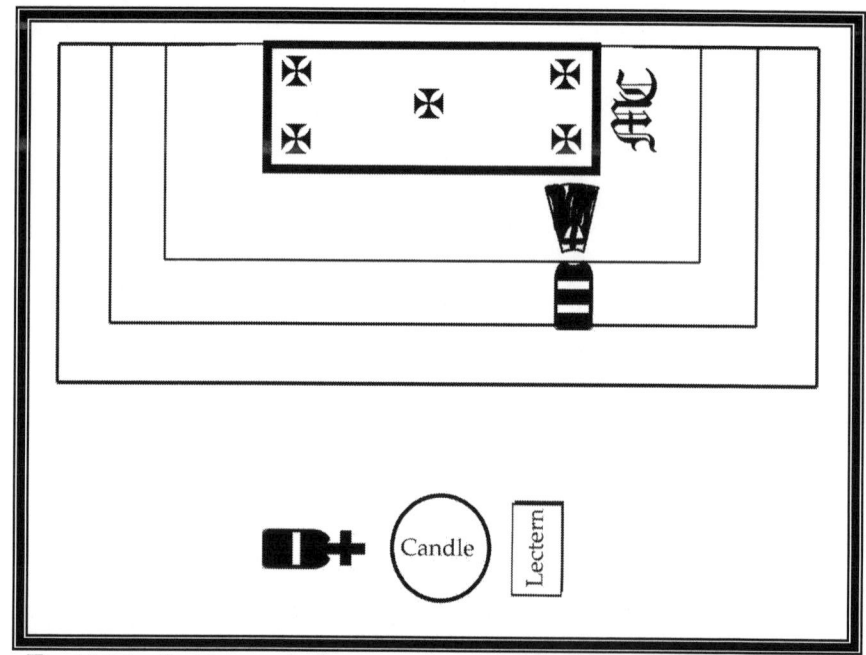

Fig. 15.25 – Positions as the Deacon receives the blessing before the Paschal Praises.

HOLY WEEK RITES

The Celebrant proceeds to the Epistle corner of the altar, while the Deacon hands the reed to an acolyte (the candles on the reed must remain lit). The Deacon takes the missal or book containing the Paschal Praises from the MC and goes to the altar, on the Epistle side, to receive the blessing. The MC then holds the book, giving it back to him after the blessing. The Celebrant stands at the Epistle corner on the predella, while the Deacon kneels on the second step. The Sub-Deacon, meanwhile, takes the cross and stands on the Gospel side, facing the Paschal candle. See Fig. 15.25.

> If the Celebrant is a Bishop: He goes to the throne instead of to the Epistle corner. The Deacon instead kneels at the throne as if receiving the blessing before the Gospel.

The Deacon rises and goes to the lectern by the Paschal candle. The MC accompanies him. The Celebrant goes to the sedilia and stands. See Fig. 15.26.

> If the Celebrant is a Bishop: He stands at the throne holding the crosier for the Paschal Praises.

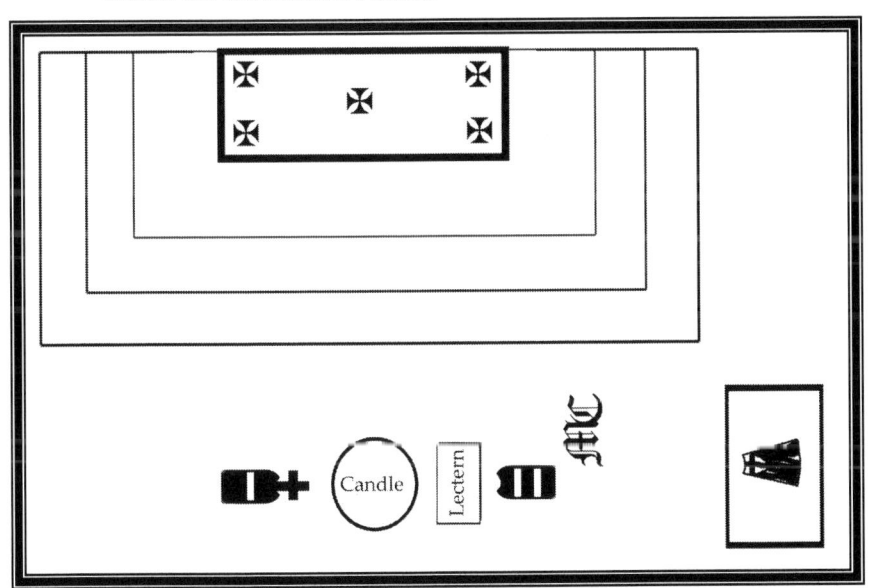

Fig. 15.26 – Positions for the Paschal Praises

If the Celebrant is celebrating this rite without a Deacon, then everything described to this point must be done by the Celebrant. He processes as usual wearing the purple cope to the new fire. A server must hold the five grains of incense. Then, before taking the reed, he gives up the purple cope and stole and takes the white dalmatic and stole (worn in priest configuration). He does as is described for the Deacon above with the reed. He kneels before the altar after giving up the reed and asks for the blessing as given in the missal. Then he takes the book from the MC and goes to the lectern. An acolyte holds the cross. The Celebrant must sing the Paschal Praises if there is no Deacon.

Paschal Praises

The Deacon, standing as in Fig. 15.26 above, chants the Paschal Praises using the chant notation given in the missal. The MC stand behind him as shown. There should be a light on the lectern so that the text may be seen. All stand as at the Gospel. A Bishop stands at the throne holding the crosier for the Paschal Praises. When the Deacon gets close to *et curvat imperia*, the Celebrant goes from the sedilia to stand in front of the Paschal candle, facing the altar, bowing (not genuflecting) to the altar. At those words, the Deacon comes to stand to the left of the Celebrant. See Figs. 15.27 and 15.28.

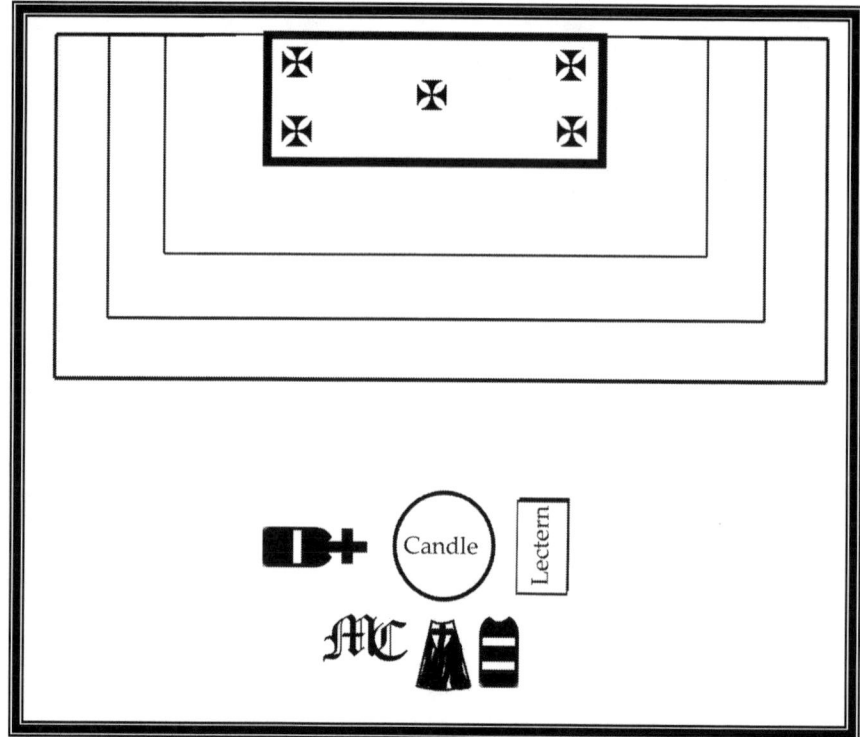

Fig. 15.27 – Positions for marking the Paschal Candle

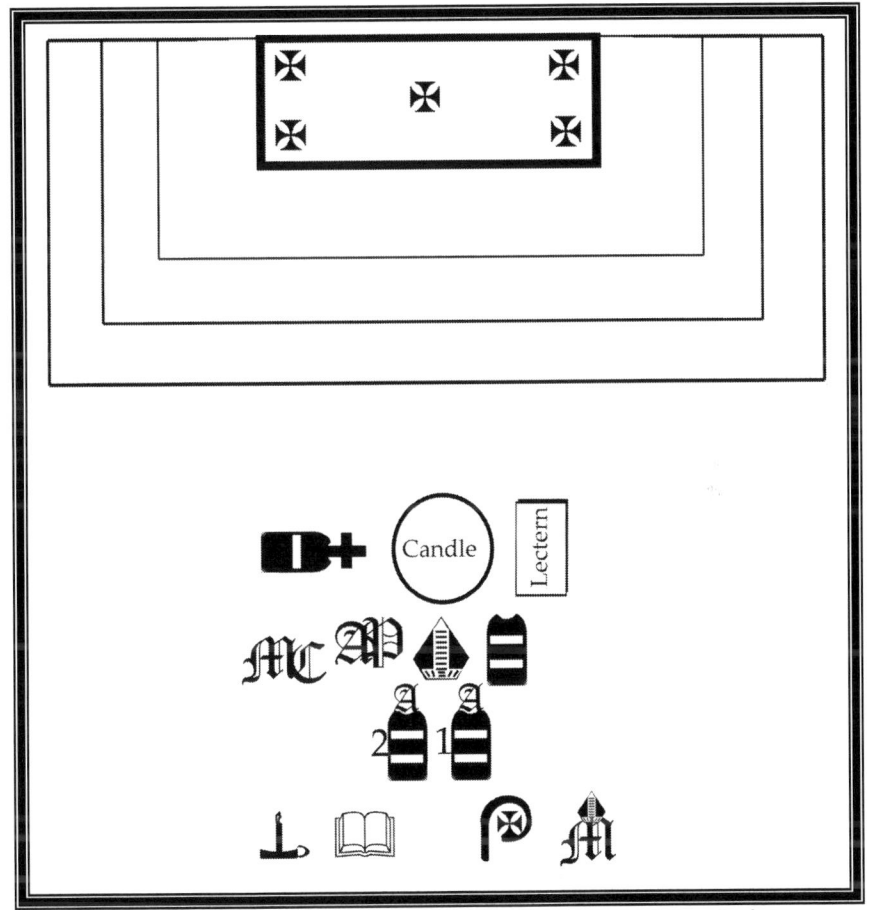

Fig. 15.28 – Positions for marking the candle if the Celebrant is a Bishop

The MC holds the candle stable. The Celebrant inscribes the cross, alpha and omega, and year as shown in the example below, Fig. 15.29. The inscriptions need not be made if they have already been made or are pre-marked on the candle. Ideally the candle will be plain, the inscriptions be made, and then any other colored or fancy markings added over the inscriptions, either at the same time or after the Easter Vigil. If no markings are made at this time, however, the Celebrant does not come from the sedilia, and the Deacon stands in the center on front of the candle, facing the altar.

```
    A
  2 | 0
  --+--
  0 | 9
    Ω
```

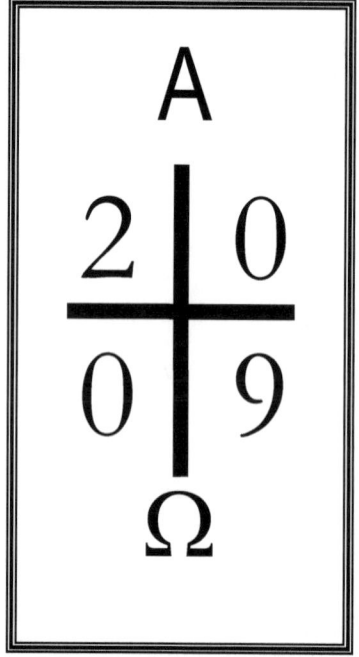

Fig. 15.29 – Inscriptions on the Paschal Candle

The acolyte bearing the grains of incense approaches. The Deacon then places the five grains of incense in the candle along the line of the cross that has just been inscribed in the following order (1 being the top of the cross, 3 being the bottom, 4 being the left end, 5 being the right end, and 2 being the center where the two arms cross):

<pre>
        1

    4   2   5

        3
</pre>

After the grains of incense have been placed, the Deacon returns to his position as in Fig. 15.26. He continues with the Paschal Praises. When he reaches the words *humanis divina iunguntur*, he goes to the front of the candle, facing the altar, as in Fig. 15.30. The acolyte with the reed approaches. The Deacon takes the reed and, using the highest candle, lights the Paschal candle. Other lamps around the sanctuary may be lit, but not the altar candles. The lights may be turned on in the church at this time.

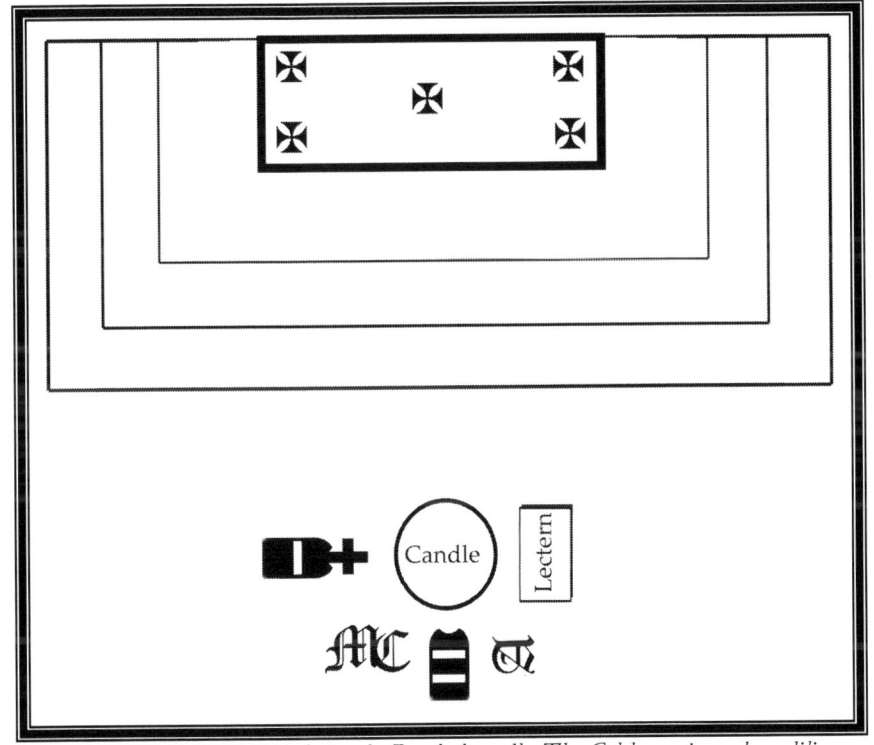

Fig. 15.30 – Positions for lighting the Paschal candle. The Celebrant is at the sedilia.

Returning to the lectern, the Deacon continues with the Paschal Praises, as given in the missal. After *Amen* at the end of the Paschal Praises, the Deacon retires to the sedilia, removes the white stole and dalmatic, and takes the purple stole and dalmatic. The Sub-Deacon deposits the cross in it stand and then goes with two acolytes as usual to read the Prophecies.

Prophecies

The Prophecies are sung in the tone of the Lessons from the chancel gate or the chancel rail, facing the people or facing the altar, according to local use and physical arrangement. The Prophecies are sung as given in the missal, without any announcement. *Deo gratias* or *Thanks be to God* are not said at the end. In between the Prophecies, the Celebrant, Deacon, and Sub-Deacon shall go to the altar and stand as in the Collects. *Oremus*, *Flectamus genua*, and *Levate* shall be sung in the usual manner, with the clergy and people all kneeling at *Flectamus genua*. Then the Celebrant shall chant in recto tono the appointed Collect. This continues in between each Prophecy. Where a Tract is appointed to be sung, the choir sings it and the Sub-Deacon returns to the sedilia and sits with the biretta like the other Sacred Ministers until it is over. Then they rise and go to the altar. At the end of the Prophecies, this is done again, as there is another Tract and Collect appointed. If the Celebrant is celebrating without a Deacon and Sub-Deacon, then he chants the Prophecies from the missal at the Epistle corner and remains there for the Tracts and Collects; or he chants the Prophecies from the various locations given as options for the Epistle in the section on Low Mass, returning to the sedilia or Epistle corner for the Tracts and the Epistle corner for the Collects.

> If the Celebrant is a Bishop: The Collects are chanted from the throne or faldstool by the Bishop. The Deacon and Sub-Deacon are at the sedilia, standing with hands joined, and sing *Flectamus genua* and *Levate* from there.

Blessing of the Baptismal Font

After the Prophecies have been sung, the procession forms to go to the baptismal font as follows:

Thurifer
Cross *(without acolytes)*
Lay Choir
Servers
Clergy in Choir
Acolyte – Acolyte
Deacon *(carrying the Paschal candle)*
Sub-Deacon – Celebrant – MC

Or for a Bishop...

Thurifer
Cross *(without acolytes)*
Lay Choir
Servers
Clergy in Choir
Acolyte – Acolyte
MC – Sub-Deacon
Deacon *(carrying the Paschal candle)* – Assistant Priest
Second Assistant Deacon – Bishop – First Assistant Deacon
Bishop's Chaplains

During the procession, the choir may chant a suitable tract. Recall that musical instruments still may not be used at this point, as the *Gloria* of the Easter Vigil has not yet been commenced. When the procession comes to the baptismal font, all stand as in Fig. 15.31. If the baptismal font is in the sanctuary, then the positions are the same and all should be positioned so that the Celebrant faces the people. In a baptistery, the participants are arranged so that the Celebrant is facing back towards the altar (though in part this depends on the physical arrangement of the baptistery). If the Celebrant is a Bishop, see Fig. 15.32.

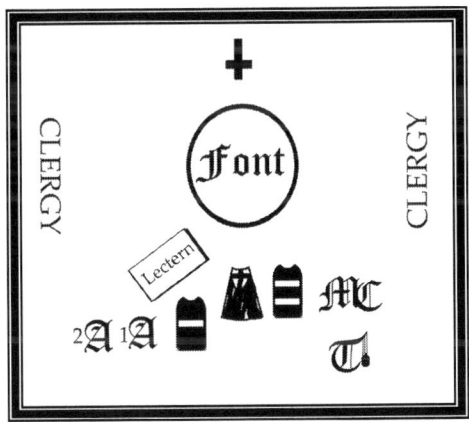

Fig. 15.31 – Positions at the baptismal font

Fig. 15.32 – Positions at the baptismal font if the Celebrant is a Bishop

The Celebrant, facing the font and with hands extended, intones *Dominus vobiscum* in recto tono. He then chants the prayer given in the missal, giving it the ending provided and following the chant into the *Sursum corda* and preface. The hand positions and actions are the same for this as at the mass. When indicated in the missal (at *gratiam de Spiritu Sanctu*), he takes his open hand and divides the water in the font in the form of a cross. See Fig. 15.33. An acolyte presents him with a towel to dry his hands.

Fig. 15.33 – Order of dividing the water

The Celebrant continues chanting the preface as given in the missal. At *non inficiendo corrumpat*, he touches the water with the fingers of his open right hand. An acolyte again presents him with a towel to dry his hands. He continues again with the preface as given in the missal. He then makes three signs of the cross over the font at *unde benedico*, at *per Deum vivum*, and at *per Deum qui te*. Then, after *super te ferebatur*, the Celebrant divides the water with his hand and scatters it to the four corners of the earth: first to liturgical east (towards the altar), then to liturgical west, then liturgical north (the Gospel side), and then liturgical south. He again dries his hands.

He continues with the chant, switching to recto tono at *Haec nobis praecepta servantibus*. After *tu benignus aspira*, he breathes three times on the water in the font in the form of a cross. This may be three times in the same location or center, left, and right. The latter is preferred. Afterwards he continues as given in the missal in recto tono. After *purificandis mentibus efficaces*, he takes the Paschal candle from the Deacon. The Celebrant dips the Paschal candle a little way into the water and, holding it there, chants in the tone of the Preface the words given in the missal. He removes the Paschal candle and then dips it deeper into the water. Holding it there, he again chants the same words as before, beginning on a higher tone. The candle is removed and then dipped all the way to the bottom of the font. Holding it there, he again chants the same words as before, beginning on a still higher tone. With the candle still in the water, the Celebrant breathes on the water in the form of a Ψ, and then sings as given in the missal. Then the Paschal candle is removed from the font and handed back to the Deacon. An acolyte may dry it with a towel. It may optionally be returned to its stand by an acolyte at this time. Or, it may be given to an acolyte to hold.

The Celebrant continues the chant in the tone of the Preface until he reaches *Per Dominum nostrum Iesum Christum, Filium tuum: Qui venturus est iudicare vivos et mortuos, et saeculum per ignem*, which is read. After this, some of the water is placed in another vessel for sprinkling the people. Taking the aspergillum, the Celebrant then sprinkles those around him as a renewal of baptismal vows. He may also go in procession, as at the Asperges, to sprinkle the faithful in the congregation, sitting in the nave of the church.

Mixing of the Oils

Taking the Oil of the Catechumens, which is in a vessel upon a table near the font, from the Deacon, he pours a little of the oil into the font in the form of a cross. Then he takes the Chrism from the Deacon and pours some of the Holy Chrism into the font in the form of a cross. Then he retains the Chrism in his right hand and takes the Oil of the Sick from the Sub-Deacon in his left hand. He pours the two oils into the font together in the form of a cross. The words to be spoken at these mixings are given in the missal. He then mixes the oil and water with his right hand and scatters it over the inner surface of the font. An acolyte presents a towel to clean his hands, and bread if needed. This towel should be purified or burned later, as it was used to clean the holy oils.

Baptism

If Baptism is to be administered, then it is done at this time. The rite is exactly the same as usual (see the Rituale Anglicanum). The various movements throughout the church given in the ritual may be done, or all may be done at the Baptistery if necessary. If baptism is to be administered, then there should be a white stole and cope for the Celebrant made ready near the baptismal font. Others need not change their vestments as a matter of convenience.

Litany

The procession returns to the sanctuary in the same order in which it went to the sacristy. The procession should be in silence. When the Sacred Ministers have returned, they lay aside their vestments and prostrate before the altar (see Good Friday above for the positions of the various ministers). Only the Celebrant, Deacon, and Sub-Deacon prostrate. The choir chants the Litany. All others kneel. When the choir begins the second half of the Litany, the Ministers rise and go to the sacristy to change into white vestments for the vigil mass. It is a fairly obvious musical change in the chanting of the Litany for this mass (see the Liber Usualis) that occurs at the beginning of the second half of the Litany. The altar candles are lit by the altar servers and the veils are removed from the crosses and images. The purple coverings about the church are removed to expose the white ones underneath. Then the Sacred Ministers and servers approach the altar while the Litany is still being chanted and recite the Prayers at the Foot of the Altar in the usual manner, with the *Judica me* and *Gloria Patri*. After, the Celebrant ascends the altar and censes it in the usual manner. Remember that still no musical instruments may be used at this point.

Mass of Easter Vigil

There is no Introit at this mass, or Summary of the Law. The *Kyrie Eleison* is chanted previously during the Litany (see above). When the Litany has finished and the Sacred Ministers are in their places for the *Gloria* (see the section on High Mass), the Celebrant intones the *Gloria* and the choir and/or congregation continues is. The *Gloria* continues just as at high mass. As soon as the Celebrant has intoned the *Gloria*, the bells are immediately set ringing. From this point forward, musical instruments and bells may again be used.

> <u>If the Celebrant is a Bishop:</u> The Gloria is intoned as usual from the throne or faldstool, with the Deacon and Sub-Deacon standing at the sedilia.

After the *Gloria*, the Sacred Ministers move to the center of the altar for the Dominus vobiscum, and then to the Epistle corner for the Collect. See the section on High Mass. There is only one collect permitted at this mass. No seasonal collects or collects ad libitum are said.

> <u>If the Celebrant is a Bishop:</u> This is done from the throne or faldstool, and *Pax vobis* may be said in lieu of *Dominus vobiscum*.

The Epistle is then sung by the Sub-Deacon in the usual manner. After the Epistle, the Celebrant ascends the altar and, standing in the center and facing the people, sings the Alleluia given in the missal. The choir continues with the *Confitemini Domino*. The Deacon proceeds to say the *Munda Cor*, and all others prepare for the Gospel as usual. Incense is used, and lights are carried. See the section on High Mass for the blessing of the Deacon and other preparations. The procession forms, and the Gospel is chanted as usual. If the Celebrant is celebrating alone, then after intoning the *Alleluia*, he prepares to chant or read the Gospel himself.

> <u>If the Celebrant is a Bishop:</u> He sings the *Alleluia* from the throne or faldstool, and all else is just as for the Gospel at a pontifical high mass.

The mass from this point is generally like a typical mass, but with some notable changes. The Offertory proceeds as usual, but there is no Offertory verse. The priest kisses the altar and, turning to the people, says *Dominus vobiscum* and *Oremus* like usual, and then immediately proceeds with the offering of the host. At the end of the *Lavabo*, the *Gloria Patri* is said. The Preface of Easter is said with the addition of the words *in hoc potissimum nocte*, as given in the missal. In the Canon, there is a proper Communicantes, and the *Pax Domini* is said, but the Peace is not given. The *Agnus Dei* is not said, and there is no Post-Communion prayer. The General Thanksgiving is omitted, and there is no Communion verse.

Immediately after the Ablutions, the Celebrant, Deacon, and Sub-Deacon sit at the sedilia while the choir chants the *Alleluia* and *Laudate Dominum* (Psalm 150). These may be found in the Liber Usualis or another suitable source. When the choir has finished this and repeated the *Alleluia*, the Celebrant rises at the sedilia and, with hands joined, intones the *Et valde mane*, sitting again while the choir continues. After the *Et valde mane*, the choir sings the *Benedictus Dominus*, with the *Gloria Patri* at the end. The Celebrant goes with the Sacred Ministers to cense the altar during the *Benedictus Dominus* in the usual manner.

The Celebrant, again rising at the sedilia, chants *Dominus vobiscum* as usual, and then chants the prayer given in the missal. Then the Sacred Ministers rise and go to the altar as for the dismissal in high mass. The Deacon chants the *Ite Missa Est*, with the *Alleluias*, as given in the missal. The Celebrant says the *Placeat tibi*, kisses the altar, and turns to the people to give the blessing as usual. The Last Gospel is not said, and the procession forms to the sacristy in the usual manner.

>If the Celebrant is a Bishop: All is done at the throne or faldstool. After the Benediction, he goes to the altar, kisses it, and the procession forms as usual.

Notes on Easter Vigil

As with Good Friday, there have been several variations on the Holy Saturday and Easter Vigil liturgy over the years. Under proper episcopal authority, this is fine, provided that the variations also reflect the meaning of the occasion. The purple of Lent changes before the eyes of the faithful to the white of Paschaltide. As we celebrate the resurrection of our Lord, we baptize the adults (and even infants) who wish to accept Jesus into their hearts. The New Covenant began with the resurrection, and we celebrate it at the Easter Vigil.

Ordinations

❧☙

Ordinations should be done in the context of a mass. The rituals for the various ordinations, as well as rubrics, are given in the Pontificale Anglicanum. This section merely gives positional charts for the ordination, which takes place at the faldstool before the altar. Variations in the below may be necessary, depending on the physical arrangements of the location.

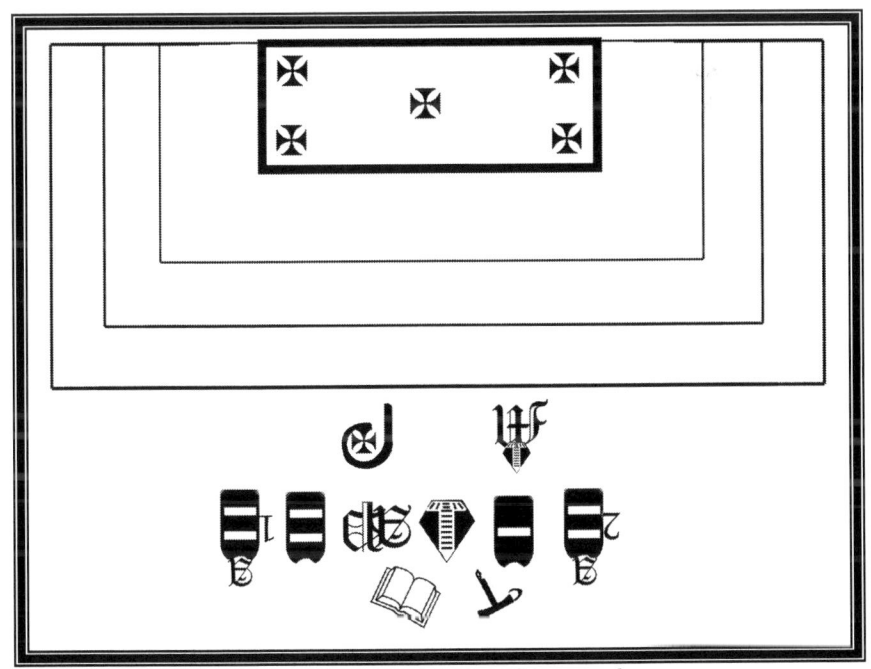

Fig. 16.1 — Positions at the faldstool for an ordination

Nuptial Masses

The Nuptial Mass may be celebrated as a votive mass when permitted by the rubrics. It may not be celebrated at all during Advent or Lent. When not permitted, the mass of the day is said (and the mass of the day may be said for a wedding anyway), and the nuptial mass is commemorated. At any nuptial mass, even if the votive nuptial mass is not done, the special prayers given in the missal in the votive nuptial mass are used when called for. The marriage rite is detailed in the Rituale Anglicanum. For an officiant who is a Bishop, additional ceremonial details are given in the Pontificale Anglicanum. Here are presented the position diagrams for a wedding officiated by a priest and by a Bishop.

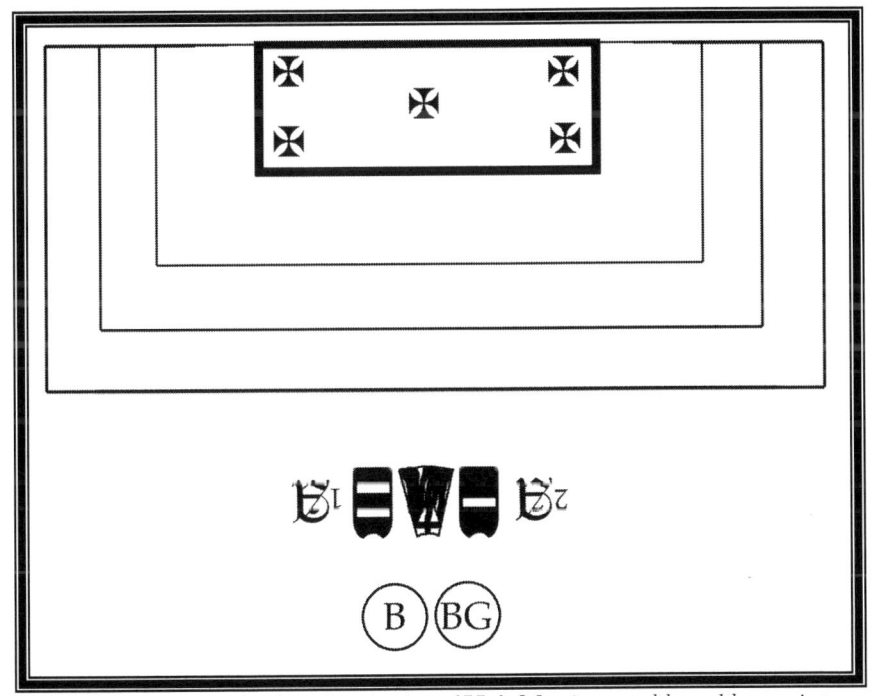

Fig. 17.1 – Positions for the solemnization of Holy Matrimony celebrated by a priest; BG is bridegroom, and B is bride.

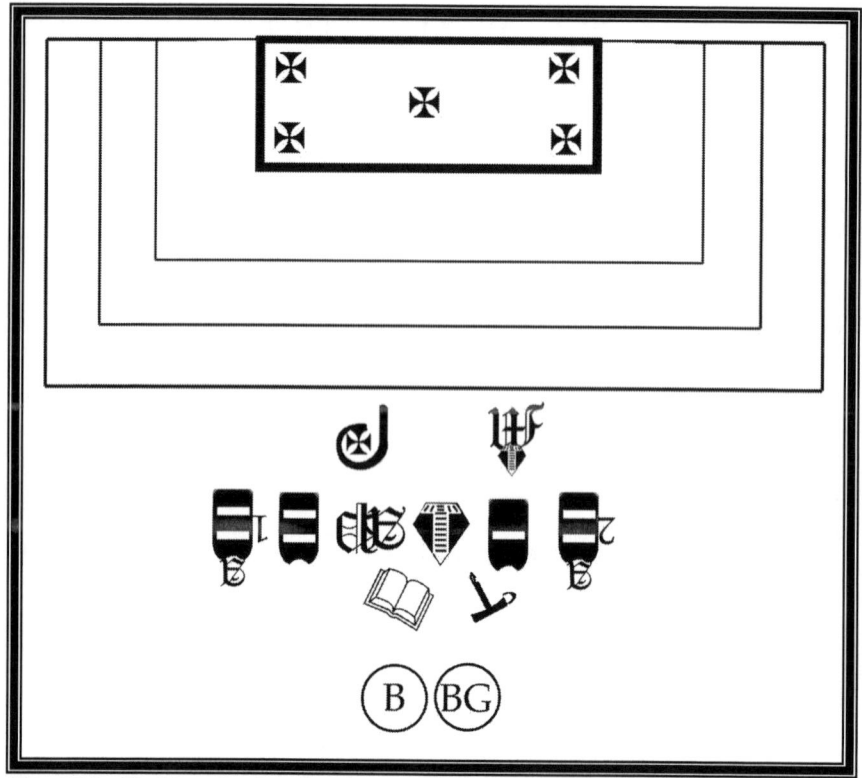

Fig. 17.2 - Positions for the solemnization of Holy Matrimony celebrated by a Bishop; BG is bridegroom, and B is bride.

In Fig. 17.2 above, the positions may be modified as needed. The Bishop sits at the faldstool in front of the altar, and the bride and bridegroom stand or kneel as called for in the ritual.

CELEBRATING WITHOUT A SERVER
೧೦೧೩

If a priest must celebrate mass without the assistance of a server, then there are some things he must do himself that ordinarily the server would do. The priest is reliant upon the faithful present to make the responses. It does take a bit of practice, and so should be reviewed in advance.

The priest processes in by himself, wearing the biretta as usual. When he reverences the altar, he removes and holds the biretta himself. He then takes the biretta to the credence table or sedilia and leaves it there until the mass is over. Returning to the front of the altar, he says the Prayers at the Foot of the Altar, saying all parts himself, through the *Confiteor*. Then he skips to the *Indulgentiam*, continuing to the end. He ascends the altar steps and then says the mass as usual. The readings he must say either from the missal or from the Book of Epistles and Book of Gospels, holding the books himself. After he reads the Gradual, he must transfer the missal himself. Then he says the *Munda Cor* in the center of the altar. For the Gospel, he may hold the book and make the sign of the cross over it, or he may lay it on the Gospel side, make the sign of the cross over it as he announces the Gospel, and then take it and turn to face the people to read the Gospel.

The Offertory presents some interesting challenges. The offering of the host is easy enough. For the chalice, he takes it to the Epistle corner or to the credence. If need be, he may bring the cruets to the altar and sit them on the far Epistle corner. At either the Epistle corner or the credence table, he pours in the wine. He may optionally set down the chalice, an then blesses the water. Taking the chalice, he pours in the water and then returns to the center of the altar. At the lavabo, he must go to the credence table, where he should have a lavabo bowl with water already in it. He dips his fingers in it and then dries them on a towel. Alternatively, he may have this set upon the Epistle corner of the altar.

The Canon of the Mass is as usual. When he gives communion, he does not have anyone to hold the communion paten. The faithful may hold this themselves, or if need be, the priest may hold the ciborium or paten under the chin of the communicant to contain any dropped fragments of the sacrament.

The ablutions are the most challenging part of celebrating alone. After saying the first prayer, the Celebrant takes the chalice in the left hand and goes to the Epistle corner or credence table, depending on where the cruets are. With the right hand (still keeping the thumb and forefinger joined), he pours some wine into the chalice. Returning to the center of the altar, he consumes the first ablution and says the second ablution prayer. He returns to where the cruets are. He must set the chalice down. He holds his left thumb and forefinger over the bowl of the chalice and pours some wine with the right hand over the thumb and forefinger of the left hand. Then he pours some water with the right hand. This he repeats for the right hand. Or, if the priest finds it easier to start the other way around, then this may be done. The remainder of the ablutions follows as usual, and he transfers the missal back to the Epistle corner (first returning the cruets to the credence table if they were upon the altar).

The remainder of the mass is as usual. When the mass is over, the priest goes to collect his biretta. He then goes to the center of the altar on the pavement and reverences the altar, holding his biretta. Placing the biretta on his head, he processes out as usual.

Celebrating Alone

֍

When a priest must celebrate mass alone (that is, with no one else present), or he wishes to do so in order to offer mass for a specific intention and no one else is available to attend, provided this is permitted under the Canons he follows, there are several things that must be changed. First, all "communication" with the faithful must be omitted, as it no longer makes sense. The basic actions are, of course, just as at any mass. It is also intended that such a

Prayers at the Foot of the Altar

The Asperges is, of course, never done when celebrating alone. The priest says the Prayers at the Foot of the Altar as usual, saying all the parts himself through the Confiteor. He skips to the Indulgentiam. He omits the *Dominus vobiscum, et cum spiritu tuo*, and *Oremus*, but says the Collect for Purity. He then ascends the altar as usual and says the *Aufer a nobis*.

From the Introit until before the Offertory

The priest reads the Introit as usual, goes to the center of the altar and says the *Kyrie*, saying the entire thing himself, and then says the *Gloria* if it is appointed. He does not say the Summary of the Law. He does not turn to the people at all when saying mass alone (as there are no people to whom to turn), and does not say *Dominus vobiscum* or *Oremus*. He proceeds directly to the Epistle corner and says the Collect for the Day and any other prayers appointed or prayers ad libitum as permitted. Then he reads the Epistle directly out of the missal at the Epistle corner. Then follows the Gradual. He transfers the missal to the Gospel side, says the *Munda Cor* at the center of the altar, makes the sign of the cross over the missal as he announces the Gospel, makes the sign of the cross on himself as usual, and then reads the Gospel. He does not say *Dominus vobiscum* before announcing the Gospel. Then he says the Creed if it is appointed. There is, of course, no sermon.

Offertory through the Sanctus

The priest reads the Offertory verse without turning round to face away from the altar or say *Dominus vobiscum*. He may, however, kiss the altar first if he wishes, it is the local custom or it is mandated by regulations.

Afterward, the priest carries out the offertory as given in the previous section, Celebrating without a Server. The *Orate Fratres* is not said. Instead the priest may say, facing the altar with hands joined, *Oro ut meum sacrificium acceptabile fiat apud Deum Patrem omnipotentem*. He may kiss the altar before this if he wishes, it is the local custom or it is mandated by regulations.

The Invitation to Communion, Confession, General Absolution, and Comfortable Words are omitted. The priest proceeds directly from the Secrets to the *Sursum Corda*. In the Prefaces in Text given in the Missale Anglicanum 2009, the first line is the final *Per omnia saecula saeculorum* of the final Secret. This is omitted at all masses except when the priest is celebrating alone. (This does not appear at all in the solemn tone an ferial tone prefaces, as these are not used when celebrating alone). The *Dominus vobiscum* is omitted. The priest continues with the *Sursum corda*, saying all the parts, and then says the preface, *Sanctus*, and *Benedictus*.

Canon of the Mass

The Canon is said exactly as usual (though there are no bells) until the *Pater Noster*. At the *Pater Noster*, he says *sed libera nos a malo* himself. Only one host is consecrated, unless he is consecrating more hosts for the purpose of reserving them. He omits the *Pax Domini*, but still makes the three signs of the cross over the chalice. The priest receives communion and proceeds directly to the Ablutions, omitting the *Ecce Agnus Dei*, etc. Ablutions are performed exactly as given in the section on Celebrating without a Server. The priest re-assembles the Sacred Vessels on the altar in the usual manner and transfers the missal back to the Epistle corner.

Conclusion of the Mass

The priest says the General Thanksgiving and Communion verse at the Epistle corner as usual. He does not go to the center of the altar or say *Dominus vobiscum* or *Oremus*, but rather continues immediately with the Post-communions. The Dismissal and Blessing are not given. After the Post-communions, the priest goes to the center of the altar and says the Placeat tibi, and then kisses the altar. From there he goes to the Gospel corner and says the Last Gospel without *Dominus vobiscum*. There the mass is ended. He takes his biretta, reverences the altar, and departs.

Public Veneration of a Relic

This should take place in the context of public liturgy, either following a mass or one of the major offices (morning or evening prayer). Additionally, the exposition may take place during the liturgy.

POSITION OF THE RELIC

The relic should be placed on an appropriate table on the Gospel or Epistle side, but not on the altar. Before it is exposed, it should be veiled with a white or red cloth (white for confessors and red for martyrs or the True Cross.) It should be carried in procession to its place of veneration and exposition following the Procession for Transferring Sacred Relics (see the Rituale). This may be done before the liturgy or after the liturgy.

EXPOSITION

The officiant should wear a cope in the color of the saint (white or red). After the liturgy is complete, the procession to bring the relic to its position is done if it is not already done. Then the officiant goes to the relic without making any reverence to it (but should reverence the Blessed Sacrament if he passes it) and removes the veil. Then, accepting the thurible from the thurifer, he censes the relic from a standing position. If it is a first class relic, then it is censed with two double-swings. If it is a second class relic, then it is censed with one double-swing. Returning the thurible to the thurifer, the officiant genuflects to the relic (first class) or bows (second class). During this time, appropriate psalms and hymns may be sung. If the procession with the relic is after the liturgy, then the Litany of the Saints is likely still continuing during this time. If the relic is of the True Cross, then the officiant genuflects before censing it.

The exception to the above is if the Blessed Sacrament is also exposed. If the procession passes in front of the Blessed Sacrament, then all make the proper reverence of a genuflection. The officiant, carrying the relic, or anyone else carrying something in the procession, instead bows low. Also, the relic is censed as usual, but it is not reverenced with a genuflection or bow.

VENERATION

After the relic has been exposed, the other clergy and laity may process to venerate the relic, during which time appropriate psalms and hymns may be sung. The officiant may also lead prayers associated with the saint whose relic is being exposed. If the Blessed Sacrament is exposed, then the relic is not venerated with a genuflection or bow, but the faithful may still come in procession to pass by the relic.

AFTER THE VENERATION

When the veneration is complete, the officiant again veils the relic. The procession proceeds as before to return the relic to its resting place. The Litany of the Saints may again be sung, or one or more psalms given for this procession in the Rituale Anglicanum or Liber Processionalis.

IF THE VENERATION IS DONE DURING THE LITURGY

The procession and exposition must be done before the liturgy begins, up to and including the censing and the officiant's veneration of the relic. The others around may venerate the relic, but need not do so. Then the liturgy proceeds as usual. The relic may be censed again after the altar is censed at the *Magnificat* (in the offices) or, at the mass, after the Introit and at the Offertory.

After the liturgy is complete, the public veneration takes places. The officiant proceeds to venerate the relic (or may delegate someone else to begin this), and the clergy and faithful may then process.

GENERAL NOTES

The clergy should either be seated or kneeling in prayer in the sanctuary or elsewhere, or in the sacristy until the veneration is complete. If the public exposition is lengthy, then the Officiant and other ministers may depart and then return to cover and remove the relic. Other clergy may also substitute in for lengthy expositions, leading prayers, etc. At the end of the exposition, the Celebrant gives the benediction with the relic in exactly the same manner as for the Blessed Sacrament, except that he does not use the humeral veil.

Made in the USA
Lexington, KY
01 February 2010